D0021596

Down to Earth

Practical Thoughts for Passionate Gardeners

MARGOT ROCHESTER

TAYLOR TRADE PUBLISHING

Lanham • New York • Boulder • Toronto • Plymouth, UK

Published by Taylor Trade Publishing
An imprint of The Rowman & Littlefield Publishing Group, Inc.
4501 Forbes Boulevard, Suite 200, Lanham, Maryland 20706
www.rlpgtrade.com

Estover Road, Plymouth PL6 7PY, United Kingdom

Distributed by National Book Network

Library of Congress Cataloging-in-Publication Data

Rochester, Margot, 1935–
Down to Earth : practical thoughts for passionate gardeners / Margot Rochester.
p. cm.
Includes index.
ISBN-13: 978-1-58979-382-8 (cloth : alk. paper)
ISBN-10: 1-58979-382-X (cloth : alk. paper)
ISBN-13: 978-1-58979-409-2 (electronic)
ISBN-10: 1-58979-409-5 (electronic)
1. Gardening. I. Title. II. Title: Practical thoughts for passionate gardeners.
SB453.R624 2009
635—dc22

2008029916

∞™ The paper used in this publication meets the minimum requirements of American National Standard for Information Sciences—Permanence of Paper for Printed Library Materials, ANSI/NISO Z39.48-1992.
Manufactured in the United States of America.

To best friends who keep me laughing
and to Dick, my dearest friend,
who shares the journey and keeps me on course.

CONTENTS

Preface xi

Acknowledgments xiii

MAKING A GARDEN 1

Down to Earth 2

The Unplanned Garden 5

Garden Like a Cheapskate 8

Regroup and Stretch 11

Getting from Drab to Chaotic . . . If You Are Ready to Go 14

Times Change 16

Going Wild in the Garden 19

AUTUMN 23

Taming the Wilds 24

Happy Accidents 27

Revving Up the Gardening Engine 30

Take Note: Plan Ahead 32

An Autumn Rainbow 35

Some Sumptuous Shrubs 38

Hydrangeas Ahead 41

Dry Shade, Oh, That Dry Shade 44

Top Tens 47

Expansion Plans 50

Fragrance, Wherefore Art Thou? 52
Covering Ground 55
Tender Loving Care 58
Queen of the Climbers 61
Add a Bunch, Subtract a Few 64
Ah, to Bed 67

WINTER 71

And Sow Forth 72
A Gardener and Her Tools 75
Hedging My Bets 78
Trees You Design Yourself 81
Lose the Blues with Winter Greens 83
Winter Pleasures 86
Lowdown on Lime 89
Over the Edge 92
Slipping into Christmas Mode 95
The Gift That Keeps on Giving 98
Cold Facts 100
Bonding in the Greenhouse 103
A Winter Stroll 105
February Itch 108
Pruning Puzzles 110
Early Risers 113

SPRING 117

Look, Look! It's a Harbinger 118
Wait, Wait! Don't Plant Yet 121
Some Swell Shrubs 124
Small Pleasures 127
An Abundance of Herbs 130
Maxing Out the Annuals 132

I'm Just Wild about Natives 135
Math Skills in the Garden 138
Knowin' When to Fold 'Em 141
Plant Now for Fall Bounty 144
The Dratted Deer 147
Drop by Drop 149
Pick a Peck of Plectranthus 151
Gray Thoughts in the Garden 153
Holes Happen 156

SUMMER 159

Slowing Down and Perking Along 160
Sempervivums Forever 163
Container Gardening 166
Going and Coming Back 168
Where Have All the Trees Gone? 171
Doing In the Deadheads 174
Summer's Peak 177
Thugs in the Neighborhood 180
Leafy Greens Galore 183
The Scent of Summer: Ginger Lilies 186
Doing Flowers and Doing Good 189
A Church Lady's Thoughts 192
Praise Be for the Good Guys 195
August and the Lilies Are in Bloom 197
Intimate Spaces 200
The Year of XXL 203
Short Stuff 206
My Garden Overfloweth 209

A GARDENER'S HARVEST 213

It's All about Wow Power 214
Who Makes These Rules? 217

Surprise, Surprise 220
Gardening Goofs: Let Me Count the Ways 223
Fleeting Pleasures 225
Sweet Surrender 227

Index 231

About the Author 241

PREFACE

Ruth, Henry, and Allen . . . My Gardening Gurus

No gardening grandmother appears in my gene pool. The first twenty years of my life were spent in big cities with urban and urbane parents. If any gardening was done, it was done by hired hands. Uninspired, no doubt. And certainly uninspiring to that pigtailed, freckled kid I was.

My life changed when, as a college freshman, I picked up the book *How to Have a Green Thumb without an Aching Back* by Ruth Stout. I discovered I was a gardener at heart and knew I would someday be a gardener in reality. Why else would that book have called my name?

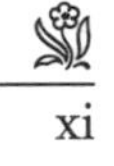

Stout, who became a gardener in middle age, toiled in the inhospitable soil of Connecticut. When she tired of toiling, she reinvented the gardening process and then told the rest of us how to do it. She not only instructed readers about the glories of mulch and compost; she introduced us to the incomparable joy of sitting on a bale of hay, fulfilled by the day's work and the next day's promise.

How to Have a Green Thumb without an Aching Back introduces the reader to an occasionally cantankerous woman who lived fully until she was ninety-six. I have a photograph of her, leaning on a pitchfork, looking around her garden, thoughtful and content. The book is a guide to intelligent, productive, labor-saving gardening but so much more.

Henry Mitchell also entered my life before I became a gardener. Again, I am not sure why I purchased *The Essential Earthman*, but once I read the first chapter, I was in love. Mitchell filled the limited space of his Washington, D.C., garden to overflowing and wrote for the *Washington Post* garden columns that are sheer genius, sometimes comic, always informative.

This is how good Mitchell is. When I became a published writer, I quit reading Mitchell because his books are packed with sentences I wish I had written myself. Feelings of inadequacy overcome me, and my own writing pales, but so does everyone else's. Rereading Mitchell's books, *The Essential Earthman*, *One Man's Garden*, and *Henry Mitchell on Gardening*, must wait until I develop a more hardened ego or I am no longer writing about gardens.

Like Stout, Mitchell's books are full of good gardening advice, but anyone can give advice. Their writing rings with perseverance, humor, and passion, and so does Allen Lacy's.

Lacy is the only author of these three mentors I had the pleasure of meeting. He spoke at a symposium I attended in 1998. Lacy knew exactly how he became a gardener. Miss Harley turned him into one by selling him (for twenty-five cents) a yellow iris fortuitously called 'Happy Days'.

Lacy has written many books, but the ones that speak to me are *Home Ground*, *Farther Afield*, and *The Gardener's Eye*, collections of columns he wrote for the *Wall Street Journal* and other publications.

Stout, Mitchell, and Lacy were gifted writers and gardeners to the core and to the heart. Their books continue to teach us to see the world differently, with what Lacy calls "the gardener's eye," and once we have it, we are forever changed.

ACKNOWLEDGMENTS

Many thanks to the people who prodded this book to fruition:

Rick Rinehart, editorial director
Taylor Trade Publishing
Rowman & Littlefield Publishing Group

And most of all, from the get-go, my cheering squad for their interest, enthusiasm, and patience:

Dulcie Wilcox, editor
Janice Braunstein, production editor
and
Michele Tomiak, copy editor

Making a Garden

Gardening has changed, and so have we. We have learned that gardening is art, not a set of rules. We are free to follow our visions, so our gardens reflect who we are and what we like . . . that is, until we change our minds.

Down to Earth

At one time I thought of myself as a lazy gardener, but I know now that I am not lazy at all. I have simply reallocated my energy.

I have discovered how to do certain jobs (such as getting rid of weeds) once and never again. I have found out how to turn sand into nutrient-rich, moisture-retentive loam. And, best of all, I have learned to let nature do much of the toil for me.

Instead of lazy, I think of myself as a leisurely gardener. At the risk of sounding smug, I have become efficient and resourceful, and I assure you that with minimal effort, you can do the same while creating a pleasurable, satisfying, undemanding garden.

In starting an ornamental garden, or what I call a mixed border, the gardener needs to begin with fundamental decisions about its location and its size and parameters. Where will it get morning sun and afternoon shade? How big should it be, and how should it be shaped?

But I think the most basic question is about the purpose of the garden. Why do you desire this garden or border? Do you want flowers for arrangements? Sustenance for birds and butterflies? A view from an interior window? A place of privacy? Or a place for entertaining?

Too often a garden begins with no objective, so the garden winds up as a hodgepodge that never quite satisfies the gardener. If you begin with a goal, a mission statement of sorts, you have a guideline for the garden's design and ingredients. Whatever goal you set, the garden should make you happy. Why else would you go to the trouble and expense?

Once the decision of purpose has been made, gather all the newspapers and cardboard you can locate. Ask neighbors and friends to save theirs for you. Flatten cereal and cracker boxes as well as cartons. People may look at you strangely as you plead for their stacks before they toss them into the recycling bin. Spouses may complain about cardboard and newspaper cluttering up storage areas. But keep the faith. You are on a mission that will change your life forever.

For this adventure you will also need a large pile of pine straw, aged wood shavings, shredded leaves, hay, dried seagrass, or a combination of any of these materials. Establish a relationship with sources of these mulching materials since you will need a regular supply as long as you garden.

When I had a garden on the coast, I gathered dried seagrass. For my mainland garden, I buy ten to twenty bales of coastal Bermuda hay every year from a local farmer who delivers it to the spot I designate. I shred and pile up leaves that fall in our yard. Leaves that fall into the garden stay right where they are. I rake up pine straw. I have been known to gather bags of leaves misguided neighbors discard. Little do they know they are dumping treasure.

Ideally, you will also have on hand some bags or a pile of composted manure, but this is not nearly as essential as the newspaper and mulch. However, it is a good investment, and once you spread a generous layer of manure on your garden, you need not do it again for years. Maybe never if, like me, you are a dedicated mulcher.

Spread newspaper and cardboard over the entire area you have picked out as your garden site. The newspaper should be eight or more layers thick. Put it right on top of grass or weeds that cover the area. Once again, if you do this right, you will never have to do it again.

The goal is to shut out light so the grass becomes compost and weed seeds are unable to germinate. The newspaper and cardboard decompose in less than a year and add humus to your soil. Humus is the material that provides texture, enzymes, beneficial bacteria, and nutrients to the soil. It also enables soil to retain moisture.

After the entire area is covered with paper, spread composted manure over it as thickly as you can. Six inches is ideal. If you do not have enough for the whole site, I suggest you spread it thickly over as much area as you can cover and do the remaining area thickly another time.

Next cover the entire area, whether you have a compost layer or not, with eight to twelve inches of mulching material. Do not skimp. One benefit of this mulch is that it hides and holds down the newspaper so that it does not blow all over and make the neighbors cranky.

Furthermore, as the newspapers decompose, the mulch becomes integrated into the soil. Earthworms move in. Beneficial bacteria and enzymes thrive. The mulch retains moisture, helps keep soil temperature stable, and provides nutrients to plants.

Let this sandwich of newspaper, compost, and mulch rest three to six months. Nature will do its work with no further effort on your part. When do you till the soil? Never. When do you get rid of those weeds and grass under the newspaper? Forget them. They are compost-in-the-making as soon as you cover them.

Make a list of plants you want in your garden: a small tree perhaps, shrubs of varying sizes, perennials of different heights that bloom at varying times, herbs, grasses, and annuals. Group plants that need shade. Some plants require moisture, while others thrive in dry soil. You will water more efficiently if you group these plants accordingly.

Waiting to plant is hard but well worth the patience. However, if you want to plant shrubs or trees immediately, cut through the newspaper layer a space large enough for the rootball. After planting, tuck in the compost and mulch, leaving an uncovered inch around the stem or trunk to avoid rotting.

As your soil becomes rich with humus and nutrients, your plants become resistant to disease and fungi. Forget about spraying and dusting. In a balanced, diverse garden, beneficial insects will thrive and so will your plants.

People frequently express disbelief when I say I do not labor long hours in my large garden. I even hear murmurs of doubt when I deny using insecticides or fungicides. But it is all true. (Or almost true. I mercilessly annihilate fire ants, whatever it takes.)

Remember the cereal commercial? "Try it. You'll like it." I suggest, if you are skeptical, that you try this soil-building, organic process in just one area of your garden for a few years. You will be hooked. You will then stroll around your garden, wondering where the weeds are, stopping occasionally to kick yourself for not taking life easy years ago.

The Unplanned Garden

No wonder I am frequently asked to speak to garden groups about "the unplanned garden." I have to face facts. I am a gardener without tape measure or graph paper, let alone a compass. My garden lacks an axis, a hardscape focus. My edges ebb and flow without pattern. Geometry is beyond me, and so is the Golden Mean (though not, I hope, the Golden Rule).

Determining an overall purpose for a garden points the gardener in the right direction. It provides a target: a place for entertaining, or privacy, or children's play. Those are goals, not plans. My objective is to create a garden that is a collection of plants overflowing with color, texture, and surprises. I have no plan except to gather diverse species and varieties that catch my attention and interest.

An efficient planner purchases plants for particular places. I bring a plant home and wander around looking for a space to put it. An efficient planner has a map. I may not even have a shopping list. But the way I look at it, lackadaisical planning gives me freedom to change my mind, to surprise myself with creative flukes, and to forgive myself for making mistakes.

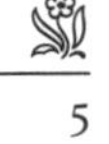

My first experience with serious lack of planning was an herb garden I started forty years ago. I placed this garden in the corner of our one-acre lot, considerably closer to my neighbor's kitchen than to my own. Of course, the garden languished from inattention. I had two children, as well as a husband and assorted dogs, and the herb garden had low priority.

A slow learner, a few years later I planted a narrow perennial border across the back of our lot in front of a hedge of redtips (*Photinia* × *fraseri*). Not good placement (since it, like the herb garden, was too far from the house), but the concept had potential. Unformed but germinating.

The hedge of redtips has gone, replaced by dark green waxleaf ligustrums to provide background, privacy, and abundant cover for birds and other critters. That strip of perennials has become a mixed border over one hundred feet in length and between eight and sixteen feet in depth, meandering around an oval of unkempt lawn that someday I may pave with flagstones.

While I may have been a gardener without plan, even as I planted that scrawny strip of perennials, I had a vision. My gardener's eye pictured a lush sweep of flowers and foliage that looked like an over-the-top bouquet of diverse textures, intertwining stems, and fabulous colors. I did not draw a plan or map, but I knew my destination.

An adept nonplanner continually enlarges the canvas. The unplanned garden is in perpetual flux—with added inches here, a few feet there, outward and onward and occasionally upward.

Because I did not know better at the time, the ground was dug up for that skinny back-of-the-lot border, but I have never tilled. Grass remains in place, turning quickly into compost; newspapers deprive grass and weeds of light; compost and mulch enrich the soil. The only digging that occurs in my garden is to prepare just enough space for plants.

This "sandwich" of newspaper, compost, and mulch incorporates itself into the soil, providing three meals a day plus snacks for earthworms and microscopic critters. I no longer fertilize. Stray weeds or groundcovers are pulled effortlessly from dark, humusy soil that began as pale, nutrient-starved sand.

This blank canvas, of course, is not prepared all at once, as a properly planned garden would be. My own garden plots grow in chunks, depending upon which way I want a path to travel, what plants are waiting to be planted, what bench or statue or birdbath needs a location. A garden designer knows from the get-go where that path will go, which plants go where, and what location is right for the birdbath.

I do not know any of these things until I see them happen. I walk the path until I bump into something, and that is where the turn occurs. My husband moves the birdbath to one place and then another. He is a fine and patient man and knows when to keep opinions to himself.

I plop the shrub or tree down in one location, change my mind, and try it somewhere else.

I try to make up my mind before I remove the plants from their pots, but sometimes they are in the ground for a season or more before I reach a decision. At one time, almost every plant in my garden was dug up and moved at least once, and some of them three times, before reaching a final location. They seemed to enjoy the attention and change of scenery. At least they did not complain.

I have learned the hard way to leave plants in their pots and move them around the garden until we hit the right spot. Sometimes they remain potted and movable for months or even a year or two.

A garden that just happens is never short of surprises. They are everywhere. Stems intertwine and foliage mingles so it is difficult to tell where one plant starts and another stops. Colors clash, but who cares? No garden planner would pair orange and pink, but Mexican sunflowers and rosy Joe Pye weed are stunning together. Cat's whiskers weave happily among rue and alternanthera. Artemisias wander at will.

Erysimum and geums, planted too closely together, bump into each other but work things out. There is room for both. Japanese anemones, bobbing on wiry stems, pop up in the most unexpected places. Dwarf pennyroyal, creeping raspberry, and dwarf veronica wander into the lawn. The garden overflows.

Even a nonplanner has guidelines, and these are mine: Locate garden spaces where they will give maximum pleasure. Feel free to expand. Forget the rules and follow your vision. Work no harder than absolutely necessary.

If I had planned my garden thirty years ago and adhered to a drawing and accompanying plant list, I would have saved myself even more time and labor. I definitely would have saved money. Who knows what I might have done with all the hours and energy I have dribbled away? Who knows what fortune I might have amassed without all those foolish purchases?

But the person who might have made that plan no longer exists. Her vision has morphed and mellowed. So has her garden. Like Popeye, "I yam what I yam," and my garden is what it is, and, after all these years, we are happy together.

Garden Like a Cheapskate

One thing I have learned in my gardening life is to make the most of my resources. I point with pride at my overflowing garden on which I have spent remarkably little, no matter what my husband thinks. With extra effort and plenty of money, I could have created this garden more quickly, but I am a patient and frugal gardener. I find "having it all" for a pittance more satisfying than instant gratification.

Paying for mature plants is more than my thrifty nature can bear. For me, a large part of gardening pleasure comes from seeing plants grow from infancy to adulthood. Planting a full-grown shrub or tree or perennial is too much like giving birth to a twenty-one year old. The child may be perfect in every way, but where is the feeling of accomplishment?

Even though I usually buy young, inexpensive plants, I watch for sales, especially late in the season when nurseries unload overgrown or tired plants to make room for new inventory. Repotting is labor intensive for commercial establishments, but I am happy to do it since I do not collect even minimum wage.

A plant that needs repotting often can be divided into several smaller plants. Recently I bought a holly fern (*Cyrtomium falcatum*) and was able to slice it into three separate crowns or clumps. For the sale price of one overcrowded plant, I now have three holly ferns.

Whether I am dividing an overgrown perennial purchased at a nursery or a crowded cluster from my own garden, the method is the same. I look at the clump of roots and emerging stems and decide how many divisions I can make.

You need a sharp knife for this operation. Locate the first possible division, and insert the knife at the top, keeping in mind that you want to salvage as much of the root structure as possible. Slice downward on one side of the division and then the other so that you wind up with a wedge like a six-inch-thick slice of pie.

Continue to slice around the clump until you have two, three, or four divisions. Go for husky chunks that will mature quickly. They are free, and life is short.

Sometimes I dig up an overcrowded perennial and pull it apart with my hands. If a shovel or trowel is not close by, I rip the plant out of the ground. My borders are full of plants that started their independence this way and have lived happy, fruitful lives in spite of my mistreatment.

I keep a plastic trough of potting mix for the next step. That way I am ready whether I have one or two plants to pot up or a dozen. My all-purpose potting mix is two-thirds commercial peat or pine bark–based mix and one-third compost or good garden soil. Toss in a couple of handfuls of lime or add a tablespoon of lime to each pot as you fill it.

Put divisions in pots large enough to allow a season or two of growth. Water well to settle the roots. Be sure the base (or new crown) of the plant is just below the surface. Put your new plants where you will visit them regularly to be sure they are watered and squirrels have not dug them up.

Of course, instead of potting up your new plants, you could put them directly in the garden. I have done this, often with the same plants I ripped out of the ground and yanked apart. Just be sure you keep the plants watered and mulched.

For me, one of the greatest pleasures of gardening is creating new plants from cuttings. Cuttings are four- to six-inch stem segments with several nodes or growth bumps where roots can emerge. The stems should be this year's growth, mature enough so that they are not flimsy but are green and bendable.

When I buy a shrub, I check for potential cuttings. I snip off as many of those four- to six-inch stem segments as I can while leaving enough foliage on the plant to assure continued vigor. For the price of one plant, I have a bouquet. "More is better" is my mantra.

Fill a six- to eight-inch-deep plastic pot or planter with coarse builders sand, vermiculite, perlite, or finely shredded pine bark. This is the medium that will hold cuttings until they are rooted. Moisten the medium thoroughly, checking that excess water drains out of the container.

Cut each stem just below a growth node (the bumpy area), and then dip it into water and powdered rooting hormone, which you can find at any garden center. With a stick or pencil or finger, poke a hole in the medium. Stick the stem into the hole, making sure the medium is packed around it.

Put the cuttings in a shady area, and keep the medium moist but never soggy. In two or three weeks your cuttings should have well-developed white roots. You will know they are rooted if they do not slide out of the medium when you give them a tug. If they slide easily, let them sit in the shade another couple of weeks and try again.

Some propagators cover their rooting containers with plastic to keep the medium from drying out and to create a moist atmosphere for the cuttings. Sometimes I do this and sometimes I do not, depending upon whether we are in a dry or rainy spell. If I lived in an arid climate or propagated indoors, I would always drape plastic over the container.

Pot up well-rooted cuttings in potting mix. Let the roots grow for a season or two. Be patient. Wait for strong foliage growth.

To make a plant or make multiple plants from one is a joyful experience. Call me crazy, but I would never be satisfied with a ready-made garden installed by a landscaper between dawn and dusk. The extended creative process and personal involvement enrich my life as no instant garden could ever do.

Regroup and Stretch

While visiting an art museum a few years ago, I was pleasantly puzzled by the work of the world-renowned abstract expressionist Jasper Johns. The card on the wall quoted Johns describing his work process: "It's simple; you just take something and do something to it, and then do something else to it."

My thoughts exactly. As a gardener, I am more gut-level opportunist than abstract expressionist, but I plant something in a space, add plants that make it look better, and then add more. No diagrams, no tape measures, no design concept other than the tall stuff goes in the back (though sometimes it winds up elsewhere), and colors should echo rather than clash (though sometimes they do clash, and the effect is quite pleasant).

My favorite garden spot, the area right outside our family room windows, was flattened by heavy equipment rearranging a forty-year-old septic system. I was presented with what might have seemed a disaster. However, I chose to view it as a fresh, if not pristine, canvas.

I tried to remember what had been in this abundant border, which plants had brought me such delight. Joe Pye weed (*Eupatorium maculatum* 'Gateway'), royal blue salvia (*S. guaranitica*), and a single baptisia re-emerged from the pale sand that had been dumped over my well-nourished sandy loam. Every other plant had disappeared.

Castor bean seeds began germinating, and I left the seedlings in place while I replanted the area. I will eventually extract seedlings I do not want and trim the remaining castor beans to provide a little shade through the summer, like "annual trees" with sturdy stems and large, burgundy leaves.

I began planting. . . . First I did one thing, then another. In a couple of weeks the border was filled with potential: tiny basils, transplanted solidago and lamb's ears, orange-flowered lion's ears (*Leonotis leonurus*), and butterfly weed (*Asclepias tuberosa*). Somehow, the color combinations meshed: royal blue, orange, yellow, and red. The palette now sizzles, though it used to be soft pastels.

Thinking ahead to my golden years, I am replacing most perennials and annuals with shrubs to cut down on labor throughout my garden. In the corner of this mixed border I planted a single *Hydrangea paniculata* 'Limelight', which will bloom in mid- to late summer, providing a respite from all those oranges and reds.

With one or two exceptions, panicle hydrangeas bloom on new wood, so they can (and should) be cut back to a foot or less in late winter to generate as much new wood and as many blooms as possible. They also tolerate more sun than mopheads and lacecaps, making them ideal for sunny mixed borders.

In the shadiest area I planted a daphne to provide entertainment in the winter. Then I did something else: an assortment of hellebores was tucked in. They will have to be moved as the daphne grows, but I will worry about that later. I wonder whether Jasper Johns does that, too.

Toward the front of the border I planted several dwarf abelias. Numerous dwarf abelia cultivars are available, but I am partial to *Abelia* × 'Rose Creek' because its conspicuous pink calyxes last all winter. I also like its compact size and shape, well suited to a mixed border.

A single variegated grass (*Miscanthus sinensis* 'Variegatus') is clustered with the hydrangea. Close to the house (definitely closer than it should be) I have placed a blue flowering chaste tree (*Vitex agnus-castus* 'Shoal Creek').

I could not help myself. Wandering through the garden section of a big-box store, I spotted a table full of 'Shoal Creek' vitexes in full bloom and bought two, one for myself and one for a friend. A vitex can reach twelve to fifteen feet, so it needs more space than I can give it in this particular border. Instead of planting it, I repotted it in a large container and will plant it somewhere else when I have come to my senses.

Vitex flower spikes are full and long and blue (or white or pink) and last for weeks, much prettier to my thinking than the blooms on a butterfly bush or buddleia. The foliage is dissected (looking a bit, I am told, like marijuana foliage). I already have a large old no-name vitex in the corner of my yard, and it is stunning. The trick is to keep a chaste tree deadheaded so it will continue to rebloom through the summer and trimmed up so that it does not turn into an oversized and ungainly shrub.

Here is another trick: when you buy a bargain plant, remove it from its pot, ruffle up the roots, cut them with a knife to loosen them, and put the plant in the ground or repot it in a larger container. Bargain plants are usually pot-bound with root systems tightly confined and unable to expand. It is too painful to think about.

But newly planted shrubs, trees, and grasses are for the future. I needed big and instant gratification in this visible border. Two fast-growing annual Mexican sunflowers (*Tithonia rotundifolia*) are just the ticket, reaching five to seven feet in height by late summer and producing bright orange single flowers until frost. Two will amply fill an area of eight feet or more, keeping in mind that castor bean "trees" (*Ricinus communis*) share the space.

Tithonias tend to fall over in late summer during heavy rainstorms, and I have learned to let them lie. They root where they fall, turn their center stem toward the sun, and keep on flowering.

I could have replanted this border as it had been originally, but disaster forced me to regroup and stretch. The garden used to be a soothing mix of pastels; now it is a zingy and cheerful bouquet.

My husband warned me for years about planting in this area, knowing that our septic system lurked below. Of course, he was right, and I knew it all along. Now I have replanted this same precarious area, which will probably need flattening again in the future. Assuming trouble is another forty years in the future, I will take the risk and enjoy the present.

Getting from Drab to Chaotic . . . If You Are Ready to Go

My garden history is full of borrowed ideas. My many gardening mentors figured out how to do things efficiently, strategies I never would have thought of myself. My own inclination is do-it-yourself, plant-as-you-go chaos.

Contrary to most of what I know about gardening, no one had to tell me how to be chaotic. I was born this way and am reminded, every time I stroll in my garden from midsummer through fall, what a wild woman I am. I prefer to think of myself as a free spirit. My garden is untidy but full of breathtaking surprises. It is a riot of color, texture, and structure. How, I wonder, did a simple soul such as I achieve such grandeur?

Often, when I speak to gardeners and show them slides of my garden, I confess that my personal Eden is never sought out for garden tours. My audience laughs, and so do I. We all know what I am talking about.

Up on that giant screen, we see the chaos that is my gardening style. It is a jungle in there and up there. By August, I have to pull plants apart to get a glimpse of soil. Stems and stalks intertwine as if they are all growing out of the same root system.

Candelabra-like seedpods of August lilies, tall salvias, cannas, and cassias shoot upward with no regard for the less stately growers around them. Not for me neatly staggered heights and subtle color combinations.

If your garden needs loosening up, if you want to go from drab to chaotic, here are the directions:

Think big. As you walk around your garden, be conscious of your posture. If your shoulders are stooped, your neck bent, your eyes cast downward, your garden is too medium, which is not surprising since most plants in home gardens are about twelve to thirty inches tall.

In a dynamic garden, eyes move up and down and up, looking for the surprises. Place *tuteurs* (latticed pyramids) and other structures for vines to climb. Select plants with height and bulk: bananas, cannas, elephant ears. In the fall, watch butter-colored cassia (*Cassia bicapsularis*) prop itself on surrounding plants as it reaches heights of seven or eight feet.

Plant big in the middle of medium. Do not feel compelled to line up tall plants or structures in the back of the border with mediums in the middle and shorts up front. Discover "see-through" plants meant to filter the view.

Plant closely so that when plants emerge and start their wandering ways, the soil will be shaded, and so will the roots. Not only is this aesthetically pleasing to those of us with chaotic taste, the overhanging foliage suppresses weeds and conserves moisture. And talk about instant gratification. Close planting quickly turns the garden into an abundant and overflowing bouquet.

Let the colors flow together like a vibrant watercolor. To my eye, burgundy creates what painters call negative space, receding but making paler shades pop. Chartreuse, on the other hand, demands attention. They make a fabulous pair, and I would not want to garden without their pizzazz.

Burgundy plants in my garden include alternanthera, hibiscus, castor beans, pineapple lily, and several heucheras, as well as ninebark shrub (*Physocarpus opulifolius*), barberry, and loropetalum.

I satisfy my longing for chartreuse with Mexican orange shrub (*Choisya ternata* 'Sundance'), which keeps its immature chartreuse foliage through the winter. *Spirea* 'Gold Flame' is chartreuse with tinges of orange.

The reseeding annual, Jewels of Opar (*Talinum paniculatum*) emerges in late spring, but the chartreuse color knocks my socks off until the first freeze turns it into mush. I allow golden-green creeping Jennie (*Lysimachia nummularia*) to ease out into the lawn, just the kind of thing a chaotic gardener might do.

Repeat colors through the garden so that, in spite of the chaos, there is continuity. Take a chance with color combinations. As with so many other facets of gardening, what have you got to lose if the choice is wrong? If the combinations do not please, remove the offender and put it somewhere else. If only all life's mistakes were so easily corrected.

A bit of pleasant chaos, or a lot of it, embellishes our gardens, just as it adorns the roadsides and fields and woods whose unpredictable abundance and texture take our breath away.

Times Change

When I taught a gardening class recently, I realized how much has changed since I became a gardener. My assigned topic was annuals and perennials, but because of the way I garden, I changed it to growing annuals, perennials, and other stuff in a "mixed border." No one seemed to mind.

A mixed border is a garden in which everything is intermingled: annuals, perennials, grasses, herbs, shrubs, and even a small tree or two. By definition it is diverse, and that is a good thing because diversity decreases the likelihood harmful insects will find a bonanza crop of whatever they like to eat.

Furthermore, diversity increases the likelihood that beneficial insects will gather to check out the plant assortment and devour their harmful counterparts in the process. Of course, if you want to invite beneficial insects to the feast, you cannot use insecticides and expect a whole lot of benefits. Insecticides are nonselective, killing the good guys along with the bad.

So I talked to my class about mixed borders and diversity and doing away with insecticides. While I was at it, I suggested doing away with fungicides as well. Some fungi are good guys, too. I occasionally use herbicides on runaway weeds and ivy but I do not feel good about it.

The point is, times have changed. When I became a gardener, I aspired to a border dedicated to perennials that bloomed in succession from early spring to hard freeze. Now I grow everything together, and we all seem to have a better time.

Furthermore, when I took the Master Gardener class fifteen years ago, organic solutions were not only not part of the course, they were not suitable topics for discussion. The organic growers among us were regarded as mavericks, and our suggestions were not encouraged. Now organic strategies are promoted as intelligent solutions and organic gardeners are no longer shuffled aside as the lunatic fringe.

Organic solutions have become cutting-edge horticulture. Herbs are cutting-edge medicine. Diversity is in, and so are mixed borders. We have come a long way in our gardens, and it seems to me we have gone in the right direction.

Ten years ago, container gardening was in; separate potted plants were out. Ideally, a container garden was a mixture of plants combined with attention to texture, shape, growing pattern, and, of course, color. This is still true of well-designed container gardens, and they are wonderful to behold.

I learned everything I know about garden design from container gardening. Something tall, something round, something trailing. Something bold and upright with broad leaves, something fine textured, something with rounded foliage. Soft pale green, greens that are almost black, chartreuse, and kelly. Shiny, matte, rippled, and smooth. I also learned to plant closely for instant gratification.

Container gardening taught gardeners to focus on foliage and make our potted gardens dramatic and bold. This is exactly what I seek to do in my entire garden—as if it were one huge container garden or bouquet.

I no longer incorporate container gardens into my borders, but I continue to fill large pots with single shrubs or large perennials. I move these pots into various places in the borders for spots of color or to fill up holes that happen over the year. Keeping these single shrubs or small trees in pots, I audition them in several places through the season before planting them in the ground.

At one time my gardening style appeared haphazard, random, even messy. But today's horticultural buzzword is "layering" and, I'll be darned, I have once again moved from lunatic fringe to inner sanctum.

Like container garden design, layering is about texture, mass, and color, so the border is intensively planted from edge to backdrop. For stronger impact, I should plant multiples (three or five or seven) of a limited number of plants, but it is my garden and I rarely meet a plant I do not want in it.

In a layered garden, plants flow into one another, so soil and mulch are hidden by foliage. A prime objective of layering is to keep the border interesting all year. Well, maybe not in winter . . . though the right selection of evergreen shrubs, ferns, herbs, and perennials can be effective and dramatic even in February.

Another change in gardening over the past decade is the addition of rocks and stonework. Large sculptural rocks are placed to look like outcroppings. Scree berms appear where lawns once spread, flat and boring. Stacked walls give a garden heft and permanence.

We purchase or create hypertufa troughs and encourage moss to grow. I suspect that alpine gardens are the wave of the future. I know just where mine will go.

I am covering the grass in the center of my wraparound garden with large, flat stones, leaving space between to plant pennyroyal, dwarf mondo grass, and succulents. In the center I intend to put a large urn with water pumping melodically over the brim and down the sides.

I did not know anyone with a water garden fifteen years ago, and now I suspect I am the only one I know without one. Tropicals we had never heard of now punctuate our borders. The leaves of common elephant ears are black and burgundy, vividly patterned and exotic. Cannas are striped and gold. Bananas rise like totem poles.

Gardening has changed, and so have we. We have learned that gardening is art, not a set of rules. We are free to follow our visions, so our gardens reflect who we are and what we like . . . that is, until we change our minds or something new grabs our attention.

Going Wild in the Garden

My favorite surprise this past week was a face-to-face meeting with a watchful toad buried up to his eyeballs in mulch. I also saw a tiny gecko, two inches long, make his way up a salvia stalk, his green skin and careful movement making him almost invisible. Earlier this summer I was surprised by a turtle strolling through the damp jungle of my closely planted garden.

Standing quietly in the garden this morning, I observed a trio of hummingbirds. Just a few feet away from me, they were scouting a clump of salvias, ready to drink deeply, preparing for the miraculous trip to Central America, where they will spend the winter. These are the kinds of things that happen in a garden that is also a backyard habitat.

Creating habitats for wildlife changes the dynamics of gardening in an amazing way. Adding plants with high wildlife value, substituting natives for hybrids, or becoming less focused on tidiness and more concerned with shelter and sustenance make a garden an intimate experience as well as a cooperative venture.

While the list of wildlife-friendly plants is almost infinite, some steal the show. Make a note in your garden calendar to start seeds of *Tithonia rotundifolia* in the spring. This Mexican sunflower, with its bright orange petals and yellow center, provides continual entertainment since it is attractive to butterflies, hummingbirds, bees, and even small birds as seedheads begin to dry.

My Mexican sunflowers (planted strategically so I can see them from the kitchen sink) are eight feet tall with strong center stems. A summer storm may knock over a plant, but the stem will make a vertical turn and continue to grow upright. Or you can cut back the plant, prop it up, and let it continue its vertical climb, blooming until November.

Perennial salvias are delectable treats for hummingbirds, butterflies, and bees. *Salvia uliginosa* and *S. guaranitica* hark back to my earliest gardening days and continue to appear each spring, entertaining the masses (as well as the gardener) until late fall.

But hybridizing never stops. A new salvia in my garden this year is *S.* 'Phyllis Fancy', an even stronger magnet for hummingbirds than my old favorites, perhaps because of its extraordinary height of six or seven feet.

I look for perennial salvias at end-of-the-season sale prices and plant them in the fall. The tops die back, but new foliage will emerge in the spring. I also seek out parsley and fennel, handsome plants that overwinter and provide sustenance the following spring and summer for butterfly larva.

Another favorite of mine, *Sedum* 'Autumn Joy', is also a magnet for butterflies and bees. I have not seen hummingbirds check them out, perhaps because they are only two to three feet tall, a little low for scouting hummers. Like salvias, 'Autumn Joy' is a perennial and can be planted now. Purchase one and make cuttings. If the plant is large, you may even be able to divide it. I am always in favor of getting the most for my money . . . and my garden.

I am also in favor of planting more trees and shrubs to provide shelter and sustenance for wildlife, as well as shade and leaves that turn themselves into mulch. Some trees that support wildlife as they enhance the landscape are bottlebrush red buckeyes, sassafras, tulip poplars, wax myrtle, and red cedars.

I grow a variety of viburnums and other shrubs for their foliage, blooms, scents, and berries. I fell in love the first time I observed *Abelia chinensis* covered by a mob of butterflies, hovering and sipping. Not ten feet way was a gawky, overused butterfly bush (*Buddleia davidii*), virtually ignored by the swarm.

A growing number of dwarf forms of *A. chinensis* are appearing at garden centers. They fit nicely in the middle or front of mixed borders and have the same charm for butterflies as the original large specimen.

Bill Hilton, Jr., educator and naturalist at Hilton Pond Center in the piedmont of South Carolina, describes trumpet creeper (*Campsis radicans*) as the perfect hummingbird plant. It blooms almost from the day hummingbirds begin to arrive in March at his sanctuary to the day they leave in October. An unregimented trumpet creeper (the common "cow itch") can be a nuisance, but it is manna from heaven to hummers. Hilton suggests growing it up a tree where it can ramble at will. I suggest harvesting those beanlike seedpods before they ripen, even if you have to climb the tree to do it.

Because I grow so many plants that hummingbirds delight in, I no longer hang feeders. Hilton does. He starts keeping them filled on St. Patrick's Day and takes them down on Halloween.

Once you become a habitat gardener, establishing an interactive relationship with creatures that share your property, you will find yourself weighing choices you make and their impact on wildlife. When you see yourself as a vital link in the natural world, your garden will give you a sense of joy and serenity that insecticides and tidiness will never provide.

For information about creating and certifying a backyard habitat, check out the website of the National Wildlife Federation, or contact your state's wildlife federation.

Autumn

A garden is not a matter of space. It is a matter of pleasing yourself with plants that speak to you. Fill your garden with color and texture and mass and, most of all, with memories of people who have given you plants and shared your passion.

Taming the Wilds

The first hint of fall is in the air. Energy surges. The inclination to thin out, chop back, divide and conquer cannot be suppressed.

This morning I pulled grapevines, passion vine, morning glories, and autumn clematis out of the section of hedge that wraps around the north corner of our yard. What are grapevines doing in my hedge? They are thugs that have escaped my husband's mini-vineyard, a series of posts and wires supporting two of his seven grapevines. As for the morning glories, they are one of Mother Nature's unappreciated gifts.

This north corner of our yard is a "wildlife garden," intended to feed and shelter wildlife and provide a spot for me to observe the action. A large hickory tree provides some shade. I have planted wax myrtles, sassafras, serviceberry, vitex, pawpaw trees, possumhaw, and lindera. A turkey oak has emerged exactly where it should. Eventually I will have to thin out this thicket, but in the meantime, it provides entertainment for the critters and me.

Off my beaten track, this area is neglected, and a glimpse at the tangled and weedy path discourages anyone but the hardiest garden trekkers. It is a jungle out there.

Over the years, dead nettle (*Lamium*) and vinca have made themselves at home, flowing over the floor of the garden. I should remove these exotics and see which natives move in with a little encouragement.

Blackberry briars have taken over the far corner, basking in the afternoon sun and cooling off under the hedge. Wild grasses have appeared, and so have weeds. I can live with these intruders. They, too, are part of the landscape. Who knows what hides beneath or finds sustenance there?

The problem is not vines and weeds. The problem is me. A serious flaw prevents me from leaving well enough alone. An empty space calls out, and before I know it, a shrub or perennial has filled the vacuum. The wildlife garden has become a mishmash of natives and exotics, and I have no one to blame but myself. *Mea culpa* and all that.

The wild garden is now home to a dozen hydrangeas because I had no other place to put them. A mock orange takes up much too much space, and so do a banana shrub (*Michelia figo*) and a Florida anise, providing little succor to wildlife other than shelter. They must go if I am to remain steadfast to my mission.

Carolina allspice (*Calycanthus floridus*) takes up too much room since it suckers eight feet away from the mother plant. Because it is native to this area and provides a thicket for shelter, I let it stay. Old-fashioned abelia is not a native but attracts bees, so it belongs.

Royal blue *Salvia guaranitica* is definitely not indigenous, but hummingbirds zero in and provide the best summer entertainment I can think of. Purple coneflower (*Echinacea purpurea*) is a native and has become a favorite, an example of how we change our minds about things as we age. I especially like the 'White Swan' cultivar, so I am not quite the purist I would like to be.

I allow Queen Anne's lace to grow wherever it wants, and more power to it. No plant attracts more beneficial insects, a significant asset in a garden without insecticides. I would love a field of it—perhaps in lieu of that useless lawn.

The same is true of butterfly weed (*Asclepias tuberosa*). I adore lemon yellow woods poppies (*Stylophorum diphyllum*), the first blooms in late winter that say, "Good-bye winter, hello spring." I allow all of these perennials to seed at will.

My first herb garden was located in what is now the wildlife garden, and remnants remain: lemon balm, comfrey, tansy, and applemint. They continue to prosper with no help from me.

You probably envision the botanical mess. My hard labor this morning was a sharp departure from my normal daily walk-through, deadheading here, pulling up groundcovers or runaway vines there. Five to twenty minutes at the most.

Today I toiled several hours, filling my wheelbarrow four times with vines, briars, and weeds. It was not an unpleasant job. I was outdoors. The temperature was in the seventies, and I felt a sense of accomplishment as I worked my way across the front of the grapevines and then along the space between the grapevines and hedge.

Tomorrow morning I will clean up behind the hedge and tackle another area. Or maybe the morning after. Eventually the job will get done, and my wildlife garden will be rid of rampant briars, inappropriate shrubs, and invasive groundcover. I will spread cardboard on the pathways and cover them with pine straw or shredded bark.

What will I do when I finish the clean-up project, assuming I live long enough to accomplish this feat? First I will take an oath to never plant another thing in the wildlife garden unless I cannot live without it. I will follow up with a promise to inspect regularly so that weeds and vines do not creep out of the mulch and win the battle. Then I will find a place to sit, watch bees and butterflies hover and birds scratch the soil and perch in trees, and be thankful I am a gardener.

Happy Accidents

If my garden had a name, it would be Serendipity or the Garden of Happy Accidents because I am continually surprised by what happens there without any planning by me. In fact, surprises often happen in spite of me. Plants appear (or disappear). Colors combined without a thought turn out to be breathtaking vignettes.

New plants are installed where I can squeeze them in, and, more often than not, they are in the right place. Plants purchased in spite of budget-busting prices turn out to be duds, and skimpy plants bought on sale become stars of the garden.

I was startled a few days ago to discover a beautiful, pristine white ginger lily (*Hedychium*) in full bloom in my wild garden. It was exquisite, fully formed and fragrant, acting as if it were August instead of November. Its appearance was not shocking, since ginger lilies are indeed planted along the wild garden path. But its tropical lushness was so out of sync with the autumn golds and rusts of sweet shrub, lespedeza, and sassafras.

I experienced the same disorientation when, a few weeks later, I saw Encore azaleas in full bloom at a public botanical garden, also in November. The pink and magenta were jarring, especially since, unlike the white ginger lily, the azaleas looked tired, ready to fade into dormancy, sort of like an aging debutante who stays too long at the ball. Fall-blooming azaleas are big sellers, so I am sure some gardeners are delighted with spring flowers in autumn. I know all gardeners have their rights (though in this case, I think they are wrongs).

I feel the same way about hydrangeas in November, though I am willing to cut the bright blue or rosy blooms and use them in Thanksgiving arrangements. 'Endless Summer', 'Penny Mac', and a few other hydrangeas in my garden bloom until the first hard freeze, and I do not think they should. In the case of flowering shrubs, to everything there should be a season, and that is that.

A few years ago I was given seeds for the six-foot-tall annual, lion's ears (*Leonotis*), and was underimpressed. The seedheads form as a series of balls stationed at intervals on a spearlike stem. They are orange but not dramatically so.

But last fall I bought the perennial lion's tail or wilde dagga (*Leonotis leonurus*), which is a whole different story. These blooms are the color of orange peel and shaggy as a lion's mane. This shrubby, branching perennial has hairy, toothed leaves and a hankering for dry soil and full sun, though being a good sport, it will tolerate moisture and some shade. Since mine was planted late, it is only three feet tall, but I am hoping for six feet in a full season.

Wilde dagga is reportedly hardy in zones 8b through 11. The bad news is that my garden is in zone 8a. No one should be surprised that I intend to mulch the plant with a thick blanket of leaves and hope for the best. Just to be sure the best is likely to happen, I have already propagated a supply from cuttings.

Throughout August and September I was entertained by a five-foot-tall *Cassia corymbosa* in my butterfly garden. This is my favorite part of the garden (unless I am looking at a different section), and I frequently assure myself that if I ever have to reduce my garden, this crowded fifteen-by-fifteen-foot space would be sufficient.

C. corymbosa was started from seeds given to me by a friend who brought them from Germany and distributed them to friends, assuring us that the plants were not invasive. And what a surprise: they are not! The blooms are small, yellow, poppylike flowers, and every stem has its share. The seeds form in beanlike pods, and I have plenty for anyone in need of another butterfly magnet.

So smitten was I by *C. corymbosa*, I could not help myself when I saw *Cassia bicapsularis* in Charleston last fall, knowing full well this cassia was hardy in zones 9 through 11, not in our zone 8. My expectations were low, but good sense has never guided my passions. I moved the pot into the greenhouse when the first hard freeze threatened.

To say it survived is an understatement. I planted it in the butterfly garden in the spring, and it grew lustily through the summer, reaching a sprawling eight feet by July. The woody stems fell over, entwining themselves in surrounding plants and sprawling over a concrete birdbath. Someone should have told me to pinch this giant back until late summer.

Talk about an October surprise! Every branch terminates with clusters of butter-colored two-inch flowers. A common name for this cassia is "butterfly bush," but ignore that. We already have too many butterfly bushes. In mid-November it is still covered with blooms. I drag people into the backyard to see this miracle, and they beg for cuttings.

Like *C. corymbosa, C. bicapsularis* grows in part shade/part sun as well as full sun. Get this: *C. bicapsularis* is recommended for highway medians and parking lots in Florida, so it is fair to assume it is drought-tolerant and tough as nails, as well as free from insect pests or diseases. To think I did not know of its existence until last fall. . . .

Of course, I also did not know the love of my life existed until I saw him standing in the middle of my college dorm lobby waiting for another girl. Just goes to show how full of exciting surprises life and gardens are.

Revving Up the Gardening Engine

Normally, September is one of my most productive months, but this year I could not get going at my usual bustling pace. Too hot, too dry, too lazy.

I did propagate a few cuttings but could not stir myself to scatter seeds, divide plants, repot containers, and all the other tasks that have always given me pleasure. In my defense, I did spend nine of my September days in Spain, another two days recuperating, and many hours packing and repacking beforehand.

But here I am in the second week of October, revving up my energy level and ready to work. At least I am not cleaning closets or canning tomatoes. My accomplishments occur outdoors, in the morning and in touch with nature.

I sow part of a packet of mixed lettuce seeds over potting mix in a shallow, round plastic container. Once seedlings emerge, I give the plants diluted liquid fish emulsion (or other nitrogen source). I could plant these seeds in the ground, but I like being able to move my lettuce garden around to catch the sun or avoid a hard rain. I can also lift it onto my potting table to cut baby lettuce leaves at the soil line, leaving the roots to grow a second and third crop.

After starting a bowlful or two of lettuces, I sow spinach seeds, hoping to supply my demand without resorting to plastic bags filled with greens trucked across the country from California.

My goal is to grow my own or at least buy local produce whenever possible. Whatever food I grow will be fresher, more nutritious, and untainted by *E. coli* and other unpalatable microorganisms. Fewer trucks will batter our roads, and less gas will be expended. I realize I may not be doing my part for the global economy, but I am not sure I want to.

Of course, a gardener does not live by greens alone. I also toss into my mixed borders seeds of Queen Anne's lace, love-in-a-mist, and poppies. One year I tossed poppy seeds in the corner of our lot where I keep potted plants and other gardening necessities.

The day after Christmas we erected a pop-up greenhouse in that same corner, and over the winter, without any moisture, those poppies emerged from bone-dry soil, grew about three feet tall, and bloomed their hot pink heads off.

After sowing my crops, I work my way around the mixed borders. I leave woodies (shrubs and trees) untrimmed until late winter but cut back perennials without seedheads, which I leave for birds and winter interest.

I root cuttings of tender perennials such as Mexican bush sage, plectranthus, pineapple sage, and various salvias so that I will have a cost-free head start getting these plants into the garden next spring.

To propagate cuttings, you follow the same process as you do with softwood cuttings. Slice off stem segments about four inches long, being sure they are still green but firm. Stems should be cut just below a node (where roots will emerge), dipped into water, dipped into a rooting hormone, and stuck into moist (not soggy) medium.

The medium holds cuttings upright and provides space for roots to develop. I use coarse builders sand, but you can also use sterile potting mix, vermiculite, perlite, or combinations of any (or all) of these. Just do not use garden soil.

A four- to six-inch-deep plastic planter with good drainage is a perfect container for cuttings. If the medium stays soggy, cuttings will bite the dust, or, in this case, the mud. Cuttings should be inserted about an inch deep.

Tender perennials, whether potted or kept as cuttings, need protection from cold and direct sunlight. I keep mine on the shady side of my greenhouse, which I do not heat unless the temperature dips below thirty-two degrees. Sometimes, when it is nippy but not cold enough to turn on the electric heater, I cover plants with white nonwoven cloth you can find in catalogs or at feed and seed stores.

Before a hard frost, I move containers of rooted shrubs and perennials into a cold frame, which I close at night. If I did not have a cold frame, I would keep them in a protected place close to the house and throw an old comforter over them if a freeze threatened.

It may be hard to believe on an October day when the thermometer may be registering ninety degrees where I live, but winter is ahead, and we will soon be pining for spring.

Take Note: Plan Ahead

If your memory is like mine, whatever you're thinking now that your garden needs or needs more of, you'll have no hope of remembering it next spring or next month.

I make cryptic notes to myself in a large calendar, hoping I am providing myself with ample clues as to what needs ordering, moving, propagating, or repeating. The trick is figuring out on which page the note should be inscribed.

For instance, one of this summer's successes in my garden was a big fat red zinnia appropriately called 'Big Red' that I raised from a packet of seeds. Sadly, all but one of the seedlings expired, but the lone survivor is a lulu, well worth the $2 packet price.

After Christmas, I will recover from the festivities by sitting down with seed catalogs. When I start seeds in January and the following months, I will pay serious attention and hope for better luck with 'Big Red'. I would love a garden full of this guy.

Okay—here's the test: 'Big Red' is blooming in October and has been since June. I will order seeds in December, and the time to start zinnias is late March indoors or late April outdoors. Where should I write a note about 'Big Red' in my garden calendar?

If you said the December page, you get an A. It will do me no good to come across a note about planting 'Big Red' in March or picking blooms in July if I have not ordered seeds in December—or January or February.

Recently I walked around my garden with my calendar, open to the September page, and made a list of plants in bloom. I counted thirty, not including the bright purple berries on the beautyberry shrubs. No wonder I love my garden best in the fall. Can spring compare to this abundance? I think not.

Of course, I always want more of the best bloomers, both for myself and for friends. Early fall is late for propagating shrubs and many perennials, but, as long as the stems are green, most propagators I know cannot stop themselves. Need more *Sedum* 'Autumn Joy'? Spirea? Fatsia? Hydrangeas? Who doesn't?

Fill a plastic pot or planter with coarse builders sand, perlite, vermiculite, or a combination of all three, perhaps adding finely shredded pine bark or peat moss. I use builders sand and normally have good luck. Good luck is defined as at least 50 percent success. I might have greater success with a vapor mist setup, but 50 percent is sufficient for me.

Snip four- to six-inch cuttings of green but firm stems (bendable but slightly resistant), and strip off all but four to six leaves at the top. Cut the remaining leaves in half, crossways, and retrim each cutting below a node (the bump on the stem where leaves emerge). Dip the cutting into powdered or liquid rooting hormone available at a garden center.

Make a hole in the sand or whatever medium you are using with a chopstick or pencil or finger. Stick the cutting into the hole. Be sure the sand is packed around the cutting. That's it.

Another way to make more is to divide, either by digging up perennials and pulling them apart or by digging around them and pulling up rooted sideshoots.

That most obliging perennial, Becky daisy (*Leucanthemum* × *superbum* 'Becky'), can be propagated all three ways: cuttings, dividing, or sideshoots. Wait until she is through blooming, about mid-October, before digging her up and dividing. However, you can take cuttings or ease out sideshoots anytime.

But Becky is not my only favorite. No plant has given me more pleasure than my plain old Joe Pye weed (*Eupatorium maculatum* 'Gateway'), which is currently five feet tall and in its second flush of pink bloom.

Joe Pye weed thrives in sun or part shade, keeping its flowers until frost and its fluffy seedheads until spring. I propagate Joe Pye weed with cuttings, and each plant spreads outward, giving a gardener an impressive clump after two or three years.

Ruellia brittoniana appeared at a nearby botanical garden about five years ago. I had never seen it until then. Now it grows in my own sunniest borders, and I am happy to see it in most gardens I visit. Ruellia is four to five feet tall and has purple petunialike flowers, explaining its common name: wild petunia.

No need to propagate ruellia. If you want to put it somewhere else or give some to a friend, pull up a clump. In fact, you will have to do so, or it will take over the border.

Last spring I bought a dwarf *Ruellia brittoniana* that is six inches tall and has been content in shade all summer, though I think it, too, would prefer full sun. It does not spread the way the tall ruellia does. To increase the bounty, I think I will have to do stem cuttings.

Patrinia scabiosifolia is a joy that keeps on keeping on, from early summer into fall, with cheerful clusters of tiny yellow flowers. However, white patrinia does not begin to bloom until early fall. Unlike yellow patrinia, which is upright with coarse, green foliage, the white is languorous and the leaves are silky. You would never know they are related. Like Becky daisies, either patrinia can be propagated by stem cuttings, division, or sideshoots.

Artemisia lactiflora is one of those plants a gardener is tempted to rip out. It flops around, taking up much too much space. However, it has elongated, creamy white flower heads in spring and then again in late summer, perfect for filling up vases as well as gardens.

I should stake this unwieldy plant, but I hate to set an example for my other floppers, so I suspect I will live with it, as is, and let 'er flop. Artemisias can be propagated by stem cuttings, or you can (and should) divide them every few years.

Walk around your garden spaces, making notes about what to add and what to pull out. An efficient way to do this is to walk around looking only at perennials; then only at shrubs. Or observe your garden in blocks for a few minutes, making notes and drawings or photographs. I actually know gardeners who do this. I wish I were one of them.

In mid-fall, we are still a month or so away from a freeze. The rain we hope will come makes this the optimum time to plant perennials and shrubs . . . and to begin thinking of spring.

An Autumn Rainbow

Soon after becoming a gardener, I realized that even in the South, spring does not last nearly long enough for me to get my horticultural fill. I needed a more extended fix, so I began planting for a late summer and fall color extravaganza.

Last week I observed like-minded gardeners scurrying around a nursery, seeking pansies, violas, and snapdragons. Some sophisticates were buying red mustard, cabbages, kale, and Swiss chard. Smart choices, though if they had thought ahead, they could have started hundreds of plants for the price of a few seed packets. But that is another chapter.

The fall color that interests me most, however, adorns plants that stay in the garden year-round and then explode with color in the fall, no extra charge.

No shrub provides more for the money than fothergilla, which produces creamy white fragrant bottlebrush blooms early in spring. During the summer, fothergilla sits sedately on the sidelines and then, in the fall, it bursts into a riot of yellow, orange, and scarlet foliage.

The three fothergillas in my garden are all *Fothergilla major* 'Mt. Airy' and are six to eight feet tall. One grows in part sun/part shade and the others in full shade all summer. Free of pests and diseases, fothergilla is easy to grow and, I am told, easy to propagate from cuttings taken in summer. However, fothergilla suckers sufficiently to provide plants for me to share with friends or donate to plant sales.

Like fothergilla, Virginia sweetspire (*Itea virginica*) also has white bottlebrush blossoms in spring. Quietly green through the summer, in October the foliage begins to turn scarlet, burgundy, and russet and is still flaming red in mid-January. This color extravaganza is spectacular in a beige winter world.

Three iteas are in my mixed border, and all are *I. virginica* 'Henry Garnet', which grows to three or four feet. One was purchased, and the other two were suckers clipped from the mother plant. Itea is a drifter, but that is okay with me. I also have *I. virginica* 'Little Henry', which is more compact than 'Henry Garnet' but not the midget I expected. Itea thrives in sun or shade.

I know some gardeners turn up their noses at *Sassafras albidum*, but if I had to choose one plant for color, it would be plain old sassafras. By mid-October, sassafras turns all shades of gold, orange, red, and purple with the first nip in the air. In contrast with some trees and shrubs that turn color one day and drop their leaves the next, sassafras holds its leaves through November, and I appreciate its tenacity.

Not only is sassafras a colonizer, it pops up in surprising places, thanks to the birds, but for me, that is something extra to like about it. Sassafras is a vigorous grower that happens to know where it wants to grow, and usually I agree. When trees emerge on their own volition, I usually leave them in place. They can always be eliminated later if they outgrow the space.

The aptly named Virginia creeper also knows where it wants to grow and, if not pruned back, *Parthenocissus quinquefolia* can be a nuisance. However, when it climbs a tree or a shrub in the fall, it is breathtakingly red, and I find myself wishing I had more of it. If Virginia creeper grows in the sun, it has purple berries, a delight to wildlife in all forms, which explains its appearance in odd places.

Virginia creeper has five leaflets, unlike that other American native, poison ivy, which has three. Virginia creeper can be tough on shingles and rain gutters, so I was surprised to see it growing up the facades of elegant manors and town houses in England. Those British gardeners are a savvy lot, and I can only imagine how gorgeous all that creepiness is in fall.

I have two shrubs that are supposed to provide the ultimate in fall color: winged euonymous (*Euonymous alatus*) and red-veined enkthianthus. So far they have both disappointed, which just goes to show you cannot always trust the experts. The lesson I have learned from this disappointment is to purchase shrubs at the time of year when they should be their showiest. Just as we should buy (but not plant) crepe myrtles when they are in bloom, we should shop for fall color in the fall.

This is not to say that enkthianthus and winged euonymous are not showy—they just have never put on a show in my garden. So far. Perhaps they were mislabeled, or perhaps my garden does not get enough sun, or perhaps the soil is wrong. I have already announced loudly that if I do not see some red soon, their spaces will go to more obliging producers. I can be merciless when it comes to color in the garden.

Taking my own advice, I intend to own a Chinese pistache (*Pistacia chinensis*) before November is over, maybe before today is over. The narrow leaves of this tree are ten to twelve inches long with ten to twelve leaflets, sort of like a mimosa. The mature height is about thirty feet. The bark is gray and flakes off to expose peach-colored inner bark.

It is the fall foliage of the Chinese pistache, however, that takes one's breath away: brilliant orange and red, like a sugar maple. The only fault, as far as I can see, is that it does not produce pistachio nuts. Even gardeners cannot have everything.

Beyond our gardens, spectacular fall color is abundant in fields and woodlands, even for those of us who live in the flatlands. No grand plan or systematic arrangement—just a panorama of scarlet and gold and orange in stunning combinations, reminding us to appreciate the glory of this season and be grateful.

Some Sumptuous Shrubs

I do not think I have ever said "redolent" out loud in my life, but it was the word that popped into my head recently when I walked out to the backyard and took a whiff. The air was permeated by the sweet scent that can only mean tea olive time.

I have had a tea olive growing in almost full shade for twenty years and never think about it until I get the feeling I am sitting in a theater or in church next to a woman who has really gone overboard with perfume. My tea olive is a garden variety *Osmanthus fragrans* that was probably a pass-along. It blooms from September to April, off and on. That is a lot of aroma, and it sure is sweet. Sometimes it is more than I can bear.

So what did I do? I planted another one, of course. A newer, fancier tea olive called *Osmanthus fragrans* 'Fudingzhu', which I suspect is Japanese for "over the top." 'Fudingzhu' is much more floriferous than the species, so it is showier as well as smellier. I planted it next to the walkway that leads to the garden in back of our house. It sets just the right tone for a garden where too much never seems to be enough.

No one pays attention to the flowers producing this overpowering scent. They are tiny and white, shyly growing in clusters between the leaves and the stems. The exception is *O. fragrans* 'Aurantiacus', which has flowers the color of orange sherbet. Though we do not usually have to worry about tea olives, which are hardy to zero degrees, 'Aurantiacus' is even hardier than the species and blooms later.

I have seen tea olives recommended as screening plants or even for hedges. I am not sure about the wisdom of this choice. Keep in mind the overperfumed lady. Think of her multiplied by six or eight or a dozen. Phew.

Also keep in mind that tea olives can grow as large as twenty to thirty feet. It is not a good shrub to plant next to the house unless you can come to grips with the probability that you (or your heirs) will have to cut it down sometime in the future. But why not live for the moment? Plant your tea olive where it will give you and your nose the greatest pleasure. You deserve it.

I am more excited about beautyberries, myself. Talk about shyly flowering. No one except butterflies and bees notice *Callicarpa americana* when it is in flower, but once those pale blossoms become clusters of bright purple beads, the expression "Wow!" leaps to mind. The berries remain after the leaves fall, that is, until the birds start chowing down.

I have a *Callicarpa americana* in the back corner of our yard, a good place for it since it does not know when to stop and is reaching out for my husband's prize grapevine. Late in the winter I will try to control its size by cutting it to the ground and letting it start over. It flowers on new growth anyway.

In the front of my wild garden is what I think is Japanese beautyberry (*C. japonica*), which should get no taller than five feet. *C. americana* 'Lactea' is a white-berried beautybush for gardens more subtle than mine. Another possibility is Mexican beautyberry (*C. acuminata*), which has black berries. There is a callicarpa for every taste.

Mine is a garden where too much of a good thing is a good thing. For instance, I just made a purchase of an Issai beautyberry (*C. dichotoma* 'Issai'), a dwarf variety with violet berries about the size of seed pearls. It should grow no taller than three feet, and I have just the place for it in the mixed border.

Short or tall, black berried or purple, beautyberries are happy in well-drained woodland soil, but they thrive in boggy areas as well. Start with a beautyberry; add an anise, a wax myrtle, some sweet shrub . . . you will have a woodland bog to brag about.

One more accommodating shrub to consider is abelia, which seems to have been recently rediscovered by hybridizers who have turned the old-fashioned *Abelia* × *grandiflora* into cutting-edge cultivars. The new varieties are more compact, growing no taller than three to four feet, so they fit well into foundation plantings and mixed borders.

Not compact at all is Chinese abelia (*Abelia chinensis*), the showiest abelia of them all, with large heads of white flowers. After the flowers fade, conspicuous pink calyxes remain, so it looks as if the shrub has two kinds of flowers.

Last spring I purchased three 'Rose Creek' abelias, dwarf descendents of Chinese abelia. They have been blooming all summer, and the shrub has remained about two to three feet tall.

Bowing just a bit to age, I am making a conscious effort to get more flowering shrubs into my mixed border. Fortunately, hybridizers are making it easy for me. Compact forms of larger shrubs seem to be the wave of the horticultural future.

Prostrate crepe myrtles are already in the nurseries, and I hear a two-foot-tall loropetalum called 'Snow Muffin' is on the horizon. In a world where bigger always seems better, it is nice to know that good things still come in small packages.

Hydrangeas Ahead

Two gardening friends strolled with me through my coastal garden when they came upon a four-foot-tall shrub covered with rose-colored blooms, eight to ten inches in diameter. Impressive, if I say so myself.

"What's that?" one of them asked. I recognized the yearning in her voice.

"A lacecap hydrangea," I replied. Of course I added the question gardeners throughout the world welcome: "Would you like one?"

The hydrangea we were looking at is as old as our house we built on the coast more than thirty years ago. It is a survivor of hurricanes, tidal floods, and other weather events that have felled many a cedar tree, wax myrtle, and my entire garden over the years.

Those fluffy lacecap blooms of *Hydrangea macrophylla* belie the toughness of shrubs so much a part of the coastal landscape that some people believe they are native to the area, though they are not. Hydrangeas thrive almost anywhere through zone six, and new re-blooming hydrangeas are being developed for even colder climates.

H. macrophylla includes both mophead and lacecap varieties. My friends did not recognize the lacecap in my yard because it is much less common than the mophead, though equally hardy.

The color of either mopheads or lacecaps can be manipulated (unless they are white). Beach hydrangea blooms are normally pink because the sandy soil is alkaline. If it is blue you are after, however, add a soil-acidifying amendment or an organic commercial product recommended for azaleas and camellias.

I do not do much tampering with nature, so I wind up with a variety of blooms ranging from rich rose to true blue, depending on how the pine straw mulch is breaking down or where the shrub is located. I have a normally blue 'Penny Mac' hydrangea next to a brick pump-house in my home garden, and the flowers are definitely pink. The cement slab is leaching, making my normally acidic soil alkaline in that space.

I read recently that the history of the genus *Hydrangea* can be traced back seventy million years. That is some pedigree, and I have no idea how it was established. Perhaps pictures of hydrangea-like flowers were found on cave walls, or petrified hydrangea wood showed up in a plowed field.

I do know that hydrangeas are native to three continents: North America, Europe, and Asia, where many plants that thrive in our area continue to be discovered. In fact, macrophyllas (mopheads and lace-caps) are native to the temperate maritime climates of eastern Asia. The world is not as divided as we sometimes are led to believe.

The best time to plant hydrangeas is in the fall, giving them several months of cool weather and adequate moisture to develop roots before the heat of summer. The planting hole should be much wider than deep. Be sure to incorporate organic material into the surrounding soil. Hydrangeas have shallow roots that move outward, so mulch the entire area with shredded leaves, pine straw, pine bark, or hay, which will continue to break down, adding additional humus to the soil.

Some hydrangeas take more sun than others. I do not think any prefer full sun, though the tags and catalogs may say otherwise. The best positioning for hydrangeas is either dappled shade or morning sun and afternoon shade. I do, however, have hydrangeas growing in morning shade and afternoon sun, but they look pretty droopy toward the end of the day. So do I.

Hydrangea arborescens is an American native that surely belongs in every hydrangea collection. In my garden, *H. arborescens* 'Annabelle' thrives in varying locations. Since she blooms on *new* wood (wood formed during spring and summer), I cut the shrubs to the ground in late February to stimulate new stems.

There is no fiddling with color with 'Annabelle'. Her ball-shaped blooms, ten inches in diameter, are pristine white and dry to a pale green. The only problem with 'Annabelle' is that her blooms tend to become weighed down by heavy rain. This is a problem most gardeners can live with. There is always a quick solution: cut off the drooping blooms, give them a shake, and bring them indoors. Two or three make an impressive bouquet.

My favorite hydrangea is *H. paniculata*, or Pee Gees, which have, instead of round or flat blooms, elongated panicle-shaped blossoms.

H. paniculata 'Grandiflora' opens pink and gradually turns white. 'Tardiva' and 'Limelight', two other paniculata cultivars, obligingly bloom (on new wood) late in summer when most hydrangeas have faded to green.

Like paniculatas, oak-leaved hydrangeas (*H. quercifolia*) produce panicle-shaped creamy white flowers. These are the least sun-tolerant hydrangeas and look best at the edges of woodland areas where the soil stays damp. An added benefit of quercifolia is their vivid fall color when leaves turn purple-red and remain attached to the plant for a long time.

Reblooming hydrangeas (such as 'Endless Summer', 'Penny Mac', and 'Dooley') bloom on old *and* new wood. This not only provides a long blooming season, but if the first buds are damaged by a late spring freeze, all is not lost.

I think of autumn not as the end of the gardening season but the beginning: a time to plan and to plant. I cannot think of a better harbinger of next spring than a hydrangea that will be covered with lacecaps . . . or panicles . . . or mopheads of blue . . . or pink . . . or white. So many choices, so much to look forward to. No wonder gardeners are such happy people.

Dry Shade, Oh, That Dry Shade

Other than beach sand and brackish swamp, no soil condition strikes as much befuddlement in a gardener's brain as dry shade.

Shade usually results from a single large tree or ceiling of understory trees that filter or eliminate sunlight. Because we have chosen not to cut down treasured old hickories that grew on our property long before we arrived, dry shade abounds in our yard, and I have made peace with it. I would not trade one hickory or oak tree for the lushest grass in my neighborhood, which, incidentally, has been practically clear-cut in order to produce one useless, high-maintenance lawn after another.

Dry shade is a difficult area in which to garden, not because it lacks sunlight but because the trees that create that shade suck all the water out of the soil, leaving little moisture for perennials, shrubs, and bulbs.

Not much to do about the shade other than cut down trees, but for me, that is not an option. I prefer to focus on providing moisture to plants growing in attractive mixed borders under the trees. Changing the texture and tilth of the soil beneath those trees is a miracle any gardener can perform.

If weeds are growing under the trees, place thick layers of newspaper over them. Do not till, and do not even think of using herbicides. You do not need them for this operation. On top of the newspapers, dump as much mulch as you can accumulate: aged compost, shredded bark, hay, leaves, pine straw, whatever is plentiful. Again, do not bother with tilling or digging. Earthworms will do the job for you.

What you are doing is accelerating the process of creating a forest floor, that soft, slightly musty-smelling soil cushion that delights us during woodland walks. This layer of soil-in-the-making captures and holds moisture for plants that may survive in dry shade but will thrive in organic material you provide. This is how a forest works. No one rakes. No one tills or double-digs.

Next to my house is a huge evergreen magnolia tree that began life forty-five years ago in our yard as a one-foot-tall potted plant picked up at a yard sale. Now much too large for our modest abode and planted too close to both the driveway and house, this magnolia gets no moisture other than whatever nature provides. It has thrived because its root system absorbs any rain that falls, leaving the variegated vinca groundcover to get along as well as it can. Magnolias have tough root systems and no mercy.

I chose vinca major as a groundcover because I observed it growing lustily underneath a beachhouse and decided that a groundcover growing in sand and solid shade could probably survive beneath a magnolia tree. The vinca has thrived for forty years, reaching out to surrounding areas the way vinca does. This year, without warning, the entire mass shriveled up and died.

I tell this story not to discourage anyone from growing vinca in ultra-dry shade. It has done its job well, and I suspect it is worn out. It happens to us all, especially if we are dying of thirst. I will let this brave patch dwindle, fluff up the soil a bit, and then plant lamium, creeping raspberry, or some other quick-growing groundcover and see how it goes. Or I may just let the leaves fall and provide their own groundcover.

Once your soil has been improved, consider limbing up shade-producing trees to allow sunlight to filter through, especially trees that are not deciduous.

The most important step in living with dry shade is selecting plants that will not only survive but thrive in the environment. Autumn is an excellent time to plant dry shade areas because roots will have ample time (and moisture) to adjust before everyone's toughest season: summer.

I was thrilled to discover that some of my favorite plants are happiest in dry shade. I deliberately moved hardy cyclamen, autumn crocuses (*Colchicum* spp.), and daffodils out of irrigated areas into dry shade, where they multiply lustily and will not rot. Wispy barrenworts (*Epimedium*) spread enthusiastically, and so do columbines, heucheras, corydalis, and hellebores. Japanese painted fern, Christmas fern, and male fern add texture and tropical oomph.

A favorite shrub of mine, *Fatsia japonica*, is happiest in dry shade, and so is butcher's broom (*Ruscus aculeatus*). I have learned to love leatherleaf mahonia (*Mahonia bealei*), whose butter-yellow flowers light up the shade in winter, as do the yellow-splotched leaves of Japanese aucuba.

A little encouragement makes life in dry shade easier to handle. When planting something new, water well and keep the soil moist until new growth and a look of contentment appear. Once your dry shade is blessed with a good steady rain, decrease irrigating and let dry shade plants show how tough they are.

When shopping for plants, read the labels carefully. Many nurseries separate shade and sun worshippers, but you need to be sure plants meant for your dry shade areas do not require moist conditions. Otherwise, they will not be happy, and neither will you after blowing your budget on plants that will die a miserable death.

One thing we gardeners discover is that there is a solution to almost every gardening problem and finding it is half the fun.

Top Tens

Most of us have played the game of deciding the person or persons we would want for company if we were stranded on a deserted island. What three books would we want with us? Or, in the case of an overcrowded lifeboat, who would we toss overboard?

Gardeners play another game. If we could have only ten plants or twenty, which would we choose? I just read a horticulture newsletter in which one author selected ten perennials that best withstand summer heat; another author selected the best fifteen plants for his garden; and a third article listed the ten best container plants.

This is what interested me most. Gardening choices are so personal. I would not have chosen a single plant those three authors selected. I know this is true because, for obvious reasons, I often ponder the need to downsize, to trade my acre of yard for a much smaller space with a limited number of plants.

I suppose what I need is a walled garden, one I am unable to climb over to plant just one more specimen I cannot bear to garden without. If I can have just ten or twenty or a hundred in that walled garden, which would they be?

I would not have a blade of grass in front or back. That goes without saying. I would need at least one large deciduous tree in back and, if I have to move, I want the street I live on to be a tunnel of overhanging trees. My borders must get morning sun and afternoon shade, and the soil will be sandy loam.

I want a water garden. Not too big. Nothing fancy. No fish. Just the sound of moving water, attractive grasses and tropical-looking plants, rocks for wildlife and dogs to perch on, and comfortable chairs where we can sit and think how good life is.

The perennials in the sunny garden would include butterfly weed (*Asclepias tuberosa*), coneflowers (*Echinacea*), Joe Pye weed, Becky daisies, native single chrysanthemums, and rudbeckia. Mexican bush sage and other salvias would have pride of place.

Beneath that large deciduous tree I would scatter at least a hundred cyclamen tubers and several hundred daffodils. The cyclamen blooms in fall and early winter, and daffodils appear from late winter into mid-spring. I want shade-tolerant, fall-blooming Japanese anemones, evergreen holly ferns, plenty of columbine (*Aquilegia*), and bright yellow woods poppies (*Stylophorum diphyllum*) to announce spring's imminent arrival.

A wheelbarrow-width pathway must amble through the garden, inviting and surprising. Birdbaths and feeders will be placed in strategic places, and rocks would serve as sculptures. Fuzzy gray lamb's ears (*Stachys byzantina*) will edge the borders, and dwarf pennyroyal must grow between pathway stones. In a small garden, every space is an opportunity.

Fatsia, the evergreen shrub that looks like an overgrown houseplant, will punctuate shady places, and so will yellow-splotched aucuba. Virginia sweetspire (*Itea virginica*) will provide bottlebrush blooms in spring and fiery red fall color. So will fothergilla.

I cannot imagine gardening without hydrangeas, but in such a small garden I would limit myself to *H. arborescens* 'Annabelle', *H. paniculata* 'Limelight' and 'Tardiva', and a reblooming blue, *H. macrophylla* 'Endless Summer' perhaps.

Rebloomers flower on last summer's growth and later in the summer on stems formed the current year. I cut back stems after they bloom in early spring to stimulate new growth, which will be old growth next spring. Too confusing? Just remember the Rule of Green Thumb: prune after bloom. Remember this, too: in late February or early March, cut to the ground hydrangeas that bloom on new wood.

I would plant viburnums for flowers and scent. I am partial to *Viburnum tinus* 'Spring Bouquet' because it blooms in winter when not much else is going on. Viburnums that take up too much room would be trimmed up as trees, opening up space below for planting and adding another dimension to the mix.

Of course, there are another dozen shrubs and perennials I would include, even if I had to keep them in pots and move them into the garden when they are their showiest.

The point is that even in limited space, we can create a satisfying, lush garden by planting plants closely, layering groundcovers, short and mid-sized perennials, and adding height with shrubs trimmed as trees. Give yourself something to see in front of your feet, at eye level, and skyward.

Just because a garden is small does not mean the gardener cannot think big and wide and tall and varied. We tend to think too moderately, and as a result, we shortchange ourselves on the pleasures we deserve. Wherever you look, there should be something to tug at your senses.

A garden is not a matter of space. It is a matter of pleasing yourself with plants that speak to you. Fill your garden with color and texture and mass and, most of all, with memories of people who have given you plants and shared your passion.

Expansion Plans

September and October are two of my most productive months. I divide, I propagate from cuttings, I start seeds . . . and, gritting my teeth, I discard plants that have disappointed. Life is too short to give time and space to flora that does not thrill—especially when garden centers are full of new treasures.

After starting lettuces and greens, such as mustard, chard, and kale, from seeds, I begin working my way around the mixed borders. While I leave woodies (shrubs and trees) untrimmed until late winter, I occasionally cut back perennials that do not have seedheads.

Winter interest is whatever thrives during January and February or dies a graceful death leaving feathery plumes, seedheads, or pods. It is a taste gardeners cultivate so that they have something to admire between December and March.

I root cuttings of tender perennials such as Mexican bush sage, plectranthus, pineapple sage, and other salvias so that I will have a cost-free head start getting these plants into the garden next spring.

Before we get our first hard frost, I move containers of rooted shrubs and perennials into a cold frame, which I close on frosty nights. If I did not have a cold frame, I would keep the plants in a protected place close to the house and throw an old comforter over them if a freeze threatened.

Unlike cuttings, which may require two or more seasons to reach garden readiness, dividing gets instant results. From one fulsome plant, a wily gardener can usually garner at least two and sometimes as many as a dozen offspring. Dig or ease out of the ground a multistemmed plant, such as ajuga, daylilies, heuchera, asters, chrysanthemums, and swamp sunflowers. Wash the soil from the root system so that you can take a good look.

If the plant has multiple clumps with distinguishable small plants, each having its own roots, pull the mass apart. Then pull some more, and then some more, until you have as many little plants as you can separate. Discard the mother plant and prepare to pamper the babies a bit.

Pot up each plant in compost-enriched potting mix, water well, and put the pots in dappled shade until the plants look perky and put out new growth. After a week or two, replant some of the divisions, share with friends, or donate some to a plant sale.

If the plant has a single stem and root ball, you cannot divide it. Since you have dug up the plant, take this opportunity to amend the soil with compost, lime, and nutrients. Put the plant back in place, water it, and you have done it no harm. In fact, you have fluffed up the soil and fed it, so the plant will probably be even happier.

If the plant has a long taproot, such as butterfly weed or baptisia, do not dig it up. Start plants from cuttings or seeds, or treat yourself to new plants. With all this seed starting, rooting, and dividing, you have saved plenty of money and deserve some treats.

Speaking of money saved, watch for sales at the garden centers. Retailers do not have the patience or labor force to divide, pot up, groom, and propagate, and so at the end of the season, they are ready to move plants out. Look for specimens that need separating or have plenty of cutting material. Do the work now, or wait until spring—but increase your stock at sale prices and you will be ready to grow.

Fragrance, Wherefore Art Thou?

With regret I have noticed that my sense of smell is no longer what it used to be. I cannot complain since my sight and hearing are intact, but I regret missing those subtle scents that add another dimension to our garden experiences. I know they are out there, floating in the air, but unless I move in close, my nose fails to pick up the haunting aromas of banana shrub, wisteria, roses, and ginger lilies.

I miss these scents and many others. No wonder. Fragrance does so much more than enhance our pleasure. It reduces anxiety and improves physical as well as mental performance. Books about aromatherapy line the shelves, and shops are full of candles and other products promising to promote well-being through scent.

I recently picked up a leaflet prepared by F. Brian Smith, an extension agent in Charleston, South Carolina, which means he gets to enjoy a lot of wonderful smells unless his nose has been seriously impaired by *eau de paper mill*, an occasional curse of that otherwise charming city.

Smith refers to a study at Sloane-Kettering Cancer Center that utilized fragrance to alleviate anxiety felt by MRI patients. Patients who got substantial whiffs of "a vanillalike scent" reported 63 percent less anxiety than those who breathed nothing but air.

He also refers to research at Wheeling Jesuit University that found athletes treated to peppermint felt higher levels of vigor and less fatigue. A third study mentioned by Smith was research at Cornell University that concluded "positive odors" can facilitate creative problem solving and other mental activities.

So all this aromotherapy theory has scientific basis, but why should we gardeners be surprised? Personal experience informs us that aromas evoke specific memories of people and places. I never smell baking bread without thinking of the mother of a high school friend who baked her family's bread three times a week. Their house smelled comforting . . . the way home should be.

Smith ranks fragrance strength by using *Daphne odora* and fragrant tea olive as the reference points of ultimate scent. He gives them both a ten. Other tens are citrus, summersweet (*Clethra alnifolia*), confederate jasmine (*Trachelospermum jasminoides*), *Wisteria sinensis* 'Pride of Augusta', and night-blooming ceris. Gardenias get a nine, moonvine and southern magnolia get eights, and winter honeysuckle a seven.

Smith also gives advice on keeping fragrance going full tilt all year long. According to him, we should be enjoying tea olives, ginger lilies, and eleagnus now, in the fall. I have no trouble catching the scents of tea olives and eleagnus. With ginger lilies I need to put my nose right into the bloom and breathe deeply, not a difficult task at all, especially considering the reward.

Since October and November are optimum months for shrub planting, I have some fragrant suggestions not planted nearly enough in my opinion.

Sweet shrub (*Calycanthus floridus*) is a native with glossy, rounded leaves and early-summer blooms with a fruity fragrance, like strawberries. But the blooms are not all that smell; the bark, leaves, and roots are scented as well. Sweet shrub (which is also called Carolina allspice) is a thicket shrub. In other words, it is stoloniferous and apt to pop up ten feet away from the mother plant.

I know this from personal experience and have done much impolite muttering about this habit. I pull up shoots that wander far and, if not for the scent, I would pull up the entire bush.

Chinese fringe tree (*Chionanthus retusus*) and the native fringe tree, Grancy graybeard (*C. virginicus*), are lightly fragrant and fabulous bloomers. The branches of Chinese fringe tree are more upright than those of Grancy graybeard. Either can be grown as a large shrub or limbed up as a medium tree of twelve to twenty feet. I have had one of each for about three years and neither has bloomed nor grown much, but I am looking forward to traffic-stopping displays in years to come. I am a patient woman.

Rice paper plant (*Edgeworthia chrysantha*) blooms in late winter and grows best in light shade. Like sweet shrub, rice paper plant has a reputation for suckering, so be warned. It grows to three or four feet in height, and in February, when we are most in need of horticultural excitement, edgeworthia bursts forth with creamy yellow flowers that look like large daphnes and smell a little like narcissus.

Skinner's banana shrub (*Michelia skinneri*) is an improvement of the old-timey *M. figo*, which is probably what you have if your banana shrub has been around awhile. Skinner's banana shrub has more abundant creamy-yellow flowers and is more fragrant than figo. An even newer michelia is *M. maudiae*, which has four- to six-inch fragrant ivory white flowers and, I am told, grows happily in full sun.

All the michelias are magnolia relatives and can be grown as large shrubs or trimmed as trees. I frequently shape large evergreen shrubs as trees so that other plants, such as bulbs or ferns, can be grown beneath. I am always in favor of diversity.

I am also always in favor of getting the most for my plant money. If a shrub is not only beautiful but offers fragrance as a bonus, it is my kind of plant and belongs in my garden.

I plan to breathe deeply, nose to bloom, and think aromatherapeutically. I can already feel anxiety slip away as my brain and body regroup for action.

Covering Ground

In spite of the rumors, I do not hate grass. I am as impressed as anyone else by lush green lawns rolling across the terrain, especially when they are populated by flocks of nibbling sheep. What puzzles me is the extraordinary effort people exert to maintain a struggling lawn in places where something else would thrive with ease.

I am delighted by the increasing number of savvy gardeners in search of grass substitutes or groundcovers. Though we may think of groundcovers as low growing and unexciting, the term includes a broad and enticing spectrum of plants. In certain situations, four-foot junipers or six-foot grasses might serve as a groundcover. The defining criterion is the ability to literally "cover the ground," preferably quickly and thickly.

Groundcovers provide necessary cover for small mammals, birds, lizards, insects, toads, and other critters. Grass does not provide cover unless, of course, it remains unmown.

Lack of hiding spaces for snakes suited my daughter-in-law just fine until I told her the old wives' tale that mint planted around the house keeps snakes away. I do not know if this is absolutely true about repelling snakes, but mints cover ground quickly, are useful for tea and juleps, and have delicious scents. I suggested spearmint or apple mint or, for enthusiastic growth and dense cover, chocolate mint.

For toughest spots, I am partial to creeping raspberry (*Rubus calcycinoides*). If this plant has a fault, it is its enthusiastic growth, hardly a sin for a groundcover. It is impervious to any abuse I have inflicted and works effectively on steep slopes to bind the soil. The brown, slightly hairy stems put down roots wherever they touch soil, so once creeping raspberry gets going, each plant covers a three-foot area quickly.

The textured leathery lobed foliage is dark green, turning reddish in the fall and winter. Its full height is four to six inches. The flowers (and drupes) are forgettable. Happiest in moist, humusy loam but tolerant of poorer soils, creeping raspberry thrives in sun to part or even full shade.

When a friend needed to stabilize a slope that tended to slide south in heavy rain, I thought immediately of creeping raspberry. A taller but equally tough plant I suggested to him was northern sea oats (*Chasmanthium latifolium*), though, unlike creeping raspberry, they are two feet tall and spread as a clump and also by seed, so they are apt to come up in surprising places.

When another friend asked about a plant to soften a stone walkway, I recommended dwarf pennyroyal. No more than an inch tall, dwarf pennyroyal (*Mentha pulegium*) used to creep out into the lawn in the center of my mixed border, squeezing out grass as it expanded. I loved this plant, which we easily mowed over when manicuring the patch of lawn.

I cannot remember why I decided to replace the lawn with stone pavers, a project in the works for over a year. Instead of having a dwarf pennyroyal lawn, I will eventually have pavers with spaces for pennyroyal between the stones.

Dwarf pennyroyal leaves are less than a half-inch in length, bright green in color, and minty in aroma. Rumored to repel mosquitoes (as well as snakes), this herb is welcome to take over the grass which, as far as I can tell, is good for nothing. Pennyroyal prefers shade, but in my garden it grows lustily in both sun and shade.

Dwarf mondo grass (*Ophiopogon japonicus*) grows to a height of six to eight inches and is a fast spreader that forms a mat quickly. Dwarf mondo grass (and regular mondo grass) does best in partial to full shade, making it an ideal grass substitute under trees and shrubs where, no matter how hopeful the homeowner is for a lush lawn, grass is not going to grow successfully.

Not to be confused with *Liriope muscari* or monkey grass, dwarf mondo grass is available in variegated and almost-black forms as well as dark green. Shorter cultivars are *O. japonicus* 'Nippon', 'Gyoko', and 'Kioto', making me think there is a growing market for something that looks like fluffy grass but grows under trees and in other shady areas.

Beware of groundcovers bent on taking over your garden . . . or the world. My biggest groundcover nightmare—perhaps my biggest gardening mistake—is a cute little plant I spotted at my favorite botanical garden more than ten years ago. The leaves are the size of a quarter and gray-green with cream-colored variation. So cute. So tempting.

I pulled up a snippet that had taken root between pavers. Not outright theft, but I wish I had not done it, a fact I am reminded of everytime I am on my knees pulling out *Glechoma hederacea*, commonly called "runaway robin," a beast with creeping stems that take root at every node. A single stolon can be seven feet long.

The moral of the story is to be careful what you plant, especially if you find it growing lustily in hostile conditions (pavement, for instance), definitely a clue that it is one tough plant.

Though not the nuisance glechoma has proven to be, lamium, vincas, and chameleon plant (*Houttuynia cordata*) also cover the ground with vigor and more enthusiasm than you might welcome.

In my garden, groundcovers get no insecticides, fungicides, or herbicides, but neither does the lawn or any other growing thing. Unlike grass, many groundcovers grow in shade. They need no mowing and are infinitely varied, unlike grass, which requires many hours and much sweat to groom to the uniformity of astroturf.

Tender Loving Care

Carrying tender perennials through the winter is not something I usually do. It seems a lot of bother taking cuttings or digging up plants, potting them, and being sure they do not freeze over the winter months. I do have a greenhouse, but until recently, I did not use it until late February or early March, when flats of seedlings number more than my laundry room can hold.

My life has become more complicated, however, by four or five plants that have entered my garden and are well worth protecting. A greenhouse helps, but a sunny porch will do even better since you do not have to trudge across the yard at midnight when the weatherman announces an unanticipated freeze.

I leave a heater in my greenhouse, ready to turn on if the need arises. I also have several old quilted bedspreads, ideal for protecting plants, both in the greenhouse and in the yard. I check out rummage sales and thrift shops for used comforters. On an icy night, a gardener never has too many, and some tender plants are definitely worth the effort.

The only fault of *Orthosiphon stamineus*, other than its unpronounceable name, is that it is hardy up to zone 9, and my garden sits smack dab in the middle of zone 8. In other words, it needs protection on winter's coldest nights.

The common name for *O. stamineus* is cat's whiskers and when you see it, you will know why. The tropical-looking white or lavender blooms have long stamens that look like a well-groomed cat's whiskers. Not just a few whiskers, but a long spike full of flowers and whiskery stamens.

A friend gave me a plant last fall and I treated it like one of the family until spring, when I put it into my sunniest garden space. Cat's whiskers actually belongs to the mint family but, to my regret, does not spread itself in mint fashion. It grows into a lank shrublike form about two and a half feet tall, and its stems (but not roots) wander outward, drifting into other plants' territories with those whiskery flower spikes.

Fortunately, cat's whiskers propagates easily (after all, it is a mint relative), so in the fall I take six-inch cuttings, strip off all but the top four to six leaves, and stick them into the plastic planter I use for propagating. Cat's whiskers have seeds, but I have never been able to germinate them successfully. The cutting container stays in the greenhouse until spring.

Here is some thought-provoking information: *O. stamineus* is the source of Java tea, used to help pass kidney stones. You may want to keep a cat's whiskers plant around for that purpose alone.

Another plant worth pampering is *Cuphea llavea* 'Bat Face', which produces nonstop dark purple-faced blooms with day-glo orange ears. Too bizarre? Forget "bat face" and think "mouse ears" or "Mickey Mouse plant," two interchangeable common names.

Often grown as a container plant, my mouse ears go into the ground. I take cuttings in fall and, just as I do with cat's whiskers, I get them rooted and potted for wintering over.

Fortunately, equally attractive cupheas do not need such tender loving care. The best known is *Cuphea ignea*, with two common names: firecracker or cigar plant. This happy plant covers itself with orange-red flowers, naturally adored by hummingbirds.

Unlike the somewhat floppy mouse ears, *C. ignea* has a neat, rounded form, about twelve inches tall and eighteen inches wide, perfect for front-of-the-border pizzazz. Because all winters, even all zone 8 winters, are not equal, I leave *C. ignea* in the ground, but I also carry over a few plants in the greenhouse to be sure the fireworks do not fizzle.

Make a note to yourself to purchase a *C. micropetala* next spring. This cuphea is covered with blooms that look like candy corn and reaches three to five feet in height. Best of all, it is hardy in zone 7. Sounds too good to be true, but I'm a believer.

I might get through summer without firecrackers, but never without alternanthera. Forget flowers. It is the foliage that makes this plant one of life's essentials.

A variety of alternantheras are available, and more appear in garden centers each year. However, the one that makes my heart leap is *Alternanthera dentata* 'Rubiginosa'. Wine-colored stems and deep burgundy leaves drift in and out of surrounding plants, adding zing wherever it wanders. It is one of those plants that, while not spectacular in its own right, makes everything else (including the gardener) look better.

Easily propagated from stem cuttings, alternanthera is the iffiest of tender plants to carry over. I pot up some, but I also keep a jar of cuttings in my laundry room where they root like philodendron and give me something to start with in the spring.

Plectranthus is one more plant I manage to get through the winter by potting up cuttings or rooting stems in water. Like cat's whiskers, plectranthus is a member of the mint family, and it spreads, but not invasively. Most plectranthus foliage is soft and woolly, but some is glossy and sleek, and some is coarse textured. Most plectranthus do not bloom, but a few do. This is an incredibly varied genus, including everything from *Plectranthus sp.*, just six inches tall and a fabulous groundcover, to *P. fruticosus* 'Purple Martin', which reaches thirty inches and has salvialike blooms in the fall.

Can't get enough coleus? I feel the same way, and this is how I assuage my greed without breaking the bank. In the spring, I shop with several gardening friends. We each get a good-sized coleus or two or three. We snip enough four- to six-inch cuttings to share, and we each go home with a baggie full of potential coleus plants as well as the plants we purchased. Like a cookie exchange, but no calories and no baking.

Queen of the Climbers

My experience with clematis is shamefully limited. The only one I grow with success is sweet autumn clematis (*Clematis paniculata*). I should say it grows itself, across an unused clothesline in my shady island bed and over a recently installed fence. I have tried to grow it up a pine tree without results, but I have seen it done and know I could do it, too, with a little more effort.

My favorite sweet autumn clematis is not in my yard but on a friend's mailbox. Whenever I pass her yard in late summer and see that mass of white blooms and think how delicious it must smell, I am reminded of my friend's mother-in-law referring to it disdainfully as a weed.

A neighbor of ours at the beach called my Queen Anne's lace a weed. In the past week, I have heard wild blue ageratum referred to as a weed. Enthusiastic procreation seems to be the distinguishing criterion for the state of weediness. I say more power to them. Bring on the lupine, goldenrod, and jessamines.

But back to the kind of clematis that is called queen of the climbers. These fancy cultivars also grow happily up and over mailboxes. Their tendrils take them up trellises, fences, and arbors, and their meandering habit will carry them through an evergreen shrub, giving it a surprising touch of color whenever the clematis blooms.

How delighted a boring holly or ligustrum must be to discover itself covered with white or blue or pink clematis blooms for a couple of weeks. Like hydrangeas, clematis vines need to be pruned at varied times, depending upon whether the blooms appear on old or new wood. If your clematis bloomed early in the spring, it blooms on old wood. The best time to have cut it two feet from the ground was immediately after it blossomed so it would generate wood for next year's blooms. If you did not do this, leave it alone and do better next spring. If you cut it back now in the fall, you will be bloomless next spring.

If your clematis bloomed in the summer, it blooms on new wood. You should cut it back in late winter at the same time you prune late-blooming hydrangeas, buddleia, and lantana. You want to generate plenty of new growth (and flower buds) during the spring.

Wouldn't you know it? Some clematises bloom on *both* old and new wood. The good news is that this means they are repeat bloomers that are at their most floriferous in late spring or early summer, but bloom again, off and on, on new shoots and old stems. Two favorites, *C.* 'Henryi' and *C.* 'Nelly Moser', are members of this puzzling group.

If you have a repeat bloomer, I suggest you prune it back in late winter like a new wood bloomer and prune some of the branches back after the first bloom as if it were an old wood bloomer.

How do you remember to do this correctly? You make a note in your calendar or journal. On the February page, remind yourself to prune all shrubs and vines that bloom on new wood.

As your old wood bloomers finish up, make a note to yourself when this happened so that you can compare flowering times from one year to the next. With your old-and-new-wood bloomers, make notes to yourself about when they bloomed so that you can think about them over the winter. I am shamefully hit and miss with my own record keeping, but it is a habit that I mean to develop.

My plain old sweet autumn clematis should be cut to the ground every year in early fall before seeds start falling everywhere, but not so early that I do not have time to admire the interesting seedpods.

I have two other clematises. One is a purple bloomer that I propagated from my neighbor's vine. The other is a *C. pitcheri* that forms yellow, bell-shaped blossoms. This one came as a freebie from a nursery when I inquired about a yellow clematis I had seen in England. An occasional free plant is a perk that garden writers with business cards can get. The yellow clematis did not bloom this year, but I have hopes for next year. Don't we all?

One reason gardeners do not grow as many clematises as we should is that they have the false reputation of being "difficult." While the pruning business is a bit puzzling, they are not fussy plants. Tradition has it that they like their bottoms in the shade and their tops in the sun, not difficult if you mulch.

Clematises thrive in good, humusy soil. Provide consistent moisture during the growing season, but not so much that the soil becomes waterlogged. Supposedly you should fertilize once a month (until fall) with a fertilizer that has high ratios of phosphorus and potassium. If my blooms were not abundant, I might consider doing so.

The most common clematis problems are stem rot and powdery mildew. For stem rot (or clematis wilt) the surest solution is to throw the plant into the burn pile. Buy a new one, the biggest plant you can find, and avoid breaking young stems. Some growers suggest planting clematis so that the top of the root ball is two or three inches below the soil surface to reduce the risk of stem rot.

To prevent powdery mildew, plant your clematis where it will get plenty of air circulation and full sun. If your intention is to grow your clematis up and over evergreen shrubs, be sure the clematis is planted in front of and a little away from the shrub.

One of my sons used to live in a neighborhood where every single homeowner grew the clematis of her choice on her mailbox. The daily walk became a treat for the neighbors instead of tedious exercise, which goes to show what good deeds gardeners often do for one another.

Add a Bunch, Subtract a Few

The trouble with most amateur landscapers is that we tend to be boring in our plant choices. Come to think of it, many pros are even worse.

We all have to get over the idea that planting a row of shrubs across the foundation is attractive or interesting. I know this is true because I have a boring row of foundation plants of my own.

I frequently drive down a street bordered by modest residences on lots of less than half an acre. They all have driveways leading from the street to carports attached to the houses. Most of the foundation plantings are single rows of the same shrub. Nothing ever happens in these landscapes. They remain static, colorless, and unentertaining.

However, several years ago I noticed the landscaping in front of one of these houses and found myself drawn to it.

The house faces east and, as I recall, has no trees in the front yard. I wish it did. But the homeowner has made use of annuals and perennials mixed in with shrubs. In the corner where the house juts forward is a clump of tall and sturdy elephant ears. Not only does this landscape change from season to season, it unfolds from week to week. I have the feeling that the homeowner has fun with this front garden and enjoys the varied textures, colors, and shapes of the plants.

Over the years, something has happened in the neighborhood. Other homeowners are sprucing up their front yards. None is like the yard next door, and I love that. A landscape design should not only adorn the house, it should express the personality and taste of each homeowner, or at least the homeowner who does the yard work. Like all gardens, it should be fun, easy to maintain, and personal.

Whether it is boring or interesting, a foundation planting that is primarily shrubs is the easiest garden to maintain. If yours has weeds, rake off the mulch and spread newspapers (at least eight layers thick) over the entire plot, fitting them around the trunks of plants you want to keep in the border. Add fertilizer or compost plus a good dose of dolomitic lime around the outside of the plants while the mulch is raked off. Water the plot well. Rake back the mulch, or replace it with fresh mulch.

My favorite mulch is coastal Bermuda hay, which I spread thickly over my mixed borders. I also use shredded leaves and pine straw. The hay is inexpensive, and the leaves and pine straw are free since they fall off our own trees. If I purchased mulch, I would opt for shredded pine bark because it is brown like dirt, not red like a bad hair color job.

Shredded pine bark also has antifungal qualities and adds humus to the soil as it decays. I do not remove mulch. I just keep adding to it. If I had a rose bed with black spot and Japanese beetles or a camellia bed with scale, I suppose I would remove the mulch and burn it every year.

Fortunately, I do not have this problem since my own garden is made up of mixed borders with diverse plants that are not disease prone. If a plant looks sickly and requires too much fussing over, it comes out and is replaced by a hardier specimen. Life is too short for coddling puny plants.

I had plans to remove my foundation plants from the front of our house and start over. I intended to subtract a row of hollies and the chartreuse dwarf spireas growing in front of them. This operation would require one of two solutions: removing huge root systems or cutting the shrubs to the ground and removing any foliage that reappears next spring. No one should be surprised that I consistently opt for the latter method.

When I told a friend about my plan to subtract, she said she planned to update her border by adding instead of subtracting. I was dumbstruck by the brilliance of her plan. I have always found adding more satisfying than subtracting in the garden as well as in the checkbook. I completely changed my approach to renovation.

I still need to subtract some hollies and spireas to make room, but by adding groups of small shrubs and replacing a few hollies with more interesting shrubs, I will achieve my goal of a mixed border, diverse in its colors and textures as a garden should be.

I will not only save labor and money, I will have a border that looks "finished" without waiting years for everything to catch up. I will have a garden that is fun to work in. The foliage of the shrubs (the "bones" of the border) will change with the seasons. Perennials, annuals, grasses, and ferns can be added as the whims of the gardener direct.

When I talk to groups about a mixed border, I begin with a fistful of plain green foliage such as boxwood, ligustrum, or holly. Then I add branches of plants with small leaves, ferny leaves, big bold leaves to see what happens when textures are combined. I add a branch from a conifer and a fatsia to make a foliar statement.

Then I add reds: burgundy loropetalum, barberry, ninebark, and smoke bush. Every artist knows that red makes greens pop. I subtract red and add golden euonymous, arborvitae, barberry, and spirea. Then, as a group, we opt for red or gold or a combination. All green is not an option if I am conducting the election.

No flowers. Just foliage with fabulous color year-round or at least three seasons. Then comes the fun part when the gardener stands back and admires the new bones of her garden. She can add winter vegetables, pansies, and snapdragons. For spring, she might add bulbs, and in summer, colorful colocasias (elephant ears), salvias, and lantana. Who is to stop her? She is an artist and the canvas is hers.

Ah, to Bed

As I walked around the garden a few days ago, after some bone-chilling nights, I mourned the passage of the last salvias. Before the frost, my collection of salvias (including my favorites, Mexican bush sage, 'Red Neck Girl', pineapple sage, 'Phyllis Fancy', and 'Frieda Dixon') looked as if they would never quit blooming. Today they are drooping shadows of their former selves.

The castor bean foliage is as limp as damp tissue, the coleus and plectranthus are mush, and the cannas and colocasias have morphed into blobs. Those six-foot-tall Mexican sunflowers have lost their orange glow. My favorite garden season has come to an abrupt end, and I have to turn my face and attitude toward the season ahead.

Putting a garden to bed for the winter will never be as much fun as waking it up in the spring, but it has its bright moments. We just have to seek out the pleasures.

I begin to work my way around the mixed borders that ramble over our acre lot, whacking back the most seriously flattened annuals and perennials. I always leave about ten inches of stem to alert me that a perennial owns a particular spot. Even with annuals, I leave roots in the ground so they become compost with no help from me.

Any plant that continues to have entertainment value I leave as is. Fall chrysanthemums still look perky, grasses are turning beige and curly, and the golden seedpods of August lilies are finally crisping up. When the edges begin to flare outward, the stalks are ready to cut for winter decorating and seed gathering.

For me, seed gathering is one of the highlights of late fall. I am fascinated by the ways seeds store themselves, and I always leave seedpods, capsules, and flowers on plants to mature as nature intends. The castor bean pouches, which look like thistles and grow together like clusters of bananas, are turning from burgundy to brown.

Mexican sunflowers and coneflowers store seeds in their flower heads. The flowers of hyacinth beans form bean pods, first purple and then beige.

Whatever kind of seeds you choose to save, wait until the pods are crisp and dry before removing them from the plant. Then bring them indoors, spread them over newspaper, and remove the seeds. If a bit of chaff remains, not to worry. Mother Nature deals with that issue. Leave them for a few more days of drying out, and then store the seeds in paper envelopes, pill bottles, plastic containers, or jars.

There is something innately satisfying in gathering seeds and, sometime later, sowing and germinating them. So resourceful, so engaging, so frugal. Like many gardening pleasures, seed gazing and gathering are addictive.

I clean up my garden the way I clean my house: in tolerable doses. I clear off the dining room table one day, sort papers another day, sweep the front porch occasionally.

In the garden, I whack off soggy plants one day, dig up and move plants another day, and cut back vines when I feel like it. No garden chore is mandatory, and none has to be done according to a timetable.

A gardening friend asked me recently whether she could root cuttings this time of the year. Of course she can. Her success rate will probably be diminished, even if she keeps the rooted cuttings in a warm location . . . but, as usual, what does she have to lose? I always stick alternanthera and coleus cuttings in a jar of water to overwinter in the laundry room. Sometimes roots appear, and sometimes the cuttings turn limp and give up the ghost, but it is always worth the try.

If stems on shrubs and perennials I want to propagate are still green and pliable, I cut the stems below a node, wet the bottom of the cut, dip it into rooting hormone, and then place it in coarse builders sand. I do the same with annuals, although they must be protected from cold temperatures in an enclosed porch, a warm room, or a greenhouse.

Evergreen plants that stay with a gardener year-round are referred to by designers as bones. Sculptural deciduous plants also provide interesting bones. In my garden, my favorite bones plants are a mix of deciduous and evergreen: daphnes, viburnums, holly ferns, English laurels, conifers, and pittosporum. The bare structures of curly willow, fothergilla, contorted mulberry, and a fig tree are especially striking . . . and I am fascinated by differences in bark, most obvious when foliage is absent.

Do not think of bones as boring. As I strolled around the yard welcoming winter, I realized the fatsia shrubs were decorated with knobby, creamy white seedheads. The gold-splotched aucubas lit up the darkest corner of the garden. Conifers were chartreuse or gold or blue-gray and lushly textured.

This is a good (though not mandatory) time of year to shake up your own garden bones and decide what plants you can add to keep your garden lush and satisfying, even when flowers fade. Take advantage of perfect planting weather and winter rains. Think in terms of texture, height, mass, and punchy colors.

As always, have fun with your garden, feed the birds, and count your blessings.

Winter

Even in winter, it is the surprises that make all the difference in a garden. We just have to look for them and, of course, plant them.

And Sow Forth

Starting plants from seed has to be one of the simplest and most satisfying endeavors in life. Put a seed in contact with soil and, given time, a seedling miraculously emerges. That is why we have trees, jungles, and weed patches.

Every year I start seeds of basil, tomatoes, zinnias, sunflowers, and other plants essential to my gardening happiness. I pore over seed catalogs from a half-dozen companies, perfect winter reading for those of us who come down with spring fever as soon as the Christmas tree is carried out the front door.

Because it is among my favorite flowers, I start seeds of columbine (*Aquilegia* 'McKana's Giant') every year. I probably already have twenty to thirty in my garden, but that is hardly enough when a gardener is in love. Though it is a hardy perennial, columbine sometimes disappears without notice, so I regard sowing seeds each year as a kind of insurance policy.

Usually I start seeds so that I can have plenty of plants without dipping too deeply into my garden budget. For instance, a single columbine plant costs around three dollars at a garden center. A packet of seeds is about the same price.

But sometimes saving money is not the main objective.

For example, I yearn for Costoluto Genovese tomatoes, described in a specialty catalog as "a unique and aromatic Italian main season tomato that is a classic component to the cuisine of the Piedmont region of Italy." I will not find Costoluto Genovese or its ilk at nearby garden centers, but I can buy twenty-five seeds (each a potential plant) for less than two dollars.

Last fall I saw a flock of birds working a dense patch of 'Purple Majesty' ornamental millet growing in the center of an oval bed of annuals. I was riveted by the sight and knew I had to replicate the magic in my own garden. I was delighted to buy a packet of fifteen 'Purple Majesty' seeds for around five dollars.

Purple from the ground up with strappy cornlike foliage and cattail spikes, 'Purple Majesty' stalks can be cut for dried arrangements, but not by me. My objective is birds swooping around the four- to five-foot stalks, nibbling at seeds and having what looks like a whale of a good time.

Last spring a friend sent me a packet of 'Empress of India' nasturtiums. She wondered whether these were the nasturtiums we had admired growing over shrubs in one of the gardens we visited together in England. I sure hope so. "Admired" is an understatement. We salivated.

'Empress of India' promises to be a scene stealer with crimson blossoms and blue-green foliage. I only need to decide which shrubs she will sprawl across. Forty-five seeds cost just over two dollars. A lot of sprawling for a pittance.

Since I am unlucky or unskilled at starting seeds outdoors, I germinate almost everything except lettuce and snowpeas indoors. After poking numerous holes in the bottom for drainage, I fill a mushroom box or similar container with plain vermiculite right up to the brim. Then I place the filled container in a pan of water, letting moisture seep through the vermiculite so it is wet but not soppy.

My goal is to spread seeds evenly across the moist vermiculite so seedlings do not come up in one or two clumps. Just like us, each seedling deserves its space.

But before I start spreading, I decide how many columbines or nasturtiums or tomatoes I want. If I choose not to germinate the whole packet, I fold the open end and seal with tape. Leftover seeds will germinate next year or the year after or, in some cases, ten years in the future.

I press seeds down gently so they have contact with the vermiculite. If seeds are large (like nasturtiums or hyacinth beans), I press them into the vermiculite. If they are medium-sized, I spread a light coating of vermiculite over them. If tiny (like columbine or parsley), I do not cover them at all.

I make myself read the packet directions to see whether the seeds require light to germinate. If so, I place them where they are exposed to daylight. If they require darkness, I cover containers with newspaper or cardboard. In either case, flats should stay in a warm location, and the vermiculite should remain consistently moist.

We have a wood stove, a relic of the eighties, and I place my flats under it. If the stove is not in use, I put flats on a warm pad or on top of a grow light my husband built about twenty years ago. Located in the laundry room, it looks like a two-shelf bookcase but has fluorescent tube lights looking down on each shelf. For no more than a day or two, I may cover the flats loosely with plastic to maintain moisture.

In three to five days, most seedlings emerge. The packet may tell you ten days or two weeks, but with almost all seeds I have germinated, the miracle occurred much more quickly than predicted.

My seedlings have never suffered from "damping off," the dread disease of germinating seedlings. I suspect I owe this good fortune to well-drained vermiculite and warmth, which hasten the process and get those little sprouts up before disaster strikes.

Once true leaves appear, I move seedlings to individual pots filled with soilless potting mix (not garden soil). I begin feeding with diluted liquid fertilizer such as fish emulsion, but unless you have a heated greenhouse, I suggest you keep your plants under a grow light or on a sunny windowsill until spring arrives.

Like so many gardening pleasures, experts sometimes make the germination process sound just short of rocket science. My advice is to think how Mother Nature proceeds and follow suit: drop seeds on a hospitable surface, keep them moist, and seedlings will emerge. It is a miracle to experience and savor.

A Gardener and Her Tools

In spite of being an excessive gardener who rarely sees a plant I do not want, I am a minimalist in almost every other way. I chose my furniture and decor forty-five years ago, and they have remained much the same ever since. My wardrobe is basic and basically black. The menu at our house is downright boring.

So I am puzzled by the number of garden tools and specialized accessories I see in magazines and wonder why anyone needs them. I look at cute potting sheds and ornate greenhouses and think how much housekeeping must be involved to keep them tidy, since everyone would want to see inside.

My own greenhouse, a plastic hoop structure, is hidden behind our garage, and that is a good thing. Though it has stood the test of time (including a bout with Hurricane Hugo) and serves my needs, it is hardly a thing of beauty.

It is furnished with five sturdy tables with wire shelving. The tables are bosom-high, and I wish my kitchen counters were as tall since my greenhouse tables require no stooping. I am convinced that backaches of most women are caused by slumping over countertops and sinks.

I heat my greenhouse with an inexpensive electric heater and keep the temperature just above freezing. When the temperature dips to the twenties, I turn on a propane heater as insurance. The fan at one end of the greenhouse is even more important than the heater. Plants need circulating air, especially when the interior temperature rises above 70. Think of your greenhouse as an oversized solar heater.

My irrigation system in the greenhouse is as low-tech as I can manage. I drag a hose into the shelter, spray water toward the ceiling, and let it shower down on the plants. Like rain.

The floor of my greenhouse is black plastic weed barrier that I would not think of using anywhere in my garden. In the greenhouse, it is effective in letting water drain out and suppressing weeds, though I do have a crop of apple mint popping up around the edges. If I had it to do over, I would have spread gravel over the weed barrier, but that should have been done before we covered the greenhouse.

Outside the greenhouse is my potting area: a fish-cleaning sink no longer used for that purpose and a picnic table where I keep a plastic tub of potting mix, ready to use whenever I find a seedling or rooted cutting or need to rescue a pot-bound plant.

I have a cold frame that I open and close manually. This is a handy storage place for potted plants and invaluable in early spring to protect seedlings and emerging tender plants. My husband built it years ago, using treated boards and a cover of corrugated fiberglass.

Those are the biggies, but equally important are pocket tools I carry into the garden, whether I am spending the morning there or just making my normal five-minute survey.

In my pocket are a pocketknife and bypass pruners. These pruners have a power gear that makes cutting easy on my aging hands. They are the most-used tool in my garden.

The same company makes power gear loppers that turn pruning into a Zen experience. I do not get a commission from the manufacturer, and other gardeners have equally fervent brand prejudices. The point is that with pruning equipment, go first class.

I have no brand preference when it comes to trowels and buy inexpensive ones I feel free to leave scattered around the garden. When I look for a trowel, it needs to be close by or I forget why I need it. Spraying tool handles with neon paint makes locating them a lot easier. Everyone knows this, though few of us can locate the spray can and the tool at the same time.

In the laundry room I have my seed-starting apparatus: a bookcase with fluorescent workshop lights attached under each shelf. I start seeds in vermiculite-filled mushroom boxes with drainage holes produced by an ice pick.

I propagate cuttings in plastic planting boxes with plenty of holes drilled into their bottoms. With propagation as well as seed starting, drainage is vital. These containers are placed outdoors in shady places where I know they will get adequate moisture.

I am asked more questions about mulching materials than anything else I write about. I use home-grown shredded leaves and pine straw. I also buy coastal Bermuda hay from a local farmer and have never had a problem with reseeding, assuring me I have purchased coastal Bermuda, a hybrid grass, and not straw or some other reseeding thug.

Because of continual mulching, I do not have weeds and rarely use fertilizer. Decaying hay and earthworms keep my soil friable and nutrient rich. I do not use insecticides or fungicides because I do not need them.

I have a large meandering garden on an acre lot, and not an inch has been tilled. I do not own a hoe or weeder. The rakes we have are used to gather pine straw. A shovel is required only for planting shrubs and trees.

These are the tools and resources that make my life easier, are multipurpose, and contribute to my pleasure and to my garden's success. Nothing is costly or destructive or harmful to the environment. And none of it needs dusting or gasoline. That is what I call simple but worthy abundance.

Hedging My Bets

After years of repeatedly spraying a hedge of redtips (*Photinia* × *fraseri*) with fungicide, clipping off denuded branches, and raking away debris, we decided life is too short. We could move or we could eliminate the hedge.

Since the attic had not been cleaned out for twenty years and we love our neighbors, we decided the hedge must go, not us. My husband relished the macho challenge of pulling each eight-foot shrub out by the roots with a winch attached to his pickup truck.

We yanked out one redtip, and our plan of attack changed. That first redtip was indeed out of the ground, but the impact on my mixed border in front of the hedge was enough to make a gardener weep. The agony of seeing that cavernous hole and the demolition of surrounding plants nurtured by me from infancy was more than I could bear.

The remaining redtips were sawed to ground level, the corpses hauled away. But then what? A suburban lot without a hedge or tall fence between neighbors is not an option.

We waited through spring and summer, nipping off redtip foliage that appeared, and that fall we went shopping for replacements. About one hundred of them.

We decided on Japanese privet (*Ligustrum japonicum*) as our hedge shrub. Not an inspired choice, perhaps, but Michael Dirr, author of the definitive *Manual of Woody Landscape Plants*, said the magic words: "actually thrives with neglect." A hedge is a hedge is a hedge, and all we were looking for was privacy, habitat for birds, and a bland background for my magnificent mixed border.

To its credit, Japanese privet has attractive glossy green foliage and creamy white blooms in spring, followed by blue-black drupes in fall.

Making a hedge is a matter of planting a shrub and then another shrub and another in a more-or-less straight line. My meticulous husband insisted that we establish a line far enough from our neighbor's boundary so there would be no question of property infringement. If the shrub of choice has an eight-foot spread, the center of each shrub must be at least four feet from that boundary line—five if your neighbor is cranky.

We established a line with a tape measure, two sticks, and a ball of string. As I recall, we started with the middle section of the hedge because that is where the mixed border is, and getting a background for this border was an urgent issue.

We planted each shrub, digging a hole at least twice the diameter of the pot in which it was growing. We separated the shrub from the pot and fluffed out the roots, cutting them with a knife if necessary so that they would grow outward, seeking nutrition and stability.

Setting a plant in the hole, we made sure it sat no deeper than it had in the pot. Then we backfilled with dirt we had removed when digging the hole. We watered each planted shrub well, being sure it was well settled and would not sink. Planting a shrub too deeply smothers feeder roots. Then we moved on to the next shrub until we became tired and bored and went inside.

By winter we had finished the hedge, keeping it watered if we hit a dry spell. We spread about a half-cup of lime on the surface around each shrub but did not add fertilizer until early spring. During the winter, we sought root development, not foliage growth.

I keep our side of the hedge trimmed to be sure sunlight reaches bottom limbs. Of course, the mixed border is too close to the hedge, so I trim off limbs that interfere with prized specimens. If I had planned efficiently, I would not have anything growing closer than six feet from the center of the hedge.

Not long ago, a friend asked about planting a double hedge between her property and a busy road. She, like me, seeks privacy, but what she really seeks is a buffer against street noise. A double hedge is a brilliant, environment-friendly solution.

I mentioned ligustrums, but my friend wants something different, something less run of the mill. Who can blame her?

I suggested *Podocarpus macrophyllus*, in front of which she could plant a tapestry hedge, a combination of shrubs lined up in a formal line or planted in a zig-zag rotation. A tapestry hedge is effective and efficient. If one shrub fizzles out or is attacked by insects or fungus, as redtips were a decade ago, your whole hedge does not have to be replaced.

Some other shrubs that would work well as a single-plant hedge, a double hedge, or in a tapestry hedge are Florida anise, wax myrtle, tea olive, English laurel, viburnum, pittosporum, conifers, and cleyera.

The important point to remember about hedges is their purposes. They give us privacy and background for other plantings. They are aesthetically pleasing and provide foliage and, in some cases, flowers and fragrance. Providing wildlife habitat should be vital to us all since our residences have displaced so much of it.

Keep in mind that a hedge is a long-term investment. It takes years to get a hedge tall enough to serve its purposes, and starting a new hedge is not something I plan to do again. Like having kidney stones or backing through the garage door, once is enough.

Trees You Design Yourself

Life is full of contradictions. I am full of them myself. My teeth clench when I see shrubs mangled into balls, triangles, and squares. Yet I find shrubs limbed up into tree forms attractive and have clipped a number of them myself in my own garden.

I began this mission when I tired of deadheading buddleias (or butterfly bushes) in my borders. I subtracted all horizontal branches lower than my chest and wound up with butterfly trees about eight feet tall, just the right height to lure butterflies and bees where I could watch them. I cut my deadheading chores in half and no longer crawl around, clipping spent blooms that no one ever saw anyway.

But eliminating tedium is not the end of the story. With this surgery, I also added height to my mixed borders and opened up space beneath the "trees" for elephant ears, iris, ferns, and other plants. What gardener is not constantly prowling for blank canvas?

This summer I saw two well-clipped vitex shrubs, one at a public garden and the other in a private garden. The first is about twenty years old so the trunk is thick and sturdy, definitely a tree, and the mass of blooms and foliage was breathtaking.

The private garden with the tree-form vitex belongs to a fellow with limited funds but a superb sense of design. He had also trimmed an overgrown Chinese ligustrum (variegated privet) into an airy, fine-textured tree. This gardener has a knack for creating an extraordinary garden with common plants used in unusual ways. He also has a collection of cast-iron tools doubling as garden art.

I have turned waxleaf ligustrums into small trees, just to gain space beneath. I have done the same to viburnums, encouraging them to put their energy into growing tall instead of wide. If only I could do the same.

At a gardening symposium I attended, the audience gasped as we watched our speaker limb up a perfectly fine loropetalum into a shapely tree. On a trip to Savannah, I was awestruck by Indian hawthorne "trees" in full bloom. In New York, I saw hydrangeas given the same transformation. The possibilities are staggering . . . and inspiring.

When I discovered my husband turning a dear old camellia into a tree by limbing it up with his trusty chain saw, I was horrified. But I was so pleased with the result, I urged him to have at it with overgrown hollies at the front corners of our house. I wish they were mushroom shaped, but that is more labor intensive than my pruning crew will tolerate. Our hollies remain free form and open, as nature intends.

You can limb up an overgrown shrub in two ways. Take one minute and a chain saw, and strip low branches off the main trunk (or trunks), being sure you leave a "collar" of wood where the branch was. In other words, do not cut off the limb flush with the trunk.

Or take a surgical approach, using loppers, a hand saw, and pruners as needed. Remove the most obvious branches first. Step back and see how things are going. Take off some more. Step back. Finish the job, keeping in mind that just about everything will grow back if the experiment is a disaster.

Surely every mixed border needs a tree or two. But we know pricey little trees grow bigger than expected, and then what to do? A common shrub already in your garden or in a pot waiting for a place to be planted can become a handsome cost-free tree in no time. A purchased Japanese maple, no matter how shapely, is just a plant . . . but a tree structured by you is a work of art.

Lose the Blues with Winter Greens

As I sorted out old slides of my garden, I was astonished to see how bare and beige the borders used to be in midwinter. I had taken these photographs to show the contrast in the garden from midwinter to spring, to summer, and then to fall. The contrast was stark . . . from drab to dynamite.

While there is still plenty of contrast through the seasons, my winter borders are not quite as colorless as they used to be. In fact, they are almost lush by comparison. Although no winter garden is a color spectacle, it can be appealing and surprising. Even in winter it is the surprises that make all the difference in a garden. We just have to look for them and, of course, plant them.

Among my favorite winter plants are evergreen ferns that continue to provide texture and variations of color in woodland gardens and borders. I am especially fond of glossy, dark green holly fern (*Cyrtomium falcatum*). Like fatsia, an evergreen shrub that looks like an overgrown houseplant, holly fern has sculptural and tropical appeal.

Another favorite, with traditional lacy foliage, is autumn fern (*Dryopteris erythrosora*). This plant contrasts handsomely with glossy evergreen shrubs such as Florida anise, sweetbox, camellias, aucuba, and cleyera. It is easy to create texture contrast in the border: pair matte and shiny, fine textured and coarse.

Although it looks a bit shabby by midwinter, cast-iron plant (*Aspidistra elatior*) is still another favorite. I must make a note in my calendar to cut them to the ground in early spring . . . or any other time, when their upright stalks need perking up. I will fertilize gingerly to promote lush upright growth. Cast-iron plant is especially attractive among ferns, and one of my most successful containers combines it with holly fern and variegated Asian jasmine.

When mahonia was pointed out to me some twenty years ago, I wondered how anyone could love this ugly saw-toothed shrub. Then I saw mahonias at a bird sanctuary, where dozens thrive. According to the docent, all but one had been planted by birds who gobble (and digest) the blue-black drupes. If mahonia delights birds this much, I knew they needed to be in my own garden.

The most frequently grown mahonia (with the common name Oregon grapeholly) is *Mahonia aquifolium.* The list of mahonia cultivars tells me that much has been done with this species since the birds planted mahonia at the sanctuary and I planted my first mahonia in our garden.

A Chinese mahonia (*Mahonia fortunei*) was a gift from a dear friend. I love the plant because it came from him, but also because it has elegant narrow leaves, slightly spiny at the edges. It also has a denser, more compact structure than grapeholly.

Chinese mahonia will reach about three feet in height, ideal for inclusion in a shady border. Oregon grapeholly will grow to four to six feet, even nine feet in favorable conditions. Both mahonias have erect racemes of bright yellow blossoms, but not at the same time. Chinese mahonia blooms in late summer and grapeholly in late winter or early spring.

Especially spectacular in winter with fragrant composite flowers at the tips of every bare branch, *Edgeworthia papyrifera* is a handsome shrub with year-round interest. Also called paper bush or rice paper plant, edgeworthia has showy bark and grows to a shapely five to six feet in light to moderate shade.

Do not forget the herbs of winter: bay, rosemary, and thyme for cooking, lavender for aroma, and rue for flower arrangements. Other evergreen herbs I am fond of are fuzzy gray lamb's ears (*Stachys byzantina*) and lady's mantle (*Alchemilla mollis*).

Each gray-green lady's mantle leaf is fan shaped and pleated to capture dewdrops that sit on the leaf through the morning. Up north, lady's mantle has fluffs of tiny, bright gold blooms, but not in the south, at least in my garden. But the absence of flowers does not matter to me at all; those dewdrops are enough spectacle in themselves.

An evergreen plant whose blooms do matter are hellebores. The bad news is that the inch-wide flowers face downward shyly, but paper-crisp bracts hang on for weeks, so even after flowers fade, the gardener has something to admire. After all, it is winter.

Commonly known as Lenten rose, *Helleborus orientalis* blooms in midwinter through spring and is the easiest to get started. Mine came from a friend who brings seed-sown hellebore babies to a community plant sale every fall.

Christmas rose, *H. niger*, is less heat tolerant, but in contrast to the earthy colors of Lenten rose, it has white or greenish white flowers that fade to purple as they age. Bear's foot hellebores (*H. foetidus*) have pale green purple-edged flowers that stand at attention above the foliage. Of course, I am in favor of having some of each.

Hellebores like humus-rich soil but benefit from an annual dusting of pelleted lime. Once they get going, they form large clumps of lustrous evergreen leaves. If, like me, you always want more, you can divide mature clumps or clear away the mulch around blooming plants so they can sow their own offspring.

Hellebores have been popular in England for the past fifty years but are just emerging as a horticultural obsession in the United States, though they have grown here since colonial days. A Virginia neighbor traded hellebore seeds from England with Thomas Jefferson, who, being Thomas Jefferson, documented the deal in his journal.

When you plant hellebores, place the crown slightly below soil level. Do not cover the lower stems with soil. Top dress with well-rotted manure or a slow-release fertilizer. If by the end of winter the leaves are tattered, cut them back to basal (ground-level) foliage for vigorous new growth.

Once hellebores get going they are long lived, but they are slow to establish, so you need to start your hellebore collection immediately. Plant them among ferns, azaleas, camellias, and other shade-loving plants. Just be sure they are placed where you can see and enjoy them, reminding yourself that winter does not last forever.

Winter Pleasures

When I saw the glossy green daphne covered with yellow flowers at a local nursery, I was smitten. It looked the size of a Volkswagen and the picture of health. Not only had I never seen another yellow-flowered daphne, I never again saw that one. Shortly after that awe-inspiring encounter, it was gone. Daphnes are like that, robust one day and kaput the next. Gardens are full of life lessons.

Do not let its relatively short life deter you from giving your garden the gift of a daphne. Just make up your mind that daphne is a short-lived but usually untemperamental shrub, and enjoy the ten to fifteen years it is with you, especially since there is plenty to appreciate in a daphne while it is among the living.

Winter daphne (*Daphne odora*) has an exquisite fragrance described as "rich orange blossom." In fact, its aroma sets the standard for garden scents. Winter daphne is a "ten," and all other fragrances are judged by comparison on a scale of one to ten. Be sure to plant winter daphne where its scent can be appreciated every day, along a shady pathway or in large containers next to an entrance.

A mounding evergreen shrub, daphne needs no pruning to retain its plump shape. Though there are larger species, mine grow to a height and width of three to four feet. The foliage is dense and glossy. Even if it did not bloom or smell terrific, a glossy green daphne would still be an asset in any shady spot.

To our good fortune, daphnes are exuberantly floriferous. Clusters of star-shaped flowers appear at the end of almost every stem, and in midwinter, my daphnes are covered with buds. They might bloom between January and early March, but whenever they open they will be welcome.

The species' blooms are about one and a half inches across and open to a rose pink. There are about a dozen daphne varieties with bloom colors from white to dark red. The foliage varies, too. *D. aureomarginata* has yellow-margined leaves and reddish purple flowers. *D. rubra* has white margins and dark red flowers.

Daphne foliage is hardy to fifteen degrees. It may scorch if cold weather is prolonged, but new foliage will appear. Daphnes are root hardy to zero degrees, so in spite of being short lived, they are tough plants. Once established, they tolerate dry soil but prefer well-drained humusy soil in part or full shade.

My four daphnes are in almost full shade from late spring to early fall. They were all propagated from cuttings taken in the spring. No one told me daphnes can be difficult to propagate, so I had no trouble getting them started. Sometimes ignorance is indeed bliss.

Daphnes thrive in zones 7 through 9, but my belief is that if you want a plant badly enough, it is well worth manipulating the climate a bit. Plants are surprisingly adaptable, especially if you do not let them read the labels or listen to experts.

Another "ten" on the fragrance scale is tea olive (*Osmanthus fragrans*), a staple in southern gardens but hardy to zone 7 and possibly even 6. If I were in too cold a climate for tea olives, I would have to have one in a container I could protect over winter.

A full-grown tea olive can reach twenty to thirty feet, but normally a gardener might expect six to ten feet. The one in my garden is forty years old and has never passed eight feet in height. A tea olive can be pruned to maintain its size and to promote branching. Frankly, an unpruned tea olive can look straggly, so occasional trimming is a good deed.

The important thing about tea olives is their fragrance. Each branch is filled with tiny creamy white flowers almost hidden among the foliage. I recommend planting tea olives in strategic places where people pass by. I have seen tea olives recommended for hedges and screens, but for me, that would be overdosing.

My newest tea olive is the cultivar 'Fudingzhu', for some reason renamed 'Nanjing Beauty'. Not nearly as large as the species, 'Nanjing Beauty' is even more aromatic and blooms off and on for nine months of the year.

Tea olives thrive in sun to partial shade. Both of mine are in too much shade, which does not stop them from scenting the neighborhood.

A third fragrant evergreen shrub for zones 5 through 8 is sweetbox, or *Sarcococca*. Pronounce it this way: sar-ko-kocka. Like daphnes and tea olives, sarcococca has glossy dark green foliage. Unlike daphnes and tea olives, its scent is subtle. Keeping in mind that daphnes and tea olives are "tens" on the smell scale, I give sarcococca a "six."

S. hookeriana reaches four to six feet in height and widens itself with stolons to about the same width. *S. hookeriana humilis* grows only twelve to eighteen inches tall, so it makes an ideal glossy green groundcover. However, when you are sarcococca shopping, look for *S. ruscifolia*, which is the most fragrant variety, has arching branches three to four feet long, and produces red berries to boot.

Sarcococca is happy in the shade, likes well-drained humusy soil, and will tolerate dry soil once established. It may defoliate when temperatures drop, but it is root hardy above zero degrees, so new foliage will appear even after a very cold winter. Sarcococca has spidery white blooms in January or thereabouts. It is hard to predict bloom time with changes in weather.

What to plant with these show-off shrubs? Camellias, evergreen ferns, soft gray lamb's ears, gingers, and, of course, winter-blooming hellebores.

Add spiky cast-iron plant (*Aspidistra elatior*) and ferns to vary structure and texture, and you have one of those "vignettes" garden designers rave about. Tuck in columbine and woods poppies for spring color and Japanese anemones to perk up things in late summer or fall.

Daphnes, sarcococca, and tea olives, along with camellias, provide a winter-long panorama of blooms, evergreen foliage, and fabulous scents. Be sure to place them where you can enjoy them every day and show them off to short-sighted friends who think nothing happens in a garden after frost.

Lowdown on Lime

Imagine the stunned silence in a room full of earnest Master Gardeners when our respected presenter spoke these words: "Forget pH." (Gasp!) "There are no acid-loving plants, only acid-tolerant plants."

This may be the most controversial statement ever uttered at a horticultural conference. If anyone else had told us we needed to "unlearn" assumptions we hold near and dear about soil acidity, we might have stopped listening and started doodling in our notebooks. But the speaker is one of the most respected and successful nurserymen in the Southeast. He has never led us astray. Our pens flew as we tried to capture every word he uttered.

We were reminded that pH means "potential hydrogen," and the scale of pH begins at zero (extreme acidity) and rises to fourteen (extreme alkalinity). When he started talking about logarithmic progression, I confess to fading away until he got back to plant stuff—azaleas, to be specific.

If azaleas are yellowing, developing skinny stems, and not holding leaves, chances are they are calcium deprived. Lime's principal element is calcium, and calcium is vital to a plant's optimum health. Before you fertilize or reach for the iron, lime your azaleas and lime them well. Two cups per plant, maybe three if you have never limed them before.

Brown patch in your grass? Aphids? Chinch bugs? Lime that lawn, applying as much as 350 pounds per 1,000 square feet if you have not been liming regularly in the past. Once your calcium level is adequate, yearly applications of 100 pounds of lime per 1,000 square feet should be sufficient in sandy soil, 50 pounds in clay soil.

Plagued with black spot on your roses? Our speaker told us about a prize-winning rosarian who applies three cups of lime in January and three cups in June to each of his rose bushes growing in sandy soil. Fungi have decreased and, with them, the necessity to pollute his yard with fungicides and pesticides.

When a customer complained about a nonblooming magnolia, the speaker advised him to buy a bag of lime (about three dollars' worth) and empty the bag around the magnolia. The tree was covered with blooms the following spring.

But, you ask, doesn't all this lime make soil too alkaline? Not likely. This horticulturist grows all the plants in his nursery in a soil mix that registers 6.5 on the acidity scale. Everything. This seems to be the optimum pH level to make soil nutrients available, but plants have been known to grow in soil anywhere between 3.5 and 8.5. That is a lot of tolerance.

The point, however, is that you should not assume you need no lime even if your pH is on the mark. Correcting pH is just one of many benefits of adding calcium. A healthy dose of calcium improves soil structure and enhances root growth, increasing moisture and nutrient retention. Calcium revs up the metabolism of the plant, stimulating vigorous growth. Calcium helps release phosphorus and potassium, two additional essential elements for horticultural well-being.

But here's the real kicker: calcium thickens the plant's cell walls so that fungi, not to mention aphids and chinch bugs, have difficulty permeating them. Remember the well-limed rose bushes with dramatically reduced black spot? The well-limed lawn with little or no brown patch?

Lack of calcium depletes energy, so by the end of the growing season, plants are pooped and new growth is downright pitiful. Adequate calcium improves flower bud set. Remember the magnolia? Stems become thicker and less brittle. Leaves do not fall off. Think about those sick-looking azaleas with yellow leaves and skinny stems.

Not all limes are equal. For years I have recommended dolomitic lime, and now I know why. Dolomitic lime contains not only calcium, but magnesium as well. Magnesium is the element that turns plants green. In fact, the only mineral element in a chlorophyll molecule is magnesium.

Gardeners often add epsom salts, which are full of magnesium. Since dolomitic lime gives optimum service with both calcium and magnesium, why not use it instead?

I prefer pelleted dolomitic lime because I do not like the powdery feel and dustiness of pulverized lime, but pulverized is slightly cheaper. Pelleted dolomitic lime is reconstituted pulverized lime, and both dissolve quickly. Whichever you buy, purchase a quality product that will give you maximum impact.

Look on the bag for a statement of one hundred mesh screen. Two hundred mesh is even better. The finer the screen, the higher the quality of the lime. I am not sure what it all means, but I have faith in the guy who told me to do this. You should, too.

Here is another surprise. It is not acidity that affects the color of hydrangeas. It is aluminum. When you lime your hydrangeas (and you should), if you want them really blue, you may need to add aluminum sulfate. I incorporate finely shredded pine bark around hydrangeas and hope this does the trick.

Blueberries? Rhododendrons? Camellias? Add plenty of lime and see what happens. Or, if you are a skeptic, add lime to half your blueberries, azaleas, and other acid-tolerant plants. Our eminent horticulturist assured us that results may show up as early as ten days to two weeks, but without a doubt, the results will be positive.

Add lime whenever you plant, about one cup for a one-gallon plant. Our speaker recommended mixing the lime with whatever fertilizer and amendments you are incorporating into the soil surrounding the root ball. For plants still in pots, add a rounded tablespoon of lime to a six-inch pot.

When to lime? The ideal time is December through February, before new growth begins. As with most good deeds, anytime is better than not doing it at all. Wait a couple of weeks after liming to fertilize. Lime regularly, especially with fast-growing crops, because it leaches out of the soil over time. Also, whenever you clean up crop residue, you remove calcium, which needs to be replaced.

Gardeners continue to learn and to change and to grow with our gardens. This hobby of ours demands resilience and an eagerness to try new plants, new strategies. Frankly, after hearing our speaker sing the praises of calcium—especially that cell wall stuff—I intend to double up on my own Tums intake.

Over the Edge

Every once in a while my husband suggests that I edge my borders with our power edger. He loves anything driven by an engine, the more noise the better. He also likes neatness and, I have to agree, a sharply dug edge between the flower garden and lawn is, well, sharp. It is a clear delineation of where the garden stops and the grass begins. Some people need that kind of definition.

Not me. I have no interest in sharp edges anywhere in my garden. I like my horticultural edges to move out into the grass as if the border were overflowing, like beneficent lava.

Whether the garden has sharp edges that stop abruptly or has irregular edges, plants placed at the front pull the border together effectively. Edges make the difference between a garden with rhythm and a border with plants stuck in, helter-skelter, without regard to tying together the vision.

Far be it from me to suggest you edge your entire garden with monkey grass or any other single plant. Why limit yourself when there are so many plants out there? Monkey grass has its place in front of a shrub border or the foundation plants, but in a mixed border, mixing it up is literally the name of the game.

Edging plants are short, so they ease the transition from border to lawn or pathway. Once you decide that you want to vary your edging rather than have a monotonous line of plants, the question becomes how to mix them so they contribute to the border as a whole.

Which plants should you use? How many should you place together so the border does not look disjointed?

I suggest you mull over the characteristics I hope you consider whenever you plant: color combinations, texture, and leaf shapes and sizes. Look at the foliage of the plant that will abut the edging, and be sure that colors blend but foliage contrasts. You do not want the abutter and abuttee to have the same size or shape leaves or the same texture. Experiment and you will see which combinations please you.

Once you decide which edging plant works best in a particular area, place a few along the front of the border. Continue planting until you decide to switch to another edging plant. Do not be afraid to mix your edging plants. Take the plunge. Like everything in the garden, plants are not permanently installed and can be moved when your mind changes.

For instance, you might plant black mondo grass or variegated carex in front of broad-leafed shrubs and perennials. Then switch to golden creeping Jennie in front of grasses or ferns. In front of dwarf glossy abelia or holly fern, plant soft gray lamb's ears, again tucking the lamb's ears around the abelia or fern. Once you find combinations you like, repeat them here and there around your border.

When asked recently about my favorite plants, I was surprised to find myself singing the praises of felt-soft gray lamb's ears. Lamb's ears are such unassuming plants and so easy to grow that I forget how much I rely on them as edging plants. They grow in sun or shade, making it easy to repeat them throughout my borders.

The lamb's ears in my garden are *Stachys byzantina* 'Helene von Stein'. Unlike other lamb's ears, 'Helene von Stein' does not flower, and that is good since I find lamb's ears flowers unattractive. The posture of 'Helene von Stein' is exactly what you would expect from such an elegant name, never flopping in the heat or shriveling in the cold. In fact, she is at her most beautiful covered with frost.

Children gravitate to lamb's ears because the large, broad leaves are so strokeable, like fine suede or velvet. Their gray color is a welcome contrast to all the greens in a garden. Lamb's ears grow in clusters, so a single plant might become three or five or seven by the end of a season. They also tuck in neatly around other plants, creating a natural flowing pattern rather than a row.

But enough of lamb's ears. The gardener's world is full of plants that make handsome edgers. Any groundcover can be an edger, but watch out. Most groundcovers grow stoloniferously. The best edgers expand, but not like rabbits . . . or mints.

I especially like heucheras with mottled purple foliage. Golden creeping Jennie (*Lysimachia* 'Aurea') is appealing because it oozes out onto the lawn or pathway. *Carex* 'Bowles Golden', a grass look-alike, makes a crisp fine-textured edger.

Dianthus and candytuft (*Iberis sempervirens*) are attractive edgers, and so is lady's mantle (*Alchemilla mollis*). I see hostas used often as edgers. Slugs like them better than I do, so I avoid them. Pulmonarias are superb hosta substitutes. The leaves have interesting spots and dapples, but their scratchy texture makes them unappetizing to slugs and deer.

It is perfectly legal to have a garden without edges, but you will be happier if you have them. You will also have more fun if you use an assortment of edging plants rather than a row of anything, even if it is a row of lamb's ears. Sometimes too much really is too much.

Slipping into Christmas Mode

So how do gardeners fill the days before Christmas? Not only do we experience the frenzy nongardeners endure to make the season bright. Not only do we have cooking to do, packages to wrap, and presents to buy. We have gardens withering before our eyes with every heavy frost and freeze.

Garnering my optimism, I take my daily amble through the borders to see what is going on and what needs doing before nightfall. Not much, fortunately. I throw an old comforter over a camellia to save blooms. I add a pitchfork full of hay or leaves to the mulch around tender plants I hope will winter over.

The daily walk is well worth the effort because every tour brings a surprise. Would you believe the *Cassia bicapsularis* still has bright yellow blooms this morning after several hard freezes? What a plant. I add forkfuls of mulch to show my appreciation.

I confess: I have still not planted all my bulbs but promise myself I will finish the job before Christmas. Or soon after. I feel guilty when I pass those bags of cyclamen tubers and Dutch iris bulbs waiting expectantly on top of the garage freezer.

I do not prune other than harvesting branches for holiday arrangements. Pruning is best left for late February or early March. My "flower arrangements" are predominantly foliar, and I like to mix up the foliage: holly, viburnum, pittosporum, ligustrum, rosemary, rue, and my neighbor's Leyland cypress.

To ice the cake, I add nandina berries, seedpods, and grasses. When elegance is required or I feel extravagant, I might add chrysanthemums, alstromeria, snapdragons, and a bit of fluff with silvery sea lavender or snow-white baby's breath.

With the garden observed and tended to and branches cut for holiday decorations, I do what everyone else does. I think about presents.

After Christmas I will head to the low country to plant one hundred narcissus bulbs, a well-deserved gift to my son and his family. We landscaped this vacation property in the fall, and the bulbs will be a fabulous surprise this spring. I want to be there when they arrive for Easter vacation and find an explosion of bright yellow daffodils.

I gave two friends sacks of woolly gray lamb's ears, and both were delighted. Gardeners are so easy to please. One recipient planted the lamb's ears around a tree in preparation for a garden tour next spring. She plans to buy black tulips from a florist and insert them in glass tubes poked in among the silvery gray lamb's ears. Normally honest people with gardens on tour bend their ethics a bit.

I visited a friend last week, and after touring his winter garden, he pointed to several clumps of hellebores. "Take as many as you want," he invited. How fortunate that I had a flat filled with potting mix in my car. One never knows when good luck will strike.

Actually, good luck strikes whenever I visit a garden, even if I leave empty-handed. I have had the pleasure of seeing a garden in the company of another gardener, fine company indeed.

Giving gifts to gardeners is easy. If your gardener is my age or arthritic, a kneeler is just the thing. It looks like an upside down seat. You kneel comfortably on the padded seat, and when you are ready to get up, you use the sides to hoist you on the way. I have one and love it. The trick is to remember to carry it with you and not leave it in the garage.

Another favorite gardening aid is a pair of gear-powered loppers. The trick with these is to stop before stripping a shrub or tree bare. That is how much fun they are to use. Gear-powered pruners are less amusing but are the most useful tool in my tote.

I have a greenhouse, but if I did not, I would ask for a pop-up plastic model (starting at $200) that folds flat when not in use. If I did not have a cold frame, I would think about building one or, even better, getting someone to build it for me.

A special plant is welcome, especially if it is something new and different and a bit pricey. For maximum effect, deliver it in a handsome pot—glossy blue pottery or faux terra cotta.

A membership to a nearby arboretum or public garden will give the recipient a year of fun and inspiration. A botanical garden is a horticultural education, especially in winter and midsummer, when our own gardens need help.

Hard to wrap but perfect presents are a pallet of stones for walls and walkways, a truckful of compost or mulch, a roll bale of hay, a fountain, or a lighting system. I personally yearn for a water garden if anyone is wondering. No fish, just rocks, plants, and a subtle gurgle.

Much cheaper but definitely welcome is a gift certificate for garden labor done by the donor or hired hands.

Most gardeners like to read about gardening almost as much as we like to garden, maybe even more when the temperature dips below freezing. Check out the gardening shelves at bookstores or, even better, ask the intended recipient. We all have wish lists.

Give yourself the gift of time off. Forget garden debris. Make big foliage bouquets using every shrub and evergreen herb in your garden. Visit a botanical garden. Collect seeds and cones from the garden and woodlands. Read, browse through seed catalogs, dream of spring. Enjoy the holidays. Pray for peace and justice.

The Gift That Keeps on Giving

I always leave the lights on the Christmas tree as I divest it of ornaments. Removing every ball and string of beads has become a contemplative ritual for me—stripping away the treasured memories each ornament represents, storing them away for the next Christmas celebration I already anticipate.

When the last ornament is stored away, the lights go off and the tree awaits arms stronger than mine to drag it out the front door or up into the attic. The storage location for the tree is under discussion. If I had the space, I would leave it stored in a closet of its own, to be wheeled out each December, lights connected, limbs ready to be adorned.

Unlike most folks, every year I have fewer ornaments to store. I ask my five grandchildren to choose a favorite or two to take home for their own trees, hoping they will remember they came from Poppa and Gargo's tree when they have children of their own. Christmas memories, I believe, are for the long haul . . . years after the toys are broken or abandoned, the jackets outgrown, the puzzle and game pieces scattered under couches and between cushions.

Each year, as the Christmas ornaments are distributed among our young families, I rely on natural ornaments, most of which are discarded in the garden when the tree comes down. Mophead hydrangeas gathered since last spring, clipped from their stems just as the blossoms become slightly crisp, are stored in the garage storage room until December. I use them occasionally in flower arrangements, but most of them are stuck into the tree wherever there is a bare spot, making the tree look full and textured.

I leave mopheads unsprayed, so they are their natural faded blue or green or purple. The elongated panicle hydrangeas are left on the shrub until they are brown and crisp, and these I spray lightly with gold paint. These blooms are placed strategically so that they thrust outward from the tree, adding a different dimension.

I collected seedpods of August lilies this summer, once they became crisp and flared at the ends like candelabra. Also called Formosa or Philippine lilies, their seedpods are naturally glossy gold and need no gilding. They look like clusters of trumpets emerging from the green branches of the tree. Be ready to gather and sow the seeds that fly out of them.

All of these natural ornaments are inserted into the tree before I hang glass beads, ornaments, candy canes, or rag dolls dressed like angels. I am thinking that eventually I will have nothing on the tree but natural materials.

I stick in stems of mountain mint and sweet Annie. Long branches of rosemary would add terrific scent. So would lavender and lemon verbena. All of these natural ornaments are shoved into the nooks and crannies of the tree. No wiring, tying, or gluing required. They are tucked in as if designed by nature . . . and pulled out to be saved or tossed on the compost pile.

The *pièces de résistance* of the Rochester tree are two skeletons of giant alliums, the size of basketballs. I had three, but the third vaporized or disappeared, chewed by a puppy perhaps. But two are enough, and one is inserted at each side of the treetop, looking for all the world like the Star of Bethlehem. The tree's angel is the friend who gave me these alliums three or four years ago. Probably time to grow some fresh stock of my own, but remembering the source of favorite ornaments is the most treasured part.

I know. I know. It is time for the tree to come down and Christmas to be tucked away for ten or eleven months. I hate to let the spirit go. So in late spring through fall, I will collect from my garden the materials for next year's tree. Once again I am reminded that the garden itself is a gift . . . one that keeps on giving.

Cold Facts

Unlike many pastimes, gardening never grows stale. Something exciting pops up regularly to surprise us: new plants, new products, new gardens to explore. I know of no other hobby so full of innovations.

One thing is certain: an alert gardener never stops learning. Just this winter I discovered two old strategies I had never tried before: hardwood cuttings taken when plants are dormant and cold seed starting.

I love propagating. The wonder of giving birth to new plants just by scattering seeds or sticking cuttings into a sterile medium never ceases to amaze me. When a seedling emerges or a rooted cutting resists being tugged upward, I am thrilled to be part of the birth process.

While I have been propagating all my gardening life from green softwood cuttings, clipped from shrubs and perennials in spring, summer, and fall, I never tried hardwood cuttings. Hardwood cuttings are taken from last spring's growth, gathered in late fall to late winter, after bark is formed and before new growth emerges. The stems look as if nothing is going on. They are dormant.

Make cuttings six to eight inches long. The upper cut should be one-quarter inch or more above a bud or node. It should also be cut on a diagonal so you can be sure which end is the top and which the bottom. Dormant cuttings look like brown sticks, and you will never know which end is up if you do not mark the tops in some way.

Bundle your cuttings together, tapping the bottom to neaten up the bunch. Many propagators tie the bunch with a string. Dip the whole bunch in water and then dust with rooting hormone to give the cuttings a better chance of success. Plants and gardeners need all the help we can get.

Dig a hole somewhere sunny. Place the bunch in the hole so that the bottoms of the cuttings have contact with soil. Fill in around the bunch with soil, being sure not to cover the tops, where you expect leaves to emerge. The bottoms of the cuttings will swell or form calluses from which, if all goes well, roots will eventually grow. This will probably take six months to a year, so be sure to mark the location of your cuttings.

Another way to do this is to dig a narrow trench about six inches deep and place each cutting separately (after dipping in rooting hormone) so that its bottom is in contact with soil. Fill in the trench with soil, being sure you leave the top of the cutting above the soil line.

Either way, do not let these cuttings dry out but, on the other hand, be sure they are not too wet. As with most gardening endeavors, good drainage is our friend.

With hardwood cuttings, you can actually cut a stem much longer than six to eight inches so, though producing roots takes longer than with softwood cuttings, you can wind up with a larger plant and can even plant the rooted cutting directly in the garden.

Among plants that do well from hardwood cuttings are buddleia, forsythia, hydrangea, mock orange, ligustrum, weigela, and wisteria. If your cuttings are from evergreen shrubs such as ligustrum or podocarpus, remove all but the top four to six leaves.

The best reason for doing hardwood cuttings is that it is the best method for propagating conifers. Cut (or tear) off side stems, remove lower leaves or scales, dip into rooting hormone, and then put into a prepared medium of sand or grit mixed with pine bark soil conditioner. Cuttings taken in early winter should be rooted by spring and potted up for a year before planting in the garden.

The other propagating discovery I have made this year is what I call "tough-as-ice seed starting." Actually, a friend found this method for me and asked my advice about medium. She found the information on the Internet and wanted to give the method a try. I do, too, since I have never had luck with sowing seeds directly in my garden.

The tough-as-ice method should work well for plants that self-seed such as castor beans, cypress vine, butterfly weed, Queen Anne's lace, and larkspur. The tough-as-ice method solves the problem of seedlings appearing in unexpected places.

The first step is to save plastic containers from the grocery store or fast-food meccas. The tops must be clear, and the container should be at least four inches deep, preferably deeper. Punch ample holes in the bottom—and the top—of each container. The bottom needs holes for drainage, the top for air circulation.

Do not use garden soil as your medium. Use vermiculite, perlite, or a packaged sterile seed-starting mix. Fill containers to the top of the bottom, if that makes sense. You do not want your seedlings down in a valley when they emerge.

Sow seeds across the medium, pressing tiny seeds into the medium without covering. Push larger seeds into the medium so they are covered about double their girth.

Place the containers outdoors where they will get at least six hours of sunlight. Because I have inquisitive dogs, I put mine up on my husband's fish-cleaning table where I will remember to check them for emerging seedlings.

With tough-as-ice seed sowing, nature takes its course, freezing and thawing seeds during winter and early spring until the temperature of the medium signals seeds that spring has arrived. When seedlings emerge, remove the container top. When seedlings produce true leaves and you are confident winter is over, pot up the seedlings or even plant them in the ground after it warms up sufficiently.

You and your offspring will be more than ready for spring.

Bonding in the Greenhouse

Two weeks after Christmas and, not surprisingly, I am thinking about gardens.

My own garden is an embarrassing mess. I have been too busy this fall talking and writing about gardening instead of cleaning out my own garden after a freeze a few weeks ago left it in tatters.

But tatters can be interesting if you look at them as remnants of last summer's glory. They are full of seeds that interest both the birds and me. They form interesting shapes, and if you like shades of beige, brown, and ecru, the colors are appealing. Best of all, however, is the ability of tatters to remind a gardener of the garden that is hovering beneath the soil. Hope springs eternal in a gardener's bosom.

When the spirit moves me, I will make my way around the garden plots, looking for surprises popping up as a result of unseasonably warm weather. Daffodils are already poking through the mulch. The hellebores (Christmas rose) will be blooming soon, followed by later hellebores (Lenten rose). The daphnes' buds are pink and plump.

I look out the window and see my faithful red and white striped camellia just starting to bloom. Some years it blooms in mid-December and camellias adorn the table set for Christmas dinner. Other years it blooms in early February, heralding spring and all that. This year, I discovered two blooms and an opening bud on Christmas morning, surely omens of good fortune and peace in the new year.

Last fall I purchased a vinyl "pop-up" greenhouse. Our old greenhouse needed recovering and I decided to pass it on to a good friend who would make better use of it and is still young enough to recover the frame. I have had that greenhouse since before Hurricane Hugo (which it withstood), and many happy winter hours were spent inside it.

The greenhouse was always too large, but my husband is that kind of builder. If some is good, more is better. If ample is adequate, extra-large is just right. But I confess I filled the greenhouse to the brim about half the years I had it, and as soon as it left the yard in our friend's trailer, I missed it.

My new greenhouse is eight feet by eight feet and nine feet tall and, according to the directions, "sets up in seconds with no tools required." Sounded like my kind of construction project. The photos on the Internet and the enclosed directions showed a woman in my age bracket carrying the greenhouse under her arm and setting it up without another soul in sight. I admired her independence and gumption.

I decided that I would wait to set up my greenhouse when my grandsons came for Christmas. I envisioned a bonding experience as we cut the straps holding the greenhouse together and watched it pop open, magically becoming the vinyl structure in the photos.

The experience was a bonding one of sorts, and the construction project has already joined the annals of the family matriarch's misguided expectations. We marched out to the site I had chosen, four of us lugging the folded-up greenhouse. Once we got started, it took one civil engineer, two grandsons, one grandpa, a granddaughter, and a daughter-in-law to get the job done in about a half an hour, not quite the cinch we had been led to believe by the gray-haired lady in the photographs.

The greenhouse is now up and ready. It really is as large as promised and has two doors and ample vents as advertised. My husband is surprised by its sturdiness, and I hope the remaining family members are pleased with their good deed. I am grateful for their efforts. What would I have done without them?

A big advantage of a pop-up greenhouse is that it can be picked up and moved to other locations and can also be placed over plants in the ground. For instance, if I have a group of budding hydrangeas threatened by a freeze, I could cover them by moving the greenhouse over them.

And if I decide I need more greenhouse, I can purchase a second one—or several—and zip them to the original, that is, if I can round up a work crew.

I use my greenhouse to protect young plants, seedlings, and rooted cuttings. But mostly I use it to keep myself connected to my garden over the winter. Like most gardeners, once we reach January, I am already anticipating spring.

A Winter Stroll

Today is New Year's Day, and I have just come in from my garden which, I am happy to say, is an interesting place to wander. Winter admittedly will never be the thrill a minute that fall is for me and that spring is for most other gardeners. But if we look, colors and shapes and textures pop out of the drabness to gladden our hearts.

I strolled around the large mixed border that surrounds an oval of unkempt lawn. The hickory tree that shades much of this area in other seasons is now bare, permitting shrubs, ferns, groundcovers, and perennials as well as winter annuals to bask in sunlight.

Most of the shrubs in the mixed garden are deciduous, but I like to look at their shapes and bark, so I do not cut them back until late February. Some shrubs, such as lantana and buddleia, have hollow stems, so you definitely do not want to cut them. If the stems fill with water and freeze, chances are the roots will not survive. Neatness is not always a virtue.

In fact, I am currently attempting to murder a lantana by deliberately cutting it back and letting those hollow stems fend for themselves. With luck, the roots will freeze, die, and, in time, turn into compost and I will not have to dig them up next spring when I am ready to plant something else.

The lantana victim is my own dear 'Miss Huff', and I have qualms about doing her in, but she has gotten too large for her location and is wandering hither and yon all over the border. Enough of 'Miss Huff' is enough. I will replace her with 'Athens Rose' or some other more mannerly lantana cultivar that will continue to attract butterflies to the neighborhood.

A shrub that seized my attention this past fall was *Itea virginica* 'Henry's Garnet', which sat around quietly, plain-Jane green, all summer (after a springtime show of fragrant bottlebrush blooms). In October, 'Henry's Garnet' turned scarlet and remains fiery red to this day. How long those leaves will hold I do not know, but I will appreciate their brilliance until the last leaf falls.

The common name for itea is Virginia sweetspire. I have three full-sized *Itea virginica* shrubs in my garden, all of them 'Henry's Garnet', though there are other cultivars. Last spring I purchased *Itea virginica* 'Little Henry', a more compact form than 'Henry's Garnet'.

I have never pruned my sweetspires, though I have pulled up wandering rooted stems and clipped them off, potting them up to plant in other places or to share with friends. If sweetspires have a fault, it is this tendency to wander, but, as a gardener who never has too many plants, I see this habit as an asset, not a flaw.

As I strolled around my garden today, I admired the daphnes with their glossy cream-edged dark green leaves. I like their naturally rounded shape, so unlike those tortured balls scalped with pruning shears. And, of course, I look forward to their blooms that will fill the air with scent in a few weeks.

In the corner of the border that spends summer in shadows is a grouping of plants that does not get the admiration it deserves until winter eliminates the distractions and shade. This grouping is elegant, diverse, rich in texture, and nuanced shades of green. It fills the bill as a "vignette," a current horticultural buzzword for a small but eye-stopping garden segment. A condensed landscape, if you will.

The backdrop for my vignette is a collection of evergreen aucuba, Florida anise, tea olive, and green and gold euonymous. This is the vignette part: two fatsias, a chunky stand of cast-iron plant, holly fern, green and yellow grasslike carex, wild ginger, columbine foliage, hellebores, and variegated lamium, all in a space of about eight feet by five feet. A vignette should pack a wallop.

Fatsia japonica is now in bloom and has been since October. The leaves of fatsia look like big green maple leaves, and the "flowers" are round spiked balls that remind me of little UFO cartoons. Fatsias can become as large as ten feet tall and wide, but mine have never grown more than four feet tall and wide, which is just as well.

My fatsias are basic green, but new cultivars have golden or white variegated leaves or lacy lobes. There is also a cross (×*Fatshedera lizei*) between *F. japonica* and an ivy, *Hedera helix* 'Hibernica'. I have one of these and planted it up against a dead, well-branched shrub, hoping the fatshedera will climb upward.

The cast-iron plant (*Aspidistra elatior*) is a broad clump of upright, spiky foliage that contrasts handsomely with fatsia leaves. The key to keeping a cast-iron plant looking sharp is to cut it to the ground when it looks ragged and to fertilize it. That is not too much for a plant to ask, I think.

Contrasting with the aspidistra and fatsia are holly ferns (*Cyrtomium falcatum*) with glossy dark green leathery leaves. This collection completes the basic vignette. The rest is frosting, the finishing touches as easy to vary as whim prompts.

The wild ginger (*Asarum minor*) is mottled green and gray. Waiting to bloom from evergreen foliage are columbines and hellebores. Lamium groundcover is a subdued green and cream, filling in spaces and pulling the pieces together.

It occurs to me that this vignette needs bright yellow woods poppies (*Stylophorum diphyllum*) here and there, and I will plant some as soon as they emerge elsewhere in the garden in February. This will give my vignette a sequence of blooms: hellebores in late winter and columbine and woods poppies in early spring. Perhaps I need to add some cyclamen for fall blooms. A garden is always a work in progress.

This five-by-eight-foot space provides an ample stage for plenty of action, sort of like a large well-filled container garden. I often declare that my next (and final) garden will be walled, so it cannot be expanded. It is gratifying to discover how much diversity can be packed into limited space . . . and tempting when I think how little upkeep is involved.

February Itch

While I have the good fortune to be free of sinus drip, migraine headaches, and most other chronic ailments, every year, as soon as Valentine's Day is over, I come down with a serious case of February itch.

I prowl around my garden looking for signs of spring and blush with shame over the shabby appearance of my borders. I cut nothing back after the first freeze last fall, so I have plenty of tall stalks, crisp beige remnants of foliage, twigs and branches, and only a hazy memory of what is planted where.

I also never got around to mulching the garden, so the mess is all out there in full view. The stone patio I began last summer is still half-finished. I ran out of stone at the same time I ran out of steam. Of course, weeds have grown up wherever the ground is bare.

I used to have a nice oval lawn in this space I am paving, but the infamous glechoma or ground ivy invaded. If I ever had a horticultural nemesis, glechoma is it. When I see it for sale, it is all I can do to keep from dumping the plants into the nearest trash can.

Some invasives, such as Japanese anemones and creeping raspberry, are worth some grief, but glechoma definitely is not. If you see it at a garden center, let your conscience be your guide. If you see it in your garden, get a blow torch.

But February itch is not about undone chores. It is about chores I am aching to do: cutting dry stalks to the ground, raking up debris, getting seeds into the ground, planting and rearranging. No matter how itchy I get, I know it is not time. Another month of winter is on its way, and installing young plants or stimulating foliage is risky business.

So what does a gardener do to get her mind off the itch? In mid-February I start seeds of Formosa lilies, parsley, tomatoes, Mexican sunflowers, and other favorites. I fill mushroom containers with vermiculite, moisten the vermiculite from below, spread the seeds across the top, and keep them warm on an electric germinating pad. Any warm place will do, but I recommend that you buy one of these pads, which are available at garden centers.

As soon as seedlings emerge, I place the containers under a grow light that holds two fluorescent tubes (plain shop lights) until they produce true leaves. If you have a sunny windowsill, that will do, but I recommend you buy or build a grow light. My husband built mine with two shelves, like a bookcase, and fluorescent tubes suspended over each shelf.

The last week in February I cut buddleia and lantana to the ground. I also cut late-blooming hydrangeas to the ground since they bloom on new wood. Hydrangeas that bloom on old *and* new wood, I prune judiciously. Some stems are cut to the ground, and others only trimmed back to a bud so I will have both old and new wood and hydrangea blossoms until next fall.

If you plan to cut back a spring-blooming plant (such as weigela or mock orange) to the ground, wait until after it has blossomed. The British call this process "coppicing" or "stooling." I recommend doing this every other year to keep large plants shapely and floriferous, a kind of tough love treatment that works.

Daffodils have been up for a couple of weeks, and I am thrilled. Every yellow bloom promises spring. Also in bloom are the bright yellow racemes of mahonia. This is a plant that grows on a gardener. I planted mine because the drupes it produces are gobbled up by birds—but the flowers become increasingly attractive after a dreary winter.

Daphnes are also in bloom. A friend recently told me that she never cuts daphnes to propagate because of their reputation as temperamental. They are not temperamental at all if you do not try to move them. That does make them cranky. But I take cuttings after the blooms are finished and keep young daphnes in constant production, so if one dies (as they sometimes do for no apparent reason), I have a substitute to move into the space.

Of course, hellebores are blooming, and so is *Viburnum tinus* 'Spring Bouquet', which has no scent but is full of clusters of pink buds beginning to open. A camellia that usually blooms in December has decided to cover herself with red and white blossoms. Better late than never, I say.

If I had planted pansies and violas in November as I should have, they, too, would be flourishing. I must remind myself to buy plenty next fall to make up for their absence this year.

Pruning Puzzles

Most suggestions I dole out are not so crucial that disaster will fall if you fail to follow them. For instance, it is best to prune at the opportune time, but plants will survive and even thrive if we put off pruning a few weeks or not do it at all. If you cut your shrubs to the ground last fall or have not pruned for the past five years, not to worry. Your plants will probably forgive you, and if they sulk, just rip them out and plant something new.

The most important reason to prune a shrub, especially a flowering shrub, is to keep the plant vigorous and healthy.

The absolute worst reason to prune is to force a shrub into an unnatural shape. There is no rationale for a square azalea or ball-shaped forsythia. Shrubs and people are not meant to have geometrical figures.

The second-worst reason to prune is to restrain a plant's growth because it would, if left to its natural inclination, overwhelm its allotted space. We have all committed this folly. It is hard to believe a small potted holly will eventually become a giant and cover the windows. Read the plant's label and, even better, do some research about the ultimate size of the shrub you are ready to purchase.

If you have not jumped the gun, go out at the tail end of winter and cut back buddleias, lantanas, abelias, beautyberry, summer-blooming spireas, altheas, and roses. These are shrubs that bloom on new wood. Pruning them on the cusp of spring will stimulate growth of fresh stems and foliage. Cut them close to the ground. The less old wood left, the more new wood you will generate.

Some shrubs bloom on old wood. Lilacs, weigela, forsythia, kerria, bridal wreath spirea, mock orange, rhododendrons, and azaleas are in this group. Wait until they are finished blooming, and then cut them back to stimulate growth over the summer and fall so you will have plenty of blooms next spring.

A few years ago, on a pleasant March day, my neighbor asked me to look at what he had accomplished with the azaleas at the edge of his lot. What he had done was cut the entire border to the ground. What could I say? I gently broke the news that he would have healthy azalea foliage this year and that was a good thing. Azalea foliage looks pretty ratty by the end of winter.

However, my neighbor would have no azalea blooms until the following spring. But our neighborhood has an azalea abundance, and next year his border will be a stunner.

The trick to knowing whether your shrub blooms on old or new wood is to pay attention. If the stems are brown and stiff, the wood was formed the previous year. If the stems are green and pliable, the wood was formed the current year. If all else fails, look up your shrub in a book or on the Internet. Do not ask someone else. Chances are she cannot remember either.

The basic rule of pruning is this: prune after bloom. Even shrubs that you prune before they bloom should be trimmed back a little once they have flowered. This is called deadheading, and if you are a faithful deadheader, your plants may rebloom. I have had crepe myrtles bloom three times in a summer because I kept the dead blooms nipped off.

Hydrangeas can be puzzling. Most bloom on old wood in the spring and early summer. First, cut back all dead branches to ground level. You can tell they are dead because they are brittle and have no green buds on them. Then trim each remaining branch back to a green bud. If a branch is growing in the wrong direction or you do not like the way it looks, cut it back to wherever you want. It is your hydrangea and, remember, it will recover from whatever you do with a pair of clippers.

Here is the puzzling part. Some hydrangeas bloom on new wood and should be cut to the ground in late winter. *Hydrangea paniculata* 'Tardiva' and *H. arborescens* 'Annabelle', for example, both bloom on new wood. 'Annabelle' blooms in late spring and summer. 'Tardiva' blooms in late summer and early fall. They are both fabulous hydrangeas that dry beautifully, and I urge you to include them in your gardens even if they do not follow the rule.

To add further confusion, a few hydrangeas bloom on both old and new wood. They are well worth the bother because they rebloom into the fall. I have dressed my Thanksgiving table with *Hydrangea macrophylla* 'Penny Mac' and 'Endless Summer.' I cut back the dead branches to the ground, cut some of the budding branches back to the ground, and trim the rest back to the first buds. This way I have some branches of old wood (for early blooms), and I will soon have plenty of branches of new wood filled with late blooms.

If all this pruning talk is more than you can bear, you have alternatives. I have a friend who has hydrangeas that are about thirty years old. She has never pruned them, and they are filled with blooms all spring and summer. These hydrangeas are at the beach, so my guess is that the wind does enough pruning to keep them perking.

You could also make a list or a chart in your garden calendar reminding you which flowering shrubs should be cut to the ground and which should be trimmed back after they bloom.

A pruning schedule is not nearly as hard as it sounds. Neither is a little rule breaking once you get the hang of it.

Early Risers

I recently attended the most academic lecture about gardening I have ever heard. My brain struggled nonstop trying to keep up with the speaker, whose thought processes leapt from one cerebral mountaintop to another.

I loved it . . . which is surprising because I am definitely a practical, down-in-the-dirt kind of gardener. The lecture was stimulating mental exercise, which, like physical exercise, feels grand when it is over and I have done the last lift.

The topic was about how we respond to gardens. What does a garden mean? How does it mean? Does it "mean" anything at all? Maybe not in this order, but the drift is probably clear.

Stay with me because here is the part that hits home: the garden, according to the speaker, offers "triggers and prompts" that stimulate our personal responses that give the garden its meaning.

This morning, as winter fades and spring inches forward, my own garden is full of triggers and prompts that stir my soul. An early riser myself, I have special affection for the garden's early risers: spring flowers that poke upward out of the ground when wiser heads know a blast of winter may be lurking.

Hellebores or Lenten roses (*Helleborus orientalis*) are triggers and prompts that straddle the seasons, bring early color to the garden, and make my heart leap with anticipation. They are the last flowers of winter and the first of spring. Hellebore foliage is evergreen and may be somewhat ratty after winter. In a rare spate of tidiness, I trim off tattered leaves, making room for new growth and flowers.

Hellebores thrive in shade or partial shade once the trees green up. They prefer rich, organic, well-drained soil that is alkaline. If you are planting hellebores now, add some dolomitic lime to the holes and write a note to yourself on the October page of your calendar to lime all hellebores in the fall.

Once established, hellebores can be divided in the spring. They also reseed at the base of the plant if the mulch is pulled back to expose bare soil. The seedlings will take three years to bloom, but we all have to start somewhere.

The true harbingers of spring for me are daffodils, and mine have been fabulous this year. I beat myself up every fall for not digging and dividing the bulbs, but it does not seem to matter. They come up the following spring as bright and beautiful as ever, though increasingly crowded.

This may be my year for digging and dividing because I have adult offspring with gardens of their own they are anxious to fill, as well as places in my own garden where no daffodils dwell. I use an organic bulb fertilizer now, as foliage begins to fade, because, as this spring ends, the bulbs prepare themselves for next spring's extravaganza.

I vow to watch the fading daffodils carefully, digging up bulbs when the foliage is brown but still visible. I will then replant the bulbs immediately, while they have my attention. If I need to delay planting, I will pot up some in good garden soil. Of course, I have made this vow before to no avail.

Just after the daffodils start blooming, another favorite mood trigger appears: *Veronica umbrosa* 'Georgia Blue'. Unlike the tall, spiky veronicas we are accustomed to, this is a prostrate speedwell that forms a dense four-inch mat of evergreen dark, shiny foliage. In early March when the daffodils are prime, little blue flowers appear in a great groundcover that appreciates frequent division. So do the recipients of those divisions.

Another spring prompt that welcomes division is the woods poppy (*Stylophorum diphyllum*). The attractive lobed, gray-green foliage has already emerged in shady areas all over my garden, and I cannot wait for the two-inch bright-yellow poppies that will appear soon. The main burst of bloom occurs early, but flowers continue to appear through the summer. The one- to two-foot clumps produce hairy little seedpods, so if the mulch is pulled back to expose bare soil, you can expect some reseeding. Share the wealth with friends because *Stylophorum diphyllum* is hard to find in nurseries.

That most elegant of spring's triggers and prompts, columbine, is reportedly short lived, so I continue to start it from seeds every winter to make sure I never am without. My favorites are the thirty-inch-tall and graceful McKana hybrids.

The seeds germinate easily. I read somewhere that they should be "stratified" or refrigerated for a number of weeks, but I have not found this necessary. Sometimes I refrigerate, and sometimes I do not. It does not seem to matter. How do these rumors start?

Last year a generous friend gave me a packet of royal blue columbine seeds she collected in Colorado. I refrigerated these to get them started, and the blooms were exquisite. This year I will pull back the mulch and see whether I can get them to reseed on the spot, as do the native red and yellow columbines (*Aquilegia canadensis*).

Here is a warning. After columbine has bloomed, the foliage is subject to leaf miners. Hold the poison. These are harmless little critters who make decorative patterns while meandering through the leaf tissue. I ignore them and find that they make their trails for a while and then disappear. If the patterned foliage bothers you, cut it off, and fresh leaves will emerge. Of course, they will also emerge if you do not trim the old foliage.

These are the early risers, the triggers and prompts, that make gardeners' hearts sing. Winter is almost over, and spring is a week or so away. Our energy rebounds, and we emerge into fresh air, drop to our knees, and crawl around looking for old friends renewing themselves after a long winter's rest.

Spring

The moral of the story is this: never work harder than absolutely necessary. Gardening should always be a labor of love.

Look, Look! It's a Harbinger

I shudder when someone asks to visit my garden in spring. I prefer visitors in summer or fall and urge them to go elsewhere to enjoy spring. That is pretty much what I do myself. I appreciate the evergreen azaleas in my own yard but could live without them since azaleas overflow my neighborhood and, of course, they all bloom in the same few weeks.

I do not feel that way about daffodils. I consistently win the daffodil growing contest in my neighborhood and since late February, my borders are filled with the bright yellow and creamy white blooms of narcissus. Unlike azaleas, a carefully chosen sequence of daffodil cultivars keeps the blooms coming for eight weeks or longer. Furthermore, they do not hog their space after strutting their stuff.

The only problem with daffodils is actually a problem with me. Every year I intend to dig up, separate, and feed my bulbs and remind myself to do so on the June page of my garden calendar. By June the foliage has withered but is still visible, so I should have no trouble locating groups of bulbs for the digging up process.

But June is a busy month, and I always seem to have more pressing things to do before my energy and interest dissipate. As a result, I have daffodils in my yard that have not been lifted and divided for twenty years. They have probably been fertilized once or twice over this period, but I would not swear to it in a court of law.

On the plus side, I know I have never fertilized daffodils in bloom or soon after they flower. At this time the bulbs are susceptible to Fusarium fungus, and nitrogen encourages the growth of this disgusting disease. So, in this case, be like me and do nothing but admire these yellow and white harbingers of spring. I used to believe I should remove the seedheads after flowering, but I have learned that this is not necessary and regret the time I wasted.

Right now I have a backlog of potted shrubs, trees, and perennials that need to go into the ground as soon as I can find the shovel and dig the holes. While I should have started this process last November, when plants went into dormancy, I still have time to settle them in before the growing season gets under way. Dawdling is not a serious sin.

I place the pots where I think I want to plant and envision how the shrub will look at maturity. Sometimes I move a lawn chair into that place so that if the plant is too large for me to picture, I have a clear indication of how it will fit into the border. I have even asked people of assorted sizes to stand in for shrubs and trees—much easier than dragging around the furniture.

Most plants are not that difficult to envision, but I like to be sure, especially with potentially large specimens. I am too old and lazy to be digging up plants and moving them to appropriate places. At one time, almost every plant in my garden had been moved at least once, and some of them two or three times. Those days are over.

After twenty-five years or so of mulching and composting, my soil is humus-fortified sandy loam. I dig a hole approximately twice the diameter of the pot but no deeper than the distance between the soil line and the bottom of the root ball. The soil line indicates where the top roots emerge from the central stem. If you plant too deeply, those top roots will be smothered and you will be disappointed in the plant's progress . . . or demise.

Loosen the roots of the plant either by manually prodding them or making shallow vertical slices along the root ball with a sharp knife. Place the plant in the hole, being sure it sits no deeper than the soil line. If it does, push some of the dirt you have removed back into the bottom, and replace the plant.

Do not fertilize plants until the growing season gets under way. I do not fertilize mine at all because I think they should get used to my soil right from the get-go. This is where they are going to spend their lives. I occasionally add compost in the planting hole and always add a handful or two of pelleted dolomitic lime, a source of calcium that enables roots to absorb nutrients.

If you have not pruned already, do it now. Prune plants that bloom on new wood, such as lespedeza and buddleia, close to the ground. If you are keeping your buddleia trimmed as a tree, leave the upright trunk(s) and remove all side branches.

Cut hydrangeas that bloom on new wood (such as 'Annabelle' and 'Tardiva') close to the ground. You want to generate as much new wood as possible. Tidy up hydrangeas that bloom on old wood by removing the oldest stems and any deadwood above emerging foliage.

If you are confused about your hydrangeas and other flowering shrubs, tag them so that you will be sure next year which bloom on old wood, new wood, or both old and new. But it is not the end of the world if you make a bad pruning decision. The plants will bloom eventually . . . though maybe not until next year.

Hold off until mid-April to put annuals, warm-weather vegetables, or tender perennials into the garden. They will just sit there pouting until the soil warms up, and that night air can be a killer.

Keep the faith: spring is coming.

Wait, Wait! Don't Plant Yet

March 20 may mean the beginning of spring on the calendar, but for most gardeners, spring begins when planting time arrives: at least a week . . . and maybe three, into April.

Hold on to your annuals, warm-weather vegetables, and tender perennials until April 7. Then take a look at the weather forecast for the following week. If daytime temperatures are seventy degrees or higher, and fifty-degree nights are predicted for the next seven days, your plants will probably be safe.

Plants respond to soil temperatures, not air temperatures, so do not let a sunny day or two fool you. We have all rushed the season and regretted it when our plants expired completely or lost their vigor, struggling through summer but never catching up. Just remind yourself that summer is a long, long season and we need not rush into it.

This is not to say we should not buy plants or start seeds, but be prepared to shelter your plants when temperatures dip. This may involve bringing them inside, putting them in a cold frame or greenhouse if one is handy, or blanketing them with row cover, a translucent nonwoven fabric. Most feed and seed stores and garden centers carry this inexpensive and reusable fabric. I usually order mine from a catalog.

This year I started two tomato varieties I have never grown before: 'Marianna's Peace' and 'Thessaloniki'. I probably will buy two 'Better Boy' tomatoes and maybe another heirloom variety or two, winding up with eight tomato plants to see us through the summer, not counting 'Sungold' cherry tomatoes, which are eaten primarily while wandering around the garden.

We used to grow strawberries and asparagus. The strawberries never met a shortcake since they were eaten by the handful whenever a Rochester got a hankering. Just one of our sons joined me in the asparagus patch, where we would snap off spears and eat them immediately before the rest of the family noticed the happy looks on our faces. The asparagus eater is my gardening son and I bet he still eats raw asparagus. I do, too.

The tomatoes I start from seed and those I buy early in spring are both potted up at least twice before they ever go out into the garden. I begin by putting them in deep four-inch pots with their root mass almost at the bottom of the pot. Then I fill in with potting mix, covering up the stems to the first cluster of true leaves. When the plants are as tall as the pot, I repot them in quart or even gallon containers the same way, with their roots close to the bottom and their stems covered up to the first growth of leaves. I fertilize every week to ten days with diluted fish emulsion.

Roots are generated all along the submerged stems, so by the time I plant them in the garden, they have large and healthy root systems. Some gardeners plant tomatoes at the bottom of holes this same way so the roots are deep and likely to remain moist. I do not do this. I plant tomatoes just slightly submerged so their root systems are warmed up quickly in the top eight or ten inches of my humusy garden soil.

Gardeners are fussier about planting tomatoes than any other plant I can think of. We each have our peculiar method and adhere to it adamantly until we see a better crop of tomatoes. Then we are likely to throw our method overboard and follow the tomato leader.

Recently, a good friend told me about his new rose planting method. You dig a hole and put the soil to one side. You dig another eight or ten inches deeper and throw that soil away. He lost me when he explained that he would fill each hole with gypsum, cotton meal, bloodmeal, and a few other ingredients, which he would then mix with that soil he had put to one side.

My friend admitted that all these ingredients were in the garage and his newly purchased rose bushes were still in their pots. If they were my rose bushes, they would be sitting in their pots next August or given away to a gardener more dedicated to hard labor than I. I am not that crazy about roses anyway, and that is probably a good thing.

The moral of the story is this: never work harder than absolutely necessary . . . especially in the garden. Gardening should always be a labor of love. It should be pleasurable and rewarding. If you find yourself stalling when it is time to deadhead or prune, figure out a way to make the job palatable.

I follow the Rule of Five, breaking down tasks into increments of five. I deadhead one perennial; and then I deadhead four more. I prune one wayward branch; and then I prune four more. Five is so doable. A row of shrubs that need pruning can be overwhelming. Five branches are manageable, even for the laziest among us.

Perhaps after five, you are ready to do another five. That makes ten branches pruned. Try another five—or go in the house and read a book. Tomorrow is another day and another five, ten, or fifteen branches.

Get shrubs, trees, and perennials into the ground before the weather gets hot and the rain stops. Shop for annuals, propagate cuttings from the pricey ones such as pentas, dwarf cleome, angelonia, and coleus, but resist popping tender summer plants into the ground before the soil is sufficiently warmed up. Giving plants a happy start is well worth waiting for.

Before you know it, we'll be complaining about the heat and wondering what to do with all those tomatoes and all that basil. Aaaah . . . for a bite of that first tomato sandwich.

Some Swell Shrubs

The older I get, the more drawn I am to flowering shrubs. They are so undemanding, so permanent, so statuesque, at least in comparison to perennials and annuals that hover at ground level and often need deadheading, dividing, or replacing.

Flowering shrubs demand little attention, and even when it is time to prune or cut one to the ground, it is not difficult to show a willing worker (paid or unpaid) how to do the job, especially if you are standing next to him with a pitchfork.

Since my goal is to replace many perennials and most annuals in my garden, I am looking for cultivars of favorite shrubs that will provide the same variations in foliage, texture, size, growth pattern, and colors that make my mixed border such a joy. A height of four feet, maybe five, is my limit, but what I am really seeking are shrubs three feet and shorter.

For example, consider the incredibly fragrant mock orange (*Philadelphus coronarius*). These old-fashioned shrubs grow to ten feet in height and width, which is all right if you own an estate or a place in the country. Because of their size and their sprawling growth habit, mock orange shrubs should be stooled or coppiced (both of which mean cut to the ground) every few years, not a job for the frail or lazy.

But *Philadelphus* × *lemoinei* 'Manteau d'Hermine' is a mini-mock orange, a two- to three-foot mound of fine-textured foliage adorned by fragrant, double, creamy white flowers. 'Snow Velvet' pushes my height maximum at five to six feet, but it occasionally repeats its bloom, a definite asset. Want to add pizzazz? *P. coronarius* 'Variegatus' has creamy white leaf margins and white flowers and is three to four feet tall.

Abelia (*Abelia* × *grandiflora*) is another old favorite that has undergone numerous transformations without losing its charms. Forget the leggy, shapeless abelias that have to be cut to the ground (remember coppicing?) to retain some order about them. Now we may choose among the three-foot-tall *A. parvifolia* 'Bumble Bee', *A.* × *grandiflora* 'Compacta', or *A.* × *grandiflora* 'John Creech.' Want something smaller? Look for 'Little Richard' or 'Rose Creek', which are only two to three feet.

I have seen two dwarf variegated abelias, and there are probably more. It is hard to keep up. 'Confetti' foliage has cream-colored margins and turns rose in winter. The foliage of 'Sunrise' has gold margins and green centers.

Remember that almost every variegated plant sprouts plain old species-green foliage, and you must cut off branches that revert. You paid extra for variegation and should hang on to it, unless, of course, you decide it is too much trouble.

If garden space is limited, fitting standard hydrangeas into mid-border or even into the back of the border is tricky because they take up so much room. Do not despair. New cultivars are on their way, and two smallish oakleaf hydrangeas are already on the market. *H. quercifolia* 'Pee Wee' has a low, mounding shape, and 'Sikes Dwarf' is upright. Both have white blooms and oakleaf foliage and are only three or four feet tall.

I have an old-fashioned weigela in the woodland area of my garden, and for about two weeks in early summer it is a stunner, reminding me of the billowing prom dresses girls wore in the fifties. All fluff. Weigela loses its charm, however, when, like the mock orange, it needs to be cut to the ground every few years to keep it shapely.

New weigelas give a gardener plenty to ponder. Think dwarf. Think purple foliage. 'Java Red' is three to four feet tall, and 'Ruby Queen' is twenty to twenty-six inches tall, a weigela groundcover that is burgundy purple with pink flowers. Wow. I can see it in the front of a sunny border, leafing out and flowering year after year with minimal effort on my part.

But one cannot live by shrubs alone—or should not want to. Mix in perennials you cannot live without. Baptisia and butterfly weed (*Asclepias tuberosa*) will always be in my mixed border, and so will coneflowers and cuphea. Certainly I will add grasses, ferns, and herbs, but they will be tucked in among small shrubs that give the garden substance and the gardener respite.

A border is not thoroughly mixed until it contains a tree—or a shrub trimmed into a tree. I have seen loropetalums trimmed into single- and multitrunk forms, becoming fabulous small trees in a border, not overwhelming but tall enough to add extra dimension to the garden as well as room to plant underneath.

When I grew butterfly bushes (*Buddleia davidii*) I always trimmed them this way. With no lower branches, there were fewer blooms to deadhead, not my chore of choice. Furthermore, the blooms were at eye level and higher, where butterflies, hummingbirds, and I could enjoy them most.

Chaste tree (*Vitex agnus-castus*) is a handsome addition to the mixed border. The fragrant blooms are blue, more elongated than those of a buddleia. Would you believe a low-growing vitex, just four to ten inches tall, is also available? Hardly a chaste tree at this size. Perhaps a chaste groundcover. The foliage of vitex, incidentally, looks like cannabis, always a conversation piece in flower arrangements.

So enamored have I become with flowering shrubs that I have taken the pledge. From here on out, I will buy only shrubs. Actually, I have made this vow before, only to succumb to the lure of perennials and annuals I do not want to garden without—sort of like vowing to diet until I am offered some chocolate cake.

No matter how old we get or how busy we are, our lives are enhanced by growing things. When we have flowers to admire and to share with friends, every day is full of surprises and satisfaction. By replacing plants that require more effort than we are willing to give, our lives are eased but continue to be enriched. And that is the way it should be.

Small Pleasures

It distresses me to realize that some awfully nice people choose not to garden. Those of us who do garden know how satisfying and therapeutic this hobby of ours is, and I am saddened that every deserving person does not share our pleasure. If everyone had a garden to love, the world would undoubtedly be a better place. It would certainly be a better place for the gardener.

Those who are wary of starting a garden think that a garden must be a major undertaking. They envision long borders of perennials or islands of tropicals. They lack time, physical ability, or energy and think that if they cannot go "whole hog," they must accept their fate as nongardeners. But what they should do is think small.

To begin thinking small, select an area that is part of your daily routine: a space by the back door, near the driveway, next to a patio, or near the children's play area. Measure a space that is manageable, perhaps as small as three by three feet.

Next to placing your garden in a convenient place, the most important step is being sure it can be watered without dragging buckets or a hose around the yard. This can be a real downer. Keep a hose nearby, or create a simple watering system with a soaker hose or small sprinkler.

As awe-inspiring as the great gardens of England are, I was most smitten by the smallest garden spaces overflowing with color and texture. In cities and countryside, if a square foot of dirt is available, it is filled with a trellised vine or rosebush surrounded by annuals or herbs. Window boxes and planters are crowded with flowers and lush greenery. Pocket gardens are squeezed into narrow spaces between buildings or between a building and the sidewalk.

Ironically, thinking small opens up enormous possibilities. For gardeners like me, a container of geraniums or even orchids will never stir my heart the way a mixed border does. I need variety, some of everything I can squeeze in. Such bounty in a three-by-three-foot space is not problematic if the gardener thinks small in terms of plant choices.

I envision a grouping of six-inch-tall forget-me-nots (*Myosotis sylvatica*), which I currently grow in a very long border. The sky-blue flowers are a half-inch across and bloom in a shady border all spring, easily divided any time of the year to share and spread.

In sunnier areas, the equally tiny Veronica 'Georgia Blue' flourishes. The little royal blue blooms begin in late winter, and the finely textured foliage is evergreen.

Mazus and dwarf pennyroyal are groundcovers that are both evergreen and ground hugging. In spring, mazus has white blooms that look like small pieces of white tissue paper. Pennyroyal is a mint and spreads accordingly but pulls up as easily as a layer of moss.

For those of us who love summer-blooming bacopa (*Sutera*), new hybrids with names such as 'Giant Snowflake' and 'Glacier Blue' are hitting the horticultural marketplace. Just six to eight inches in height, they are ideal for containers but adapt happily to a garden setting as well.

Envision this three-foot-square garden blooming year-round with delicate-looking but hardy epimedium in late winter. Think small with violas in fall and winter and violets in the spring. Imagine miniature 'Tete-a-Tete' daffodils and dwarf iris popping through.

Include tiny herbs such as thyme. Plant a rosemary or lavender for upright interest. Trim it as a topiary, and your miniature mixed border has a tree. Include a small conifer or myrtle. If plants outgrow your garden, dig them up and move them, or trim them back to appropriate size, like a bonsai.

Do not be stymied by shade or sun. Try what you like, no matter what kind of light your little garden gets, and see what happens. We are not talking about major expense or exertion of labor . . . and isn't that pleasant?

The most fun I have had thinking small was with a container garden that began with a pair of miniature Adirondack chairs. I filled a shallow round plastic container with planting mix, plopped in the chairs, and I was off and running with my first "fairy garden."

Possibilities abound in fairyland. I planted cuttings and seedlings to serve as shrubs. I trimmed some into tree shapes, added a fence, little rocks that look like boulders, mirrors to serve as ponds, and tiny terra cotta pots. At craft stores I have found bird houses and tiny garden tools. Christmas ornaments such as miniature tricycles and sleds are enjoyed year-round in a fairy garden.

My granddaughters and I can rearrange and replant our fairy gardens at will. Sometimes they are peopled by Winnie-the-Pooh characters and other times by doll house families. I am constantly on the lookout for minuscule fairies and gnomes.

While I use plastic containers for fairy gardens because they are moved often, I adore hypertufa troughs planted with succulents. They need little water, and propagating is a cinch. Just pick up the plants (or pull them apart) and move them, like sculptures that grow.

I long for a water garden but am reluctant to take the big step because I cannot decide where to put it. What I need to do instead is take a little step by putting a simple and inexpensive water garden where I think I might like it. If it does not work out in a particular location, I have not exerted much labor, time, or expense, so moving or eliminating it is no big deal.

Big can be scary, costly, and permanent. Small is manageable and unthreatening, a bite and then another bite. We all need to think small at times because life is full of small pleasures, especially gardening pleasures, that no one should miss.

An Abundance of Herbs

I like living in a country that dedicates a week to celebrating herbs. I am not sure who decides these things, but I am happy herbs are getting their due since not long ago, growing herbs was considered kind of quirky. When I began gardening, herb plants were hard to locate, and I started mine from seeds or ordered from catalogs produced by folks who lived on mountaintops.

Herbs, by definition, are utilitarian. They are used for cooking, curing, dyeing, and scenting as well as repelling and attracting insects. When I point out an herb to a visitor, I am always asked what I do with it. No one asks what I do with fothergilla or petunias, but invariably I am quizzed about what to do with lemon verbena, borage, or anise hyssop.

What I do with herbs is what I do with every plant I grow: I enjoy them. If they bloom, I am grateful. I delight in the foliage textures and colors. I wallow in their scents, breathing deeply the heady aromas of lemon and licorice and pineapple. As I pull up chocolate mint gone astray, I inhale the odor of a peppermint pattie.

I began, like most herb growers, with a traditional herb garden: a carefully defined rectangle set apart from the rest of the garden. I prepared the sandy soil with plenty of compost, limed it well, and filled this patch with a variety of herbs that flourished but failed to thrill. While the herb garden was pleasant to inhale, it was not exactly breathtaking to look at.

My interest in the herb garden diminished, and the herb garden itself disappeared.

This is not to say I gave up herbs. It was the herb garden I left behind.

Now I grow herbs in my mixed borders. Along the edges I use woolly gray lamb's ears (*Stachys byzantina* 'Helene von Stein'), gray santolina, thyme, and green and white pineapple mint. Dwarf pennyroyal creeps from the shady border out into the lawn, and I let her roam.

Lemon verbena wanders upward and outward. In the sunny end of the border, lemongrass forms a four- or five-foot clump, and lemon balm lines the pathway in the woodland garden. If you love the fragrance of lemons as much as I do, you must plant lemon marigold (*Tagetes lemmonii*), the most aromatic lemon herb of all. Just brush by it accidentally and the air is filled with lemon.

In midborder, I grow parsley and rue with lacy blue-green foliage that makes flower arranging a snap throughout the year. Both are fodder for swallowtail caterpillars. So are dill and fennel, which grace the back of the border with feathery foliage.

Here and there in the front of the border is another butterfly magnet, 'Siam Queen' basil, blooming in shades of pink to burgundy. My favorite basil for tomato sandwiches and salads is Genovese basil, a fabulous bouquet for the kitchen. When cooking becomes unbearably boring, just poke your nose into a vase full of basil, and life improves immediately.

Among tomatoes I plant southernwood and garlic chives, both reputed to discourage nematodes. In the bed closest to the kitchen, I grow lots of parsley, a bay shrub (*Laurus nobilis*), thyme, and rosemary. I like to keep them handy for the soup pot should I have a cooking spell.

Lavender goes in the leanest, driest soil, rewarding me for this neglect with an abundance of blooms that keep their scent for years. Think Mediterranean. I mulch lavender with a blanket of white pebbles that reflect the sun to keep the bottom leaves dry and the roots moist.

Apple mint grows with manageable abandon. It does not spread as rampantly as many mints but grows year-round inside my dirt-floored greenhouse without a drop of water. Most mints should be grown in pots to keep them contained, but the four I grow (apple mint, chocolate mint, pineapple mint, and dwarf pennyroyal) are allowed to wander at will.

Herbs grow lustily despite drought, downpours, heat, and neglect. I add a generous dose of lime when planting herbs but never fertilize them. I never spray herbs or anything else. In fact, an important reason to grow herbs is to attract beneficial insects to your garden so that spraying is unnecessary.

Herbs thrive in Spartan conditions, making them a confidence builder for the gardening novice. They cost little, smell wonderful, look attractive, have no calories or fat grams, and procreate lustily, giving their gardener a super return on her passion.

Maxing Out the Annuals

The trouble with annuals is that they are here today and gone in a few months, never to return. This flaw is troublesome to frugal gardeners, who want plenty of everything but are unwilling to pay for a dozen angelonias, alternantheras, pentas, or coleus. Fortunately, the problem is easily solved through the magic of propagation.

I buy a single specimen of four or five different coleus: short ones with small leaves or tall growers with large leaves in a variety of dynamite colors: metallic red, deep burgundy, chartreuse, and green and gold. I select my purchases carefully, focusing on the quantity of stocky stems that will give me as many coleus as I want for borders and containers.

From these few coleus plants, I clip three- or four-inch sturdy stems, removing all but the top four to six leaves. I reclip each stem just below a node, dip it in water and then in powdered rooting hormone, and finally stick it in a pot of sand, perlite, or vermiculite. The purpose of this medium is to hold stems upright and provide an anchor for roots that will soon form. I place the pot of cuttings in a shady, warm spot, and in a week or two, I have a collection of well-rooted coleus stems.

I pot up each new rooted stem in commercial potting mix, keeping them all moist and out of direct sunlight. When they start putting out new foliage and are well rooted, they are ready to go into the garden for the summer. I could root coleus in water, and sometimes I do, always potting up the rooted stems until new foliage appears.

Another annual that roots easily in water is alternanthera, a group of plants growing in popularity, and for good reason. You should have no trouble finding a variety of alternantheras in local independent nurseries. If you cannot find any, make your wishes known. This is called consumer demand, and it works.

The most common alternanthera, and my favorite, is *A. dentata* 'Rubiginosa'. The foliage is deep burgundy, and so are the stems that, as they grow, start winding outward into the neighborhood, emerging in the middle of a clump of something else. No matter where it pops up, it is right where I want it, but I welcome surprises, especially in the garden. Of course, you can limit alternanthera's meandering by growing it in a pot alone, or if you are looking for pizzazz, combined with chartreuse or orange.

As with coleus, buy one alternanthera and snip cuttings. If they flop by the next day, you have cut them too soon and need to wait for stronger stems. Clip each cutting below a node, dip in water and rooting hormone, and stick stems into the medium of your choice. Or put the stems into water.

Pot them up and you will soon have masses of deep burgundy alternanthera, making dramatic statements wherever you choose. Like coleus, its flowers are negligible and I cut them off. It is foliage that matters to me.

Two other annuals priced like perennials are pentas and angelonia. Unlike coleus and alternanthera, the flowers are the focus. Look for pentas with stature, worthy of cloning, eighteen inches tall with rounded clusters of bright pink or red blooms. The heck with the price (which might be as high as six or seven dollars). Start snipping as soon as nonflowering stems are sturdy and three or four inches long.

Do the same with angelonia. The hard part with propagating angelonia is finding stem tips without flowers on them. You will see these annuals with names like 'AngelMist' and 'Angelface', but they are all angelonia and come in purple, purple and white stripes, rose, and white.

Angelonia begins blooming in mid-spring and continues until frost. It reaches eighteen to twenty-four inches in height with spikes of little orchid-shaped blooms. Angelonia thrives in heat and sun and looks best planted close together, which is all the more reason for creating plenty.

Cuttings of these and most other annuals root easily, and in fact, you can make several cuttings from a single stem. Just be sure four to six leaves are at the top and a node is at the bottom.

On the bulletin board above my desk is a hodgepodge of reminders and papers I cannot decide how to file. Photographs of idyllic pathways are stuck here and there. My favorite image is a silvery grouping of white *Hydrangea paniculata* 'Tardiva', an upright dwarf blue spruce, and a clump of variegated grass. In front of this combination, edging a brick path, is fluffy blue-gray artemisia and knock-your-socks-off *Petunia integrifolia*, as magenta as can be.

Years ago, this hot petunia (a hardy annual in my garden) reappeared every spring without my having to replant. Then it disappeared. Fortunately, a friend gave me cuttings, so I once again have the pleasure of its company.

Mass-market petunias do not interest me, perhaps because too many other people plant them in abundance. I enjoy theirs and save my own spaces for blooms that call my name—loudly, in the case of *P. integrifolia.*

This plant is petite but powerful, with masses of small magenta, black-eyed blossoms. Just six inches tall, it grows outward with determination, forming a mat two to three feet wide. Like alternanthera, it is apt to weave its way into and up through neighboring plants. It blooms without rest until frost, never looking bored and straggly like other petunias.

Other annuals easily propagated are salvias and sweet potato vines. Plant the mama plant in the garden or in a pot, and snip cuttings until your lust has quelled. The principle here is to buy one and make the most of it. You will soon have a sufficiency for your own garden and plenty to share.

I'm Just Wild about Natives

I was late to jump on the native plant bandwagon. However, once I discovered that native plants are not only historically and horticulturally significant but are every bit as beautiful and soul stirring as the fanciest imported "exotics," I was smitten. And when I realized how essential native plants are to native wildlife, I could not believe I had waited so long to fall in love.

Before I came to my senses, I had regarded natives as plain-Jane kinds of plants, admittedly tough and drought resistant but lacking pizzazz. But once I began to focus on coneflowers, columbine, milkweed, sassafras, possumhaw, and other natives, I discovered their colors, distinctive structures, and aromas. Because their qualities are subtle, native plants invite close examination. Growing them has enriched my garden and made me a more perceptive gardener.

Unfussy by nature, I have always planted randomly. Mixed borders have been my specialty by default. I like plants. Lots of them. Different ones. As a result, I achieved diversity without really trying. Exotics (nonnative plants) cohabit comfortably with natives designated for my geographical location. Bees, butterflies, lizards, toads, and many beneficial insects drop by for sustenance and shelter. Hummingbirds buzz in and out.

My relationship with natives began when I decided to create a backyard habitat. I focused on plants that attracted wildlife to my yard and discovered that most of them were either natives or cultivars of natives. I provided nectar plants for butterflies, hummingbirds, and bees as well as foliage for insect larvae. My parsleys were nibbled to skeletons, and I rejoiced. I added fennel, rue, dill, and milkweed.

I hung a feeder and planted a variety of salvias for the hummingbirds' delight and mine. I discovered that hummingbird attractors do not need to be red. In fact, the best hummingbird plant in my garden is royal blue *Salvia guaranitica* (anise sage), which is invasive but worth controlling. A hummingbird magnet that is more manageable is *S.* 'Phyllis Fancy' with pale blue flowers. This salvia grew about six feet tall in my garden last summer and bloomed from spring through fall, luring hummingbirds all the while.

Red buckeye (*Aesculus pavia*), a handsome native suitable for a shrub border or as a specimen tree, is an early bloomer, an important consideration when your garden is a haven for wildlife. Another early bloomer, trumpet creeper (*Campsis radicans*), is often described as the perfect hummingbird plant because of its structure and long blooming period. This vine can be invasive but, like *S. guaranitica*, it is worth the chase.

Discovering plants that satisfy the varied appetites of garden wildlife is not difficult. Larval food is the most urgent need and the most difficult to supply. Many plants, even some exotics, provide nectar, but larvae require specific foliage, primarily that of natives, that they can digest. Lists of suitable annuals, perennials, vines, shrubs, and trees are available in books, on the Internet, and from native plant societies in every region of the country.

The single rule regarding a wildlife garden is that no insecticides be used. I do not spray even insecticidal soaps or other organic concoctions on either native or nonnative plants. Approximately 98 percent of insects are beneficent or beneficial, and I am of the no-kill persuasion. Because of the built-in diversity of a wildlife garden full of native plants, chances are that insect damage will be minimal anyway. The only plants chewed in my garden, I assume, are nutrient sources for bugs and other critters. They are welcome to chomp.

Once I began recreating my garden as a wildlife habitat and I focused on native plants, I realized that being an eco-friendly gardener actually takes less effort than being an eco-oblivious gardener. Once established, native plants need minimal irrigation and no winter protection. They are resistant to diseases. Because I use no chemical fertilizers or poisons, my mulched soil is continually enriched by earthworms, insects, and microorganisms.

No gardener has to opt exclusively for natives, though once we begin focusing on natives and their minimal care, purists often choose to have exclusively native gardens. I have taken a more inclusive approach. Rather than ripping out treasured exotics, I intersperse natives, creating biodiversity a plant at a time. As plants die or fall out of favor, they are often replaced by natives. Another possibility is to create new borders, especially along the perimeters of our yards, clustering shrubs and small trees native to the area.

My naturalist friend who encouraged me to develop my wildlife habitat garden urged me to allow a tenth of my garden to "go wild," and I did. A corner of our lot was designated as a natural area. Whatever wildflower or grass or tree emerges from the earth is allowed to grow without any help from me, other than an occasional thinning out of vines and brambles. It is untidy, a downright mess, and definitely not for everybody, but in some ways it is the most interesting segment of the garden. So full of surprises.

I believe that we can have an impact on protecting our natural heritage. A single person can create a backyard wildlife habitat, providing food and shelter sources that development has erased. A single person can be a model to her neighborhood. A single person can have a diverse and bountiful garden with plants native to her area, easy to maintain and a pleasure to see.

My friend knew she had a believer when she heard me say, "Oh good. Something is eating my *Asclepias tuberosa.*" Tolerating imperfections, I am doing my part, small as it may seem, in preserving a world I want my grandchildren and their grandchildren to share and to treasure.

Math Skills in the Garden

As I struggled through high school algebra and geometry, I was continually assured by my teachers that I was learning essential skills that would lead to success and personal happiness. This was an intimidating promise for someone who never understood anything beyond a straight line being the shortest distance between two points. The time when two trains might meet as they hurtle toward and away from Chicago remains a mystery to me.

Fortunately, the mathematical processes we use as gardeners are perfectly obvious. We divide to make more plants. We multiply to make more plants. We subtract to make our plants shapely and lush. And we all know about adding more plants, more space, and more pleasure.

The traditional rule is that spring-flowering perennials should be divided in autumn and fall bloomers in spring. While I understand why fall bloomers should be divided in spring, since I would not want to divide them while they are blooming, it seems logical to divide spring bloomers either before they bloom or immediately after.

The truth is that I divide everything I want to divide when I feel like it. I prefer dividing in spring when plants are four to six inches above ground, but I often divide in midsummer without disaster. Frequently I divide plants as soon as I get home from the nursery. Two or three plants for the price of one seems a shrewd deal to me. I am a whiz at this kind of math.

Because my garden continually enlarges, I often move to the front an older midsize plant that used to be in the back of the border. Once I have it out of the ground, it seems sensible to turn an overcrowded clump into individual plants.

If the number or size of a perennial's blooms has diminished, the clump is probably overcrowded and stressed and is ready to be divided. If the center of the clump looks like a doughnut hole, this is a sure sign the plant needs dividing. If the plant has become too big for its allotted space, divide it.

Dividing provides new plants (at zero cost) to spread around your borders or to share with friends who might be inspired to do their own dividing and sharing.

If the plant to be divided has mature foliage, subtract by one-half to two-thirds to reduce stress. Dig the clump out of the ground. Dig deeply to save as many roots as possible. Wash off the roots so that you can see what you are doing, and with your fingers, pull the rooted segments away from one another. When you replant the segments, group two or three together as you pot them up . . . or, for more plants, pot them up singly.

If your fingers cannot separate the rooted segments, use a sharp knife, clippers, a saw, or a hatchet. Do what you have to do. You may lose some roots or even some plants, but you will still end up with more than you started with.

Another way to divide is to ease baby plants from the outer rim of the mother plant without disturbing her a bit. This is the best way to divide sedums and is the method I use throughout the season on clumpers such as Becky daisies (*Leucanthemum* × *superbum*), patrinia, forget-me-nots, and lamb's ears.

I have seen pictures of plants being divided with two back-to-back pitchforks, but that is more effort than I want to exert. I myself have ripped shallow-rooted plants right out of the soil and immediately replanted them in a new location or handed them to visitors along with a plastic bag.

Discard dead-looking stems and roots. Keep new divisions moist and shaded in their new locations until they begin growing. Do not fertilize, but incorporate compost where the mother plant was removed and the babies are being planted. At this point you want root growth, not excessive foliage.

Gardening subtraction is even easier than division. Sometimes plants do not work out as we had hoped. They fail to flourish, or they attract harmful insects or become diseased. They spread too rapidly, or we just do not like the way they look. If they are unhealthy, pull or dig them out of the ground and discard them, preferably by wrapping them in a plastic bag and tossing into the garbage so they will not infect other plants. If they are healthy but not right for your garden, pot them up and pass them along to a good home.

Gardeners also subtract by pruning and deadheading. Deadheading perennials is essential but not difficult. I deadhead with bypass pruners or hedge shears, depending upon how much time I have or how much deadheading I have to do. I can clip off one branch or one deadhead at a time with the pruners, but with hedge shears I can lower an entire plant by one-third or more with a single whack.

Deadhead to encourage repeat blooms and fresh new foliage. Stagger the height and bloom time of perennials by lowering some and not others.

Last summer I deadheaded butterfly weed (*Asclepias tuberosa*) three times and was blessed with a succession of bright orange blooms before I let the plant go to seed.

I cut autumn bloomers such as swamp sunflowers and asters in half in mid-July to keep them from falling over before they flower.

Math is not nearly as difficult as I supposed. Keep your plants properly divided, subtracted, multiplied, and added, and you, too, will know the thrill of success and personal happiness, just as my teachers promised.

Knowin' When to Fold 'Em

Sometimes gardening is like poker. Knowing when to throw in a hand is a basic skill. Take hostas, for example. Slugs love them. Deer find them delectable. And gardeners find them irresistible. Sooner or later, the hosta bug bites most gardeners. We begin buying one or two at a nursery or plant sale, or we are given one by a generous friend. Before we know it, we are in love, and although well aware of the risks involved, we amass as many hostas as our space and pocketbooks permit.

Hostas are the dream plant of gardeners with a yen to collect. Hundreds of hostas fill nurseries and catalogs devoted to this single plant and, of course, the hosta devotee wants them all, even if it means ripping up the shade garden, starting a new border of hostas, or getting a job to support the hosta habit. Hostas can put a strain on a gardener's budget. I have seen a single hosta priced at fifty-five dollars, and I know people who will pay the price to satisfy their passion.

I no longer recall where my first hostas came from since they were with me only a brief period before succumbing to slugs. All it took to ravage my hostas was a few days without a pan of beer for the slimy little creatures to fall into or a dose of slug bait spread thickly around their outer leaves.

Deer do not mess around just nibbling hostas. They eat the entire plant, lick their lips, and look for another. Netting and fences are effective until a wily buck finds an alternate route. Repellents work but need to be replenished consistently.

My hostas were pleasant looking but nothing special, so when I ripped them out, freeing up space for less vulnerable plants, there were no tears or gnashing of teeth. If they had been those lush three-foot-tall blue-leafed fifty-five-dollar specimens, I would have been undone.

Let this be a lesson to us all. When a plant is more trouble than it is worth, get rid of it. Life is short and replacements plentiful, even for hostas.

What do slugs eschew and deer avoid? What has hostalike foliage with the added feature of undersides that feel like hairy sandpaper? What has fancy spots and streaks and silvery leaves and flowers that change color from pink in bud to blue, and other blooms in shades of white, purple, and red?

Pulmonaria, a genus with common names like spotted dog, lungwort, Mary's tears, and thunder and lightning, is the answer to all the questions above and maybe to our prayers as well. Like hostas, they have patterned foliage and look best on the outer edge of a border or massed as a dramatic groundcover. Also like hostas, they grow best in shade and humus-rich, moist soil. Although they prefer cool air temperatures, they have thrived in my hot, humid garden.

Unlike those long-gone hostas, I do remember getting my first pulmonarias and being less than optimistic about their ability to survive since they began life at a nursery in Oregon and had come to live in my hot, muggy southern garden.

I planted the two little pulmonarias (misplacing their tags and therefore their identities) at the front of the shade garden, and both spent the summer expanding into two-foot-wide clumps. Pulmonarias double and even triple their size in a year. In good soil they need no fertilizer. I mulch mine with compost of shredded leaves, but I have read that too much mulch may lead to crown rot.

Pulmonarias are among the earliest perennials to bloom and are welcomed by the first bees of the season. Later in spring, they are relished by low-flying hummingbirds. Their blooms appear in clusters of small, flared bells on short stems. Most pulmonaria blooms undergo an intriguing transformation: beginning pink when in bud and turning blue as they mature. Other pulmonaria blooms are white, red, purple, and wine.

Although hybridizers are focusing on pulmonaria blooms, the flowers will never be a thrill to me. For me it is the foliage, varying from almost no pattern at all to distinct white splotches and streaking. Some pulmonaria foliage is iridescent, as if thinly coated with silver foil. My favorites are *Pulmonaria* 'Trevi Fountain', a silver-spotted stunner with clusters of cobalt blue flowers, and 'Silver Streamers', with ruffled edges on the silvery lance-shaped leaves. 'Milky Way' has heavily spotted leaves and wine to purple flowers. 'Moonshine' has shimmering silver-white rounded leaves, each bordered by a thin, dark green edge. The foliage of 'Raspberry Ice' is variegated mint green and creamy white.

As with hostas, the expanding choice of pulmonaria cultivars makes collectors salivate. Plant them as you would hostas, combining them with hellebores, Japanese anemones, ferns, Solomon's seal, and other shade plants. There's no reason not to plant them with hostas themselves if you are not ready to give them up.

Those little pulmonarias planted two years ago are ready to divide, a job I will do on a cool fall day. I will dig up the plants and divide the thick rhizomes, or I will cut the clump in half with a sharp shovel and ease one of the halves out of the ground.

When shopping for pulmonarias in garden centers or catalogs, read the labels or descriptions carefully, looking for mildew-resistant varieties as well as sun tolerance if you do not want to confine them to shady borders. Chances are, once you get started with pulmonarias, you will want them everywhere.

While pulmonarias may never reach the magnificent heights of those fabulous hostas seen in garden magazines, they are much less likely to break your heart when devoured by slugs and deer or break your budget with outlandish price tags.

Plant Now for Fall Bounty

A few weeks ago a friend in Charleston e-mailed me in desperation. Her son and his bride-to-be want to have their rehearsal dinner at the family home in mid-November and, of course, she is panicking about her garden, which is quite a nice one. "Nice," however, is not what a mother of the groom wants. She longs for "spectacular," and so would I.

Fortunately the party is to be in Charleston (zone 9) and not the midlands of South Carolina, where we are apt to have a freeze by mid-November. In a string of e-mails (as I thought of plants she absolutely must plant immediately), I suggested my favorites that look good in my garden the month of October, assuming November in Charleston will still be balmy. My friend panicked just in time. If she wants her garden to look fabulous in November, she needs to plan and plant now . . . and so should we all.

Taking center stage in my own fall garden are cassias. The bright yellow flowers are a mainstay in my garden, beginning with *Cassia corymbosa*, which begins blooming in midsummer and continues through fall. *C. corymbosa* tops out at four or five feet in height, a relatively subdued "shrub" that fits comfortably into a sunny mixed border. On the other hand, the much flashier *Cassia bicapsularis* reaches seven to eight feet in height. The stems drift every which way, mingling quietly with neighbors, until October, when this multi-stemmed shrub explodes into breathtaking bloom and, depending upon when the first hard freeze hits, may continue until Christmas.

I started *C. corymbosa* in my garden years ago from seeds given to me by a friend. My first *C. bicapsularis* was purchased in Charleston a few years ago. It was love at first sight and, though I was sure it would not survive winter in the midlands, I had to have it.

I kept it in my greenhouse over the winter and moved it into the garden in the spring. I propagated several more from cuttings so that I could have this fabulous plant everywhere. That was three years ago, and *C. bicapsularis* has returned in triumph every spring without ever again being sheltered in the greenhouse.

I call castor beans (*Ricinus communis*) the signature plant of my garden. I love the rich burgundy color, the large palmate foliage, and the stature of this annual—grown from seed and seven feet tall by late summer. As I do with cassias, I trim them up as tree forms and spot them here and there like oversized exclamation points.

Between cassias and castor beans, I have a combination of burgundy and butter yellow, calling out for orange . . . or blue . . . or purple. Pizzazz is the guide word for a fall garden. Mexican sunflowers (*Tithonia*) cannot be found in a nursery, but with a packet of seeds you can have a dozen or more plants that by summer's end reach six to eight feet and are covered with orange-red daisylike blooms. Your reward will be fabulous color as well as a crowd of butterflies hovering gratefully over these sunflowers. If the plant falls over in a late summer storm, let it rest. The former top will take a skyward turn and continue to produce flowers and nectar until a hard frost.

Most perennial salvias continue to bloom from midsummer until frost, but my favorite salvias, pineapple sage (*S. elegans*), *S. madrensis* 'Red Neck Girl', and Mexican bush sage (*S. leucantha*) do not even start blooming until late summer or fall. Plant them all and add red, butter yellow, and purple to the spectrum. Need some blue? I recommend royal blue *Salvia guaranitica* as well as the paler blues of 'Anthony Parker' and 'Phyllis Fancy'.

The best way to get started with Mexican bush sage (or any salvia) is to buy a plant early in spring. Choose a specimen with plenty of potential cuttings, plant it in the garden (giving it ample space), and begin propagating as stems firm up. That way, for the price of a single plant, you will have almost enough Mexican bush sage . . . or 'Red Neck Girl', or any other salvia you covet.

Fall-blooming daisylike chrysanthemums are a nuisance all summer, wandering here and there, taking up valuable space. I cut these perennials back in midsummer to keep them reined in. Nag your local nurseryman, the one who welcomes you as a serious gardener and customer, about a supply of pink 'Ryan's Daisy', bronze 'Miss Gloria', or butter yellow 'Gethsemane Moonlight'.

The last to bloom are New England asters, such as 'Fanny's Fall Aster', 'Purple Dome', and the fragrant climber, *Aster carolinianus.* As with chrysanthemums, you may be tempted to rip out asters in July, but have patience. You will welcome the cheerful blooms when days and nights get frosty.

Even without an imminent wedding, plan and plant now so your fall garden will delight until you are ready to call it to a halt. For me, this happens when the last flowers grace our Thanksgiving table, reminding me how blessed I am to be a gardener.

The Dratted Deer

I have put off writing this chapter for at least twenty years. It always seemed like being the referee in the middle of a standoff: gardeners on one side, Bambi on the other.

Living in the middle of a subdivision whose woods have disappeared, lot by lot, I am not personally affected by the ever-expanding and always-hungry deer population. As a result, my garden is never pruned to ground level by dratted deer, nor is a favorite tree, the expensive and coddled one, chewed to a nubbin.

On the contrary, I am pleased to see deer emerging from someone else's woods or browsing in a field. An awe-filled moment occurred when I sat on the screened porch of a Low Country house a couple of years ago and was startled to first hear, then see a herd of deer running lickety-split across the wooded backyard, no doubt chased by a dog or irate gardener.

Whenever I visit that house, I purposely rise before dawn and move silently to the porch, hoping to catch a few deer nibbling on the shrubbery. I know they are there because I hear them shuffling through the marshy ground. If I make a sound or someone turns on a light, the deer take flight. Otherwise, they remain at their tasks until the soft morning light makes them pleasingly visible.

My deer delight is not shared by most gardeners. No subject brings more ire than deer on the chomp. I get phone calls and e-mails pleading for help. I am stopped in the grocery store or the post office by angry gardeners who have lost their prized specimens to nibbling deer. Deer are in their gardens, on their porches, leaping over fences, wherever the most prized plants grow . . . or grew.

What to do? I am of two minds on this issue: one mind says to garden with the deer (in other words, give up the struggle and enjoy sharing their habitat). The other mind says figure out ways to outsmart them. After all, we are the ones with bigger brains.

I like to think that planting smart allows us to enjoy the deer and our gardens as well. And why not?

It does not take a large portion of those brains to tell us to plant what deer do not eat, keeping in mind that, if deer are hungry enough, they will eat anything growing. Wouldn't we all?

It makes sense to begin a deer-discouraging garden with shrubs (or bones) that, according to gardening guru and Virginia nurseryman Andre Viette, are never or rarely eaten by deer. A perfectly acceptable garden can be created with plants on his list: aucuba, chokeberry, barberry, buddleia, common boxwood, spice bush, false cypress (*Chamaecyparis*), inkberry, American hollies, Chinese juniper, mountain laurel, kerria, beautybush, mahonia, and nandina.

These plants are, according to Viette, sure bets. For the risk takers among us, his list also includes some "iffier" shrubs, but be warned. It is a matter of deciding which plants you cannot live without and, with luck, you can have them . . . at least for a while.

But gardeners cannot live by shrubs alone; we want more. Perennials that appear on Viette's list include yarrow, alliums, amsonia, anemones, native columbine, artemisias, butterfly weed (*Asclepias tuberosa*), baptisia, plumbago, chrysanthemums, crocosmia, coreopsis, coneflowers, Joe Pye weed, euphorbias, and geum.

There are more: hellebores, bearded iris, red-hot poker, tiger lilies, mints, bee balm, miscanthus, salvias, ferns, pulmonaria, rosemary, sedums, solidago, veronica, and lamb's ear.

Gee whiz, a gardener could create Eden with these plants alone. And, when she is through, she can lie in her hammock watching deer stroll through her yard on their way to visit neighbors who continue to fight the battle.

Drop by Drop

My personal verdict is still out regarding global warming, but I have no doubt we should live (and garden) as if a climate crisis were pending.

This realization was brought home today as I drove down my street, located in a suburban development with 1970s landscaping: broad expanses of grass, a row of shrubs across house foundations, a well in almost every backyard, and inefficiently placed watering systems.

Several irrigation systems were already in action in early spring. Not only was still-dormant grass being watered (though it had rained the day before), but driveways and the street itself were getting their share of the wet stuff. If my irrigation system were up and running, it no doubt would be doing the same dumb thing.

I learned recently that an average American uses 100 gallons of water daily. Twenty-five percent goes to watering lawns and gardens. According to EPA estimates, half the water used on landscaping is wasted because of evaporation, runoff, and overwatering.

Fifty percent of my readers are probably saying to themselves, "But I have a well. . . ." I have said this myself until I came to grips with reality. We own the well and the pump as well as the timer and pump house . . . but water we pump from our wells, as well as from lakes or ponds, belongs to all of us.

We can argue about this issue, just as we argue about melting ice floes, but why not behave as if it were true?

I want to do the right thing, but, as usual, I do not want to work any harder than necessary. In a month or so, our irrigation system will be turned on. Waiting as late as possible to irrigate makes sense. Why water until necessary? Why not encourage the grass to produce a deeper root system than the usual one inch? Surely a four- to six-inch root system is better prepared to take care of itself should we experience a drought.

Since we installed our irrigation system, we have watered the entire acre yard (minus the house site) three times a week for an hour. This summer we will cut back to two times a week and water a sample site until a rain gauge indicates it has received one inch of water. Then we will set the timer for all six stations.

Consider this startling information about watering overhead during daylight hours: 30 percent of the moisture is lost to evaporation. Watering early in the morning or at night reduces usage by 25 percent, or 11,000 gallons per year per family. Now how hard is that?

Our overhead irrigation system is not installed underground, so it is easy to manipulate. I intend to be more careful about where water is landing, preferably on the grass and garden rather than the driveway or street. We have always been ahead of the norm when it comes to evaporation since our system is set to start the cycle at around three o'clock in the morning, finishing up by eight.

This summer I intend to use more soaker hoses in the garden areas, decreasing evaporation at least in the borders. That does not solve the problem entirely, though we will feel good about wasting less water than we have in years past.

My handyman husband has never been one to allow leaks, so I do not think we can improve there. However, I was startled to find myself dumping a bowl of water (used for washing grapes) down the drain. I decided to place a two-gallon watering can by the sink and dump water into it instead of down the drain. An hour later I had to take a full can of water outside to empty where it can do some good. Admittedly this involves some effort, but I am feeling downright smug about my conservation success. Some efforts are worth exertion.

I have always been a mulcher, placing about four to six inches of hay, shredded leaves, or other mulching material on my borders every spring. As a result, my soil is full of organic material and my roots are cooler and moister than they would be if the top surface were bare.

I am a compulsive showerer, and that is a good thing for a gardener to be, especially in the summer. A timer might decrease dawdling. However, my goal is to conserve water, not attain sainthood.

I would never urge anyone to work harder in their garden, let alone do it myself. Other than taking the watering can outside, nothing about my conservation plan requires increased effort. But consider the result if we all do something to conserve, and think how good we will feel as, drop by drop, we save the world.

Pick a Peck of Plectranthus

With a name like plectranthus, you've got to be good. While *plectranthus* sounds more like a dinosaur or a disease than a plant genus, it is, in fact, a happy horticultural clan with a common denominator. It grows with enthusiasm but stays within bounds. The bounds are just big ones.

Plectranthus, like salvia, thyme, and rosemary, is a member of the mint family. Frost-tender natives of Asia, South Africa, Australia, and the Pacific islands, they thrive in hot, humid climates and are happy in sun or partial shade. They appreciate moisture but tolerate drought. One more reason to love plectranthus: deer do not find them tasty . . . yet.

As if having a moniker like "plectranthus" is not enough, plectranthuses are tagged with species names such as *fruticosus*, *madagascariensis*, *forsteri*, *coleoides*, and *argentatus*. Do not let this confusing nomenclature stop you from snapping them up at your local garden center. No plants are easier to grow.

Since I am a gardener of limited memory and pronunciation skills, I choose to divide plectranthuses into two groups and leave it at that: trailing and upright.

The best-known trailing variety is Swedish ivy, a boring houseplant that has been around longer than I have. Fortunately, every plectranthus I have met propagates as easily as Swedish ivy. Stick tip cuttings in a medium such as sand or perlite to hold them upright, and in a week or so, you should have rooted stems ready to pot up.

Several years ago, on a visit to my favorite botanical garden, I was smitten by Cuban oregano, my first experience with the plectranthus clan. Like lamb's ears, a whole different species, the soft, fuzzy, variegated leaves of Cuban oregano call out, "Pet me, pet me." The muted green foliage edged in cream makes it an elegant front-of-the-border foil for dark, glossy foliage. And here's the kicker: it spreads obligingly, so a single Cuban oregano planted in spring may be a yard wide (but just ten to fifteen inches tall) by August.

Even more exciting is another trailing plectranthus, 'Purple Majesty', which has thick, crinkled dark green foliage. The leaf surface has a metallic glow, and the undersides are purple. As with all plectranthuses, the first freeze dooms 'Purple Majesty' left outdoors, so I bring in a pot to winter over.

The upright plectranthuses that bloom in late summer are the ones that quicken my gardening greed. I want them all, and I want plenty of each.

Last summer a friend gave me a rooted cutting of 'Purple Martin' that eventually grew thirty inches tall, and I have been propagating from that single plant ever since. 'Purple Martin' does not have the thick, woolly foliage I had come to expect in a plectranthus. Instead it has textured, light green foliage (similar to lantana) with a golden sheen and purple flower spikes that bloom late in summer, just when I need them most.

Last summer I discovered 'Mona Lavender' in another friend's garden and was thrilled to find some at a local garden center. Like 'Purple Martin', it blooms from late summer to frost with purple flowers at the ends of deeper purple thirty-inch stems.

I am currently on the lookout for 'Erma', which will reach four or five feet in height and has pink flowers. And then there are 'Vanilla Twist' and 'Athens Gem', promised for the near future.

I am not the only one with an appetite for plectranthus. More than 250 known species exist, and hybridizers, no doubt, are working their magic, developing plectranthuses to every gardener's liking. As usual, I like them all.

Gray Thoughts in the Garden

When I traveled to Italy and France, I was warned ahead of time that there are not many gray-haired women in either country. I was surprised to find that this is true: European women "of a certain age" go to great lengths to deny the passage of years and hair color. Like wearing white walking shoes or a jogging suit, gray hair, I was warned, would make me look American.

Of course, looking American wherever I am is quite all right with me. It is who I am. A silver-haired American, in fact. Not surprisingly, I think of gray not as a sign of age and deterioration, but as a mellow veil that comes with experience, a kind of filtering lens. In my garden, gray and silver plants provide the same mellowing effect. Masses of green foliage and brightly colored blooms are interrupted by clumps of soft gray artemisias, rue, germander, and santolina. Used judiciously, gray rests our eyes but can draw as much attention as the hottest pink or red or blue.

Throughout my garden I have clumps of perennial lamb's ears (*Stachys byzantina*) at the front of the border in both sun and shade. Lamb's ears have a woolly texture that delights children. They find the softness irresistible. I do, too. Stroking lamb's ears foliage is like petting a puppy.

My favorite lamb's ear is *S. byzantina* 'Helene von Stein' because her oversized whitish-gray leaves hold up well in both rain-soaked or drought conditions. I have seen other stachys become a pulpy mess by midsummer. 'Helene von Stein' does not bloom, and that is all right since lamb's ears blooms are unattractive woolly spikes. Lamb's ears also remain presentable year-round.

Lamb's ears have been in my garden as long as I can remember. I am sure I started with a single plant because that is the way almost all plants in my garden began. Each lamb's ear spreads itself into a clump-shaped colony. I pull out leaves that become discolored or tired looking and yank out chunks as the colony spreads. Few people leave my garden without a few lamb's ears, even if they do not know they want them.

Speaking of front-of-the-border perennials, another gray favorite is lady's mantle (*Alchemilla mollis*) started from seed years ago, before I knew they were difficult to germinate. Ignorance can, indeed, be bliss. Once alchemilla plants become comfortable and increase in size, they are easily divided.

As with lamb's ears, I grow lady's mantle for the foliage and not the mounds of bronzy gold flowers I see in catalogs but never in my borders. Alchemilla leaves are shaped like lobed fans and collect shiny drops of rain or dew that look like fairy tears. Some things are even better than blooms.

In midborder, painted ferns (*Athyrium nipponicum*) grow to about eighteen inches. While lady's mantle and lamb's ears are matte gray, painted fern is shiny silver. I grow them in part to full shade wherever I am looking for a bright spot of texture.

Artemisia 'Powis Castle' flourished in my garden and then disappeared without a wave good-bye. Like mounds of lace, the finely cut foliage grows about three feet tall and wide and does its best in full sun, though I grew it in shade, perhaps accounting for its demise. I believe it is time to try it again.

A. ludoviciana 'Silver King' is the artemisia to grow for flower arrangements, both fresh and dried. Cut it when the silvery white "beads" form. These are flower heads, and once they open, Silver King's prime has passed. Be advised and be wary.

A. lactiflora is another flower arranger's delight, with creamy white flower heads and ferny foliage. It can be annoying if the gardener is fussy, however, because it flops over just about the time it is ready to bloom. My recommendation for all artemisias (except the bright green *A. annua* 'Sweet Annie') is to cut them back by one-third to one-half in midsummer.

Mountain mint grows about two feet tall and prefers shade but will grow in sun. I plant it where it can roam, but if you are the tidy type, put it in a pot. Choose a big pot because you will want plenty. The foliage is gray-green and, as it dries, it acquires a silvery hue. The fine-textured flowers are gray-green buttons less than an inch across, and the minty aroma lowers the temperature ten degrees.

Rue (*Rutus graveolens*) is an herb with lacy gray-blue foliage, and I do not understand why everyone does not grow it. It grows in sun or part shade, reaching two feet in height, and keeps its foliage through the winter. It produces clusters of negligible yellow flowers that I snip off. The foliage is spectacular enough. Letting it bloom would be gilding the rue.

Mexican bush sage (*Salvia leucantha*) is not a dependable perennial in my garden, so I root cuttings and nurse them through the winter in a protected environment. Occasionally I am surprised when it returns from last summer's roots, but the cuttings are insurance.

I would not want to be without Mexican bush sage, which grows four to five feet in height and begins to bloom in late summer, continuing until frost. The long purple flowers definitely are the stars, but before they appear, the willowy gray-green leaves add texture to the middle or back of the border.

Silvers and grays are dynamite in a white garden, softening whites just as they intensify dark colors and blend the hot colors I favor. Most grays are drought tolerant, and downy grays are deer resistant.

Work grays and silvers into your borders and you will be charmed by the cooling effect. Do not be surprised to be so enchanted by the effect that you toss the hair-coloring kit into the trash and enjoy what silver does to your own aura. A lot can be learned in a garden.

Holes Happen

Holes happen in the best of gardens. One day the garden looks perfect; the next day a shrub keels over, perennials fade, a fern shrivels. Chasms open in the border, inevitably when guests are on their way.

We know we should rise above such disaster, especially since the rest of the garden looks fine. But a hole in the border is like a pimple on the nose. No matter how good the rest of you looks, that blemish is an eye-catcher.

While I think loosely, I plant tightly. My borders tend to overflow and intermingle, so when a hole occurs, it is obviously a hole and not one of those spaces designed to let the eyes rest.

Like all ideas that have improved my gardening ways, the concept of substitution is not one I devised on my own. I visited a garden last fall and the owner, a rose specialist with a fabulous mixed border, pointed out plants that remained in black nursery pots but were placed in the garden as if they were part of the grand design.

She claimed to have started leaving plants in pots (sometimes for years) until she decided definitely where they should go. I know how she feels. I have plants in my own garden that have been moved twice and even thrice before getting settled permanently.

How much easier it is to move pots around, even if the plants must be repotted each year, than to dig the plants out of the ground and move them elsewhere.

I now keep a collection of potted substitutes to send in when the starting lineup needs pepping up, like a coach with a bench full of players eager to get into the game. I keep conifers, both youngsters and full grown, in pots, not only to use as substitutes, but to make them appear bigger than they are. Planting them in pots instead of in the ground makes them instantly two feet taller and less likely to get lost in the shuffle.

Ferns are excellent fill-ins, adding instant texture and fluff. Autumn fern and holly fern are my favorites, two different textures but both evergreen and happiest in shade. Cinnamon fern, Japanese painted fern, and royal fern take the sun, so a pot of each is handy for slipping into a sunny border.

Because I like their large ovate leaves, I purchased three English laurels (*Prunus laurocerasus*). I planted one laurel as a screen behind the pump house, but the other two I planted in handsome lightweight pots. One is toward the back of the mixed border. The other waits in the holding pen for stardom.

I reserve a couple of reblooming hydrangeas in pots for instant color and two small loblolly bays (*Gordonia lasianthus*) for their sculptural shapes. Mexican bush sage and pineapple sage thrive in pots, waiting for their bloom time in late summer.

When a large daphne withered overnight in late winter (the day after I took its picture because it was so gorgeous), I had a large sweetbox (*Sarcococca hookeriana*) waiting in the wings. I bought this plant in midwinter, sharply reduced because it needed repotting. Just the kind of plant I love. I invested a little labor repotting it in a larger, taller container, and this summer I will take at least a dozen cuttings from this well-rooted beauty.

Replacing a dead plant with a potted one makes good sense. That daphne died for a reason, and the soil is no doubt contaminated. I dug out the daphne, filled the hole with compost, and placed the pot of sweetbox where the daphne had been, but on top of the ground.

Because I plant primarily for foliage, sometimes my borders lack the oomph that color provides. Large pots of orange Mexican sunflower, yellow cassia, blue and red salvia, multicolored coleus, and other annuals and perennials add needed pizzazz. When flowers fade, move the pots to the back of the border, cut them back with hedge shears, and when they are rehabilitated, move them back to front stage.

I would not be satisfied with a garden of containers. I prefer plants in the ground, where they belong. But moving pots in and out of the borders not only fills holes; it keeps a garden dynamic and diverse, an endless source of horticultural surprise.

Summer

There is an artist in each of us,
just waiting to escape into our gardens.

Slowing Down and Perking Along

Mid-August is mid–garden season for me. Everything is planted where it is going to stay until fall, and with a little maintenance, the garden and I are good to go until first frost. When I say "a little maintenance" I am talking about five minutes to a half hour in the garden most days of the week, just to keep things perking along and looking good.

The mophead hydrangeas continue to bloom sporadically and will do so until November. So does 'Annabelle'. I clip 'Annabelle's' blooms as they turn pale green and a little crisp to share with friends for winter arrangements or Christmas tree fluff.

Late-blooming *Hydrangea paniculata* 'Limelight' is in full bloom, and *H. paniculata* 'Tardiva' should be in full bloom within a week. Though 'Limelight' is reportedly lime green, in my garden both hydrangeas have bright white elongated blooms that are spectacular cut flowers. Like 'Annabelle', 'Tardiva' and 'Limelight' need to be cut close to the ground in early spring since they bloom on the current season's growth. Cutting them to the ground generates more foliar growth, and the more new wood, the more blossoms.

If you have any of these hydrangeas or others you notice blooming late in summer, jot a reminder on the February or March page of your garden calendar. The hard part is remembering which plants are which, so mark them with flagging or labels.

I trim hydrangeas when I want flowers for arrangements and to remove shabby blooms. Cutting them back stimulates new growth for cuttings. For cuttings, and summer is the ideal time to propagate hydrangeas, I use stems that have not bloomed. The stems should be green rather than woody, slightly pliable but not floppy.

When the cutting puts out new growth and resists being pulled out of the medium, it has roots and is ready to pot up in potting mix. Leave rooted and potted hydrangeas or other shrubs in a shady area, keeping the plants moist but not waterlogged.

Once you have successfully rooted cuttings, you will be hooked. Hydrangeas are an ideal first venture because they root so easily and start putting out new growth quickly. If you root cuttings in July or August, you will be potting up in October and planting new (and free) plants next spring or the following fall. What a deal. And what a delight to have a supply of favorite plants for your own garden and to share with friends.

I deadhead or cut back all herbs, perennials, and annuals (including coleus) to remove spent blooms and to stimulate growth. Doing this assures me that they will continue to thrive, and many will rebloom. Even plants that do not rebloom will have healthier and more abundant foliage after an enthusiastic shearing. Kind of like getting a good haircut.

The biggest discourager for gardeners is the weed problem. Unless you are like the enthusiastic if eccentric gardener I met last spring who regards weeding as therapeutic, it is awful to weed a bed thoroughly and come back in a couple of weeks and have to start all over again. No gardener should face this travail, largely because it is unnecessary.

Because I mulch all my beds and borders, I rarely see a weed. The first time I mulch a bed, I begin by spreading eight layers of newspaper either tucked around the plants or over the entire surface if it is not planted. It is much easier to do this over the entire surface, even if it means removing plants temporarily. You go through this process only once if you do it right.

On top of the newspapers, I put a layer of compost or manure if the soil needs amending. On top of the compost, I put a layer of mulch: coastal Bermuda hay, shredded leaves, shredded pine bark or seaweed, whatever organic material is cheap and accessible. When do you do this? Certainly before you quit gardening in disgust. There is no wrong time to make life easier for yourself and to save your sanity.

Coastal Bermuda hay, my favorite mulch, is available from local farmers or feed stores. If you can find spoiled hay, unsuitable for animal fodder, you should be able to cut a deal. Coastal Bermuda (not to be confused with scratchy, seed-filled straw) is pleasant to handle, smells delicious, and does not reseed because it is a hybrid.

Another way I avoid laborious weeding is by planting everything close enough so that the foliage of the plants shades and cools the soil. This crowding excludes sunlight, so weed seeds do not germinate and, even if they did, there is insufficient room for them to flourish . . . and who notices if they do?

I have to confess to one kind of "weeding" with no one to blame but myself. Over the years I have deliberately planted some groundcovers that cover the ground with zeal. I pull out yards of chocolate mint, lamium, and English ivy. I knew better than to plant these nuisance plants but did it anyway. And probably will do it again.

I try to think of this labor as exercise and emotional therapy that comes from successfully doing mindless tasks. Now, in mid-August, these deliberately planted vines are taking over the borders, using up not only space but water and nutrients. I spend at least five minutes a day pulling out these vandals. I never eradicate them, but I do discourage them from taking over the neighborhood. The happiest gardeners know that perfection is not required—or even attainable—in a garden.

The most important thing to do at this time is walk around your garden daily and take care of the small tasks: deadheading, weeding, and digging up and discarding as you go. But even more important than getting things done is giving yourself the pleasure you deserve.

Sempervivums Forever

When people complain that they would like to garden but do not have the time or space or energy, I advise them to think small and easy—advice that seems pretty bland when most of us dream of long mixed borders of fabulous colors and textures.

But small and easy have become cutting-edge horticulture, thanks to revived interest in succulent plants. Your grandmother's hens and chicks, stonecrops, sedums, and agaves are being featured in elegant coffee table books, in garden magazines, and on the patios of designer houses.

Succulents have become the darlings of horticultural trendsetters—and here's the best part—they are inexpensive, easily available, almost self-sufficient, and fun to collect and combine.

Succulents are plants that have adapted to arid temperatures by developing thickened gelatinous leaves, stems, or roots that store moisture. Where they store water defines what kind of succulent they are: leaf succulents, such as aloes and hens and chicks (*sempervivums*), stem succulents (*cacti*), root succulents, and caudiciform succulents (*sedums*), which store water in both roots and stems.

The most interesting succulents are sempervivums (a combination of two Latin words that mean "always living"). The name fits. Only two mistreatments are likely to kill them: too much moisture and too little sun. Excellent drainage and light are the keys to succulent contentment.

Native to mountains in central and southern Europe and Asia Minor, sempervivums are rock plants, thriving in thin, gravelly soil or taking hold of fissures in the granite cliffs. The genus includes approximately forty species, all of them forming tight rosettes in close colonies.

The common name, hens and chicks, stems from their similarity to a mother hen setting on her brood of chicks, each chick a miniature of its mother. Another common name is houseleeks, but the origin of this name is less obvious since a houseleek does not look like a leek at all.

Sempervivum tectorum, the botanical name for houseleeks, means "growing on roofs," and they were, in fact, grown on thatched roofs as fire protection. This is not as absurd as it might seem. A California landscaper told me recently her place of business is surrounded by massed beds of succulents to suppress fires.

Considering the spate of devastating forest fires, I wonder why Californians have not traded their lawns for carpets of succulents. They are so much more interesting and need no mowing at all and minimal watering . . . but lawn lovers are a devoted and stubborn lot.

Sedums (the caudiciform succulents with water-storing roots and stems) range in size from *Sedum* 'Ogon', no more than an inch tall, to *Sedum* 'Autumn Joy', which is two feet tall. Low-growing sedums (such as 'Ogon', 'Green Mantle', 'Goldmoss', and 'Blue Spruce') make ideal groundcovers in a dry garden or under plants in a mixed container.

Sedum 'Autumn Joy' has long been a star in my mixed border, with blooms that begin a creamy white and morph over the summer to deep rose. Their blooms are broccoli-like clusters of tiny star-shaped flowers, attractive to bees and butterflies though they have no apparent scent.

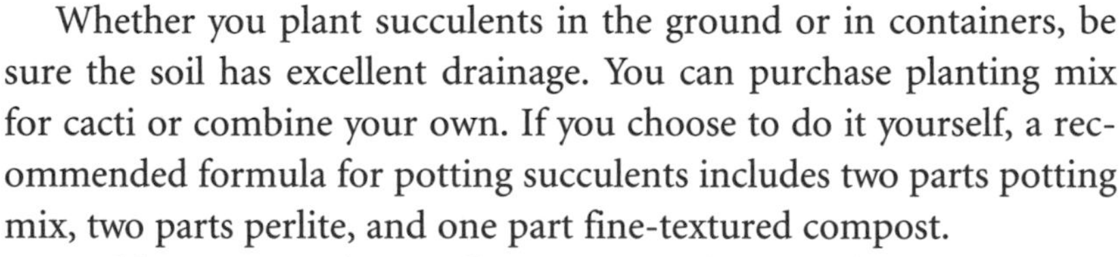

Whether you plant succulents in the ground or in containers, be sure the soil has excellent drainage. You can purchase planting mix for cacti or combine your own. If you choose to do it yourself, a recommended formula for potting succulents includes two parts potting mix, two parts perlite, and one part fine-textured compost.

I add coarse sand as well as pea gravel to regular potting mix. Some growers use poultry grit or vermiculite to facilitate drainage, which is the key to success.

I mulch succulent plantings (in containers or in the ground) with pea gravel so the bottom leaves do not become wet and spongy. To accelerate growth, I might fertilize sparingly in spring with an all-purpose granular product or diluted liquid fertilizer.

While succulents like to be dry, they do need water: every seven to ten days in spring and summer, twice a month in winter if the plants are indoors. Water thoroughly when the soil has dried out. Never let succulents or cacti sit in water for prolonged periods. They will never forgive you.

To propagate succulents, cut or pinch a snip of stem or a rosette, and let it callous over for a few days. Stick the calloused end into potting mix, but do not water for a few days, and do not press the soil down. Give it air. Water sparingly until signs of growth appear.

Once the cutting has roots, pot it up or stick it into a container where you are growing succulents. Succulents look elegant potted singly, but I think their sculptural forms are made for mixing.

They are also perfect for planting in terra cotta or, even better, stone or hypertufa containers. Rusty buckets, old boots, chimney tiles, or even weathered cinder blocks make useful and eye-catching containers. Add moss for instant aging.

Look for succulents in nurseries, garden centers, and catalogs. Buy a variety of textures, colors, foliage, and plant sizes. Play with combinations. You cannot go wrong.

One warning, however: be prepared to become a collector, an addict, a sempervivumphile. You will not break the bank or your back with these babies . . . but you will have the delights of a diverse and textured garden with minimal time, energy, and space.

Container Gardening

No one's breath is taken away by the originality of my container gardens. I have the same harum-scarum approach to "doing" containers that I have toward interior decorating, garden design, and wardrobe accumulation. It is dumb luck when things actually go together. As a result, my life is full of surprises, and I like it that way.

For instance, I just put together a combination of purple fountain grass (*Pennisetum setaceum* 'Rubrum'), *Alternanthera* 'Purple Knight', orange *Calibrachoa* 'Superbells Tequila Sunrise', and asparagus fern, following the formula of "something tall, something fluffy, and something dangling." Two identical pots are sitting on my front porch, and I hope they manage to make a reasonable statement about my taste, color sense, and zest for life. At least I got them done before mid-July.

The pots are large enough for three or four plants. I filled them with moistened potting mix and pawed out four indentations large enough for the plants, and that is as complicated as container planting gets.

If the potting mix does not contain fertilizer, I scratch some slow-release pellets into the soil surface and give the container a drink to settle everything. I also cut back all the plants by half or more to stimulate foliage growth and flowers.

The trick to keeping a container garden looking good starts before you select your plants. Be sure the plants are compatible regarding the need for drainage, sunlight, and moisture. You set yourself up for failure if you try to combine bog plants and cacti in the same pot, or hostas and zinnias.

The plants I chose for my porch containers agree about drainage, sunlight, and moisture. They will live happily together from now to the first hard frost on my front porch as long as I remember to water the soil deeply once a week. The filled pots are not so heavy that I cannot move them into dappled shade when summer cranks up. Portability is the point, I think, of doing containers.

My neighbor has two large and handsome pots of red geraniums paired with smaller pots of purple petunias. Container gardens do not have to be contained in a single container. A bevy of potted plants can be combined into gardens as well.

In fact, my favorite pots are filled with single plants or a single plant and groundcover. I move these around the garden over the course of the year, depending on where they are needed. For instance, when a large daphne died a quick death four years ago, I had a big pot of sweetbox (*Sarcococca hookeriana*) to put in its place. Suspecting the daphne expired from root rot, I did not want to put another plant in the same soil. The pot of sweetbox still sits on the surface, quite content with life as a substitute after all these years.

Sometimes a hole occurs in the garden, and it is a relief to have a potted something to fill it up. Or a section of the garden looks bland and boring. A snappy variegated ginger, a clutch of brightly colored cannas, or a pot of red geraniums can give the garden instant pizzazz.

Usually I move a potted plant around because I cannot decide where I want it permanently placed—I mean actually planted in soil that will serve as its home until it outgrows its spot or, like the daphne, expires.

I know I should think about design before purchasing plants, but that is not my nature. I do not have a design. I have earth to be filled with plants that speak to me. What little I know about garden design, however, I learned from filling containers with plants that look good together, moving containers into areas that are lacking, and combining containers of plants that, like my neighbor's geraniums and petunias, look snappy together.

Creating container gardens (and gardens of containers) teaches a gardener about combining textures, colors, shapes, and growing habits. Unlike mature trees and shrubs, container mistakes are easy to correct or toss away . . . teaching the most important lesson of all: there is an artist in each of us just waiting to escape into our gardens.

Going and Coming Back

Two things are going on in my garden. One: I am getting ready to leave it, and two: I am making sure I have plenty to enjoy when I get back.

To prepare for my absence, I water well and mulch, looking for dry spots the hoses do not reach. I mulch with coastal Bermuda hay until the leaves start to fall. I purchase the hay (about ten to twenty bales a year) from a local farmer, and you should do the same. Coastal Bermuda hay, a hybrid grass that does not reseed, is grown for stock animals. If I had a cow or a horse myself, I would let it eat my grass and save the hay for mulch.

We use pine straw primarily for mulching shrubs in front and in back of the house. Pine straw does not decompose quickly, which is beneficial for large shrubs and hedges where mulching is a once-a-year or every-other-year task.

In the mixed borders where plants are continually growing, I want a mulch that feeds the soil. Coastal Bermuda hay breaks down quickly and adds tilth as well as nutrients to the soil. (Think of tilth as fiber that holds moisture and adds micronutrients and beneficial bacteria to the soil.)

Hardwood leaves break down quickly, too, and once they start falling, they become my mulch of choice. That rich chocolate-brown layer looks and smells delicious.

If leaves (or pine straw) land in the garden, I leave them there to disintegrate on their own. I do not know why people rake out their borders. It does not make sense. Some folks have an overdeveloped need for tidiness and should get over it.

Leaves that fall on the lawn are sucked up and shredded by the lawn mower. My husband dumps piles of shredded leaves in various places around the yard, and I spread them around plants. I rarely fertilize anything. I cannot remember the last time I did so. The decomposition of the mulch and the presence of earthworms and microorganisms enable the soil to take care of itself. The soil retains nutrients and moisture. The plants thrive, and I save money and time, as well as muscle power.

As I spread mulch (a pleasant activity allowing me to focus on the plants as I strew), I wonder about people who put big plastic bags full of raked-up leaves at the curb for the trash collector. I suspect they are the same people who rake out their borders. I assume they then purchase mulch by the truckload or in more plastic bags. Go figure.

Preparing for my venture away from home, I pull out plants that crowd more desirable specimens. For instance, I have a stubborn crop of chocolate mint that winds its way here and there until I realize I have lost sight of the phlox and crocosmias and caryopteris. I have a crop of elephant ears (*Colocasia* 'Illustris') that are gobbling up Siberian iris. As I thin out beds, I make editorial decisions about what to keep and what to extract.

Here is the hardest part about leaving a garden: pruning back plants by one-third or so. It is painful to the gardener, but not, as far as I know, to the plants. Cutting back plants stimulates new growth so that, when we return from our trip, the garden will be refreshed and in bloom.

Trimming back top-heavy plants such as castor beans (*Ricinus communis*) and Mexican sunflowers, mainstays of my late summer garden, makes them less likely to fall over if a storm should occur while we are away. I cut all the blooms off cleome and coneflowers and most of the blooms off salvias, leaving enough for hummingbirds and bees that find them tasty.

I do not cut back shrubs at this time, except lantana and vitex, which will rebloom. If I had butterfly bushes (*Buddleia davidii*), I also would cut the blooms off them.

Before leaving on my trip, I place new cuttings in a shady area. I ensure the medium is moist and, if we are experiencing drought conditions, I cover the cutting boxes with nonwoven cloth (such as Reemay) to conserve moisture. I take a last walk around before we leave, assuring myself that I have done what I could to care for my garden while I am away.

Sometimes a gardener has to say good-bye, no matter how gorgeous the garden looks or what will happen while we are gone. My mother-in-law, a dear woman who lived in upstate New York, did not visit us during winter months because she could not leave her furnace.

A friend would not go on a fabulous garden tour of England because she was sure her own garden would not survive.

I decided years ago I would never let a possession keep me from people I love or places I want to see. As much as my garden delights me, I know it will be waiting when I return . . . and, if not, I know how my garden should look and how to recreate it. Even better.

Where Have All the Trees Gone?

As long as I can remember, I have longed to live on a street lined with large deciduous trees that form a tunnel over the road. I have been a tree hugger from the get-go.

For more than forty years, we have lived happily in a neighborhood that once was a pine forest where tall longleaf pines were interspersed with mature hickories and oaks as well as varied understory trees. My husband chose our lot because those hickories indicated to him that beneath the sandy soil was a layer of clay and moisture. Unfortunately, no tunnel of trees shelters our road.

On our acre lots, we and our neighbors created 1960s landscapes with large lawns, shrubs across the foundations, and too many azaleas and boxwoods if you ask me. Most of us retained as many trees as possible, eliminating just enough to build comfortable houses as well as provide space for playing baseball and hide-and-seek and for gardens and garages.

Over the years, trees were cut down because they were diseased or threatened rooftops. Then, quite suddenly as I recall, one by one our neighborhood trees started disappearing, not because of safety concerns or dented cars, but to provide sunlight for endless acres of grass. The pursuit of the perfect lawn began.

As we all aged, more trees fell to eliminate the labor of raking leaves and pine straw.

But my husband and I held on to our trees to the point where our landscape has become unique by attrition. When I give visitors directions to our house, I tell them to look for the yard with plenty of trees. They have no trouble identifying it. Our neighborhood is on its way to treelessness.

After years of debate, we ourselves cut down a handsome hickory tree in the backyard because the hickory nuts bombarded cars parked in the driveway. They would ricochet off the roof, sounding like a meteor shower. I gave way eventually when guests started parking their cars out on the street or in our neighbors' yards. But I miss that tree every time I look out my kitchen window. It is my biggest arboreal regret.

Still a tree hugger after all these years, I am glad to admit it. I have hugged a good many people who have done considerably less for our environment than trees. Their capability to clean up after us and beautify the world is incomparable.

Think of this. Trees clean the air by removing dust and particles. They absorb ozone, carbon monoxide, and sulfur dioxide and release oxygen back into the atmosphere. Trees reduce flooding and runoff and prevent soil erosion. An impressive list of tasks . . . but if trees are no longer among the living, if we succeed in clear-cutting our neighborhoods, woodland areas, and commercial properties, who or what will be around to pick up the slack? Which tree will be the tipping point?

Closer to home, where our wallets reside, trees save us money by reducing utility bills. The evaporation from a single large tree can produce the cooling effect of ten room air-conditioning units running twenty hours a day.

Furthermore, trees increase property values of both residential and commercial properties. I wish the clueless developer in the town where I live had realized this before he bulldozed several huge old oak trees, as well as every other living thing, on a prospective commercial property. Then he put this bleak vista on the market, where it continues to sit, vacant and barren.

I respect property rights, but how presumptuous and shortsighted this developer was to assume that no one would be interested in a building site on a major highway with those irreplaceable trees. If a buyer required that the trees be removed, that might be understandable. But the trees that made the site unique and desirable are gone forever. So is a buyer who might have considered those trees an asset.

I may be short on business savvy, but even I can see that if trees increase property values, eliminating trees surely decreases them.

Across the road from my favorite botanical garden is a neighborhood of sensibly sized houses that might be attractive to someone like me. I could walk in the garden, perhaps volunteer in the greenhouse, and enjoy tending fabulous plants in an ever-changing collection.

However, I cannot imagine living there. The developer has eliminated every mature tree on the site. What are these people thinking?

Across the street, not thirty feet away from the denuded neighborhood, are thickly timbered woodlands, which no doubt face the same destiny.

I know trees have life spans and homeowners (who also have life spans) have valid reasons to cut down trees in their own yards. However, I think we have a responsibility to replace what we have removed from our personal environment. I have replaced hardwoods we have cut down with understory natives such as holly, sassafras, Grancy graybeard (*Chionanthus virginicus*), and wax myrtle, as well as a nonnative fig tree and several vitexes.

Trees, it seems to me, belong to us all in some mystical way. I find myself drawn to the concept of community forests where trees in home landscapes, schoolyards, cemeteries, churchyards, and commercial sites are protected and viewed as an ecology we must share, respect, and treasure. A world without trees is too terrifying and disheartening to contemplate.

Doing In the Deadheads

While I usually adhere to the gardening premise that too much is almost enough, sometimes too much really is too much. This morning I took my hedge clippers and whacked an expanding bed of Mexican petunias (*Ruellia brittonia*) in half. With the same serious clippers, I then sheared my favorite *Salvia guaranitica* by one-third, eliminating with one fell swoop dead brown flowerheads as well as perky royal blue blooms, much beloved by hummingbirds. I was merciless, but life is short, and I do not intend to spend much of mine clipping off one dead bloom at a time.

The process of removing spent blossoms from plants is called deadheading. It is a tidying up process, but deadheading is also done in hopes that plants will rebloom. Most plants assume, once they have flowered and produced seeds, that they are through for the year and go on vacation. But not in my backyard.

Even novice gardeners know annuals need to be deadheaded regularly so that they will continue to flower in an effort to reproduce themselves with seeds. A dried zinnia or snapdragon is full of seeds which, in the normal botanical cycle, will become zinnias and snapdragons in the future.

Plants, like insects and other critters, regard reproduction as their purpose in life and will go to extraordinary ends to be sure the job is done. As long as they are deadheaded, zinnias, marigolds, and most other annuals assume their seeds have not matured and will keep on trying until the first hard frost.

Some annuals are adept at sowing themselves. Plant cleome and you are likely to have cleome for the rest of your life without effort on your part. 'Lady in Red' salvia does the same, and so does cypress vine. The champion reseeder in my garden is a burgundy castor bean plant whose offspring pop up in the most improbable places. I allow a few to stay, trimming them up like trees. I call them the poor woman's Japanese maple.

This self-sowing habit of some plants is another reason for deadheading. If you do not want cleome all over your garden, just cut off flower heads as they fade. The plant will look better, and seeds will never mature.

Many perennials also rebloom if deadheaded. Coneflowers (*Echinacea*) and butterfly weeds (*Asclepias tuberosa*) will produce a second and even a third crop of blooms. So will gaura, heuchera, and phlox. Alas, false indigo (*Baptisia australis*) will not rebloom, so let seedpods dry on the stem, and plant the seeds in potting mix. Even crepe myrtles, a very large perennial to be sure, will rebloom if seedheads are cut off.

Cutting back plants may be done for reasons other than encouraging reblooming or preventing population explosions. You can control the height and width of plants so that they do not overwhelm their neighbors or flop over because they become leggy or top-heavy. Since I do not like them, I remove heuchera and pulmonaria flowers to focus on the plants' much handsomer foliage.

A neat trick to perform is to stagger blooms so that all your daisies or mums or sunflowers do not flower at one time. Cut back half or a third of the stems so that their flower formation is delayed.

If a plant is badly infested with insects or fungus, cut it back to healthy foliage or, if necessary, to the ground. Struggling roots will have less plant to support, and you will have less plant to coddle. New growth will emerge, and, if it does not, all you have lost is a plant that would have died anyway.

The traditional method of deadheading is to carefully cut off each stem that supports a dried bloom. This is time consuming and far too tedious for me. Life flies on, and there are more enjoyable things to do.

My deadheading is emphatic and quick. My weapon of choice is a pair of top-quality hedge clippers with which I whack away across the top and sides of a plant. To prevent its ultimate collapse in October, on the Fourth of July a clump of swamp sunflowers (*Helianthus angustifolia*) is reduced to half its original size in seconds. In early summer, before blooms form, *Sedum* 'Autumn Joy' is reduced by one-third. Coreopsis is sheared when there are more dried seedheads than fresh flowers.

The only tricky part of cutting plants back to manipulate bloom and foliage growth is figuring out when to do it. The best guide to deadheading I know is the book *The Well-Tended Perennial Garden* by Tracy DiSabato-Aust, who presents meticulous lists of plants that should be treated in specific ways at various times.

As for me, I regard the deadheading and reshaping process a matter of personal preference. In other words, gut feeling guides my clippers. I have never killed a plant by hacking away with the hedge clippers, but I might die of boredom deadheading one bloom at a time. No matter how disfigured a newly clipped plant may appear, the plant renews itself quickly, and I survive to slash another day.

Summer's Peak

When Joe Pye weed reaches full bloom, my garden is at its peak. I find myself taking pictures from every angle and at various times of day to catch the perfection of this six-foot-tall perennial that tops itself off with rosy pink fluff, about eight inches in diameter, between early July and mid-September.

As usual, when I like something, I want it everywhere. My favorite patch of Joe Pye weed (*Eupatorium maculatum* 'Gateway') is just outside the French doors leading from the den (clearly visible from my reading chair). Joe Pye can also be found in my mixed border in front of the back hedge as well as in the "wild garden" in the northwest corner of the yard.

Once started, Joe Pye weed thrives and expands outwardly into a fat clump. In my large garden, the clump can expand as far as it wants to go. A thicket of Joe Pye weed would thrill me. The way I keep Joe Pye weed blooming over several months is to pinch some plants when they are about three feet tall in early June. This results in branching out and somewhat smaller flowers, though the plants themselves will still reach six feet in height.

Cutting back plants in early June (in contrast to pinching) results in shorter plants. Since unlike many tall plants, Joe Pye weed remains erect in spite of wind and heavy rain, it need not be cut back to stay upright. However, I cut back stems to stagger heights so that all the blooms will not be six feet in the air.

Do not bother deadheading since Joe Pye weed will not rebloom, but the fading flowers remain attractive until frost. Attractive, that is, if fluffy beige seedheads appeal as much to you as they do to me.

Joe Pye weed grows best in the sun in moist locations. Be patient. It takes three years for plants to reach maturity. If, like me, you want Joe Pye weed in varied places, in spring, ease small plants from the outside perimeter of the clump. Pot them up or plant them immediately wherever you want big and pink in your garden.

The Joe Pye weed in my garden is surrounded by royal blue *Salvia guaranitica*, not quite as tall as the eupatorium but close. Below the Joe Pye weed is golden rudbeckia, red pentas, white coneflower, and deep purple alternanthera. A burgundy castor bean "tree" (with branches stripped to shoulder height) pops upward. Velvety gray lamb's ears edge this border to quell the color riot.

In contrast to the dull, dark green foliage of Joe Pye weed are the bold, glossy giant leaves of elephant ears (*Colocasia esculenta*). The addition of big shiny shapes to a border (or foundation planting) adds plenty of pizzazz and aplomb to what might otherwise seem ordinary, if not downright dull.

A few weeks ago I visited a friend's garden and was surprised by her collection of huge green elephant ears scattered throughout her garden. "I fell in love with elephant ears this year," she told me. I know the feeling. When love (or lust) hits, we want lots of whatever has caught our fancy.

What my friend did not know when she bought her colocasia bulbs (at a pretty fancy price, I bet) was that elephant ears reproduce like rabbits, so instead of each bulb producing one stem, it has produced five. And next year, my friend needs to expect ten, passing along some of the surplus to me I hope.

The return of elephant ears to garden glamour is good news. Of course, the current wave of stylish elephant ears is a far cry from the old three-foot-tall grass-green variety. Now we can have elephant ears with black or rhubarb-red stems and leaves, or foliage with creamy white stripes or splotches. You will pay a hefty price for a premium colocasia bulb (as much as twenty-five dollars), but keep in mind that you will soon have five and ten and fifteen.

In my garden I have a growing collection of *C. esculenta* 'Burgundy Stem', whose heart-shaped leaves are waxy green with a purple sheen and up to two feet long. The stems are five feet tall and a burgundy so intense it seems black. After one year, I have three separate clumps of 'Burgundy Stem'.

I have considerably more *C. antiquorum* 'Illustris', which is not as tall or spectacular as 'Burgundy Stem' but effective as an emphatic groundcover. I have a grouping under a crepe myrtle at the edge of my mixed border. It shares the space with spring-blooming Siberian iris, a combination which works out well since colocasia does not emerge until mid-May.

The twelve- to twenty-four-inch leaves are purple-black veined with green. 'Illustris' has an expansive nature, so after a year you will have plenty of small plants to move and to share.

Colocasias are happiest in sun to light shade and are winter hardy in zones 7 and 8, where I garden. Alocasias, which look the same but are not winter hardy, need to be dug up and overwintered inside, which is not an option in my garden or in my life.

As summer draws to a close, my garden is a riot of color and texture. Plants merge into one another. Some of the colors are obviously out of place or have outgrown their territory, but so what? I will do better next spring, but I will make other errors. These happy (and even unhappy) accidents keep me surprised, enriching my garden and my soul.

Thugs in the Neighborhood

I had to laugh when I read the article "Thugs in the Garden" in the newspaper's garden section a couple of weeks ago. Ten invasive plants were listed . . . and six of them are in my garden, invited there by me. An invasive plant, by definition, spreads aggressively and is especially problematic when it spreads into a new habitat and overwhelms the native plants growing there.

But one gardener's "thug" may be another gardener's pet. Some gardeners become upset by any plant that meanders beyond its parameters. As a rule, I am not one of them. I don't even recognize the parameters until the plant has wandered well beyond them. When the meandering goes too far, I lean over and rip out the offending plants. Now how hard is that?

I have written *ad nauseum* about my arch-enemy plant, glechoma, which is in a class by itself among invasives. Glechoma is scary because it swallows up entire lawns given the opportunity. I will fight to its death and show no mercy.

However, many plants defined as invasive have redeeming qualities, like friends who are annoying but also kind, generous, funny, and usually good company. They enrich my life, so I overlook whatever they do that irks me and focus on their redeeming qualities . . . exactly what I do with so-called garden thugs.

The first plant listed in the "Thugs in the Garden" article is *Salvia guaranitica* (blue anise sage), which in my garden grows to shoulder height. Stems are tipped with royal blue tubular flowers full of what must be absolute manna to hummingbirds. I no longer put up a feeder because the hummingbirds pass it by in favor of those blue blooms. Of course, I also plant cupheas, pineapple sage, and other tubular plants so that hummers have diversity in their diet, but *S. guaranitica* is the beaks-down favorite.

I had the life-altering experience of standing next to a mass of this exuberant salvia when a hummingbird buzzed up to dine less than eight inches from my face. I know the blooms are blue, and hummingbirds probably know it, too, but lack of redness does not diminish their allure.

As usual with a plant I like, I have planted this salvia in several places, and that probably is a mistake, but so far I am able to keep up with it. I am in my garden for at least a few minutes most days, and if an area looks too crowded, I pull up rooted stems and either put them in a brush pile or pot them up and, with fair warning, give them to friends who are happy to take them home.

Imperial taro elephant ear (*Colocasia* 'Illustris') is next on the list and is probably the most requested plant in my garden when folks come to visit in the summertime. This elephant ear grows to about two and a half feet to three feet and is best grown in masses with some sunlight. The velvety leaves are burgundy black with green veins.

In my garden, I have several massed groupings of *Colocasia* 'Illustris'. The most dramatic grouping is beneath a fuchsia crepe myrtle. Siberian iris bloom in the same location before the elephant ears emerge in late spring.

Like *Salvia guaranitica*, colocasias, roots and all, pull out of the ground with little effort. Sometimes I pot them up for plant sales, but usually I just put a bunch in plastic grocery bags and pass them along to grateful visitors.

The third plant on the list is *Clerodendron bungei*, which is stunning and tempting. Mine arrived with something else because I know I never deliberately planted it. Its roots wander aggressively and, for me, it does not have enough redeeming qualities to make me want to keep it. It also has a funny smell. Remember what I said about "invasive" being a matter of personal judgment.

But also on the list of thugs is Jewels of Opar (*Talinum paniculatum* 'Kingswood Gold'), a well-behaved necessity in my garden. It has wiry stems full of tiny red-pink seedheads that have a reputation for generating "a carpetlike mass." Not in my backyard, however, probably because I mulch thickly, preventing seeds from germinating.

Jewels of Opar grow in manageable clumps in sun or shade. I might discover less than a dozen seedlings between late spring and fall, and I immediately pot these up for friends who beg for them. The foliage is vibrant chartreuse, adding pizzazz, especially in shady places. *Talinum* is listed as an annual, but clumps seem to come up in the same places every year, right where they should be, at the front of shady borders.

Virginia creeper (*Parthenocissus quinquefolia*) is also listed in the article about garden thugs. To illustrate my point about invasiveness being a state of mind, I saw handsome manors and townhouses in England with Virginia creeper artfully trained on their mellow old walls.

I pull Virginia creeper out with my hands and pruners when it invades desirable neighbors. It is a native plant, recommended for wildlife habitats, a good example of a nuisance with redeeming qualities.

Japanese fleece flower (*Polygonum cuspidatum*) is like clerodendrum—absolutely gorgeous when it blooms and tempting to gardeners. People have begged me for a rooted stem, but I am reluctant to pass this thug along. Not able to let go completely myself, I put a stem in a large pot, hoping to confine it there. But I still have fleece flower popping up in my garden. I chop it back, hoping to control it, but late in the summer it is heart-stoppingly beautiful.

It is a jungle out there . . . full of temptation and wandering roots. I believe we can afford to live with invasive but engaging plants if we are vigilant. However, we have a responsibility to keep up our guard against bullies who push themselves into territory where they do not belong, no matter how attractive their redeeming qualities may be.

Leafy Greens Galore

In mid-August, I already dread winter, when the thrill of crisp and cold days has gone, borders are beige, and garden tasks are as dull as housework. When summer's end is in sight, my thoughts turn to vegetables: lush, leafy "greens" that are blue-gray, burgundy, and deep rich purple, and greens from kelly to almost black. Envision three-foot-tall mustards aptly named 'Red Giant' and 'Purple Osaka'. Picture kale called 'White Peacock', 'Nero di Toscana', and 'Russian Red'. Imagine a clump of red-streaked tatsoi emerging from a blanket of snow.

Leafy greens are not only edible, full of vitamins and fiber, they are incredibly beautiful and turn a winter garden into an object of beauty. As usual in my garden, I want more plants than I can afford, so I start my collection of fancy greens from seeds. Nothing could be easier or more frugal. For the price of a single giant red mustard at a nursery, a packet of seeds will produce a flat of fifty to a hundred seedlings. While all greens are easy to start from seeds, mustard is especially quick and confidence building: it takes one minute to plant, germinates in two or three days, and is ready for the garden in six to eight weeks.

I start seeds in plain vermiculite available in small or large bags at any garden center or feed and seed store. I use foam mushroom containers and poke holes in their bottoms with an ice pick. I place filled containers in a pan of water until the vermiculite is thoroughly moistened but not soggy. I remove containers from the water, being sure that the holes are doing their job. Drainage is crucial.

I sprinkle seeds across the surface and then press them down to be sure they make contact with the vermiculite. I put the container in a warm place. I do my germinating in the laundry room and use an electric pad specifically made for starting seeds, but any warm place will do.

When the first seedling emerges, I move the container into bright light. I use a grow light with fluorescent tubes, but sunlight works as well. Just be sure the vermiculite does not dry out, or your seedlings will be kaput.

When seedlings form true leaves that look like mustard or kale or whatever I have seeded, I dump the container over and pull the seedlings gently apart (holding leaves, not roots). I put each seedling in a separate container or into six-packs filled with commercial potting mix, not garden dirt.

I put the containers somewhere outdoors that gets morning sun and afternoon shade. If nights are cold, I will need to bring the containers inside. That is why I start my greens in August. I fertilize with half-strength liquid fertilizer at two-week intervals until my seedlings reach plantable size.

Just when I am getting sick and tired of tending to their needs, the "greens" are ready to go in the garden. The only problem will be where to put a hundred mustard plants that will grow three feet tall and wide. My answer is "everywhere." Brighten up foundation plantings, fill up containers, intersperse in the border, share (or trade) with other gardeners.

When nights turn cool (and they will), I start my lettuce crop. Lettuce growing for me begins in late summer. By August I am eager to see tiny lettuce leaves emerge, heralding the end of the heat wave. I purchase seeds of lettuces with names like 'Red Butterworth', 'Ruby Red', 'Deer Tongue', 'Red Lollo Rosso', and 'Oakleaf'. I order packages of mesclun mixes of lettuces and greens to be picked in their infancy.

Unlike leafy winter greens, I begin lettuces outdoors from the get-go. I fill shallow bowl-shaped containers measuring at least two feet across. Buy several because once you get started, one will not suffice.

Fill the containers with three parts potting mix (not soil) and one part packaged or well-aged manure. Wet the mixture thoroughly so it is moist but not soggy. Sprinkle seeds across the top. Do not worry about spacing. Just cover the surface as evenly as you can. Press the seeds down with a piece of board or wax paper.

Do not bother covering them. Keep in mind that seeds of lettuce and other greens germinate quickly when exposed to light. I place my containers in dappled shade until I see the first seedlings, and then I move the basins to locations where they get at least four hours of morning sun.

Portability is the major advantage of planting lettuces in containers. You can move them around so that they get ample sunlight through the winter, because you will be growing these salad greens from fall through spring. If an ice storm threatens, you can move the whole container into shelter and save your crop. However, I have left containers out to face the elements, and the lettuces continued to thrive once the weather improved. If I lived in Minnesota, I would still grow lettuce in containers, but probably only in fall and spring.

Another reason to move containers about is that they are handsome additions to the winter border as well as the deck or patio. A big, round basin of colorful foliage, glossy, green, red, rough textured, and silky is a sight to behold, especially in January, when not much else is going on.

Keep scissors handy because that is how the crop is gathered. When leaves are at least two inches high, trim them off just above ground level, or if the container is overcrowded, pull up enough plants to make a salad. Then give your salad greens time to revive and produce the next set of leaves. Be sure you reap when the greens are young and tender, and continue to do so until the plants bolt or stop producing.

Tip the potting mix out when your lettuce crop is finished, and mix it with some fresh potting mix and manure. Spread fresh seeds over the surface and the next crop is under way.

Once you grow your own greens, tired store-bought salad makings and winter greens are hard to swallow. But that is how gardening is. The personal touch makes all the difference.

The Scent of Summer: Ginger Lilies

For the past month I have had the pleasure of observing an apricot-colored ginger lily growing just outside the kitchen door. In spite of its name, it looks nothing like a lily, and the flower does not look like the typical ginger lily we know and love. The inflorescence, or bloom cluster, is a sixteen-inch stiffened bottlebrush, kind of like a tall, thin artichoke, topping off a five-foot-tall stalk with leaves marching up each side, like the foliage of cornstalks or bamboo.

Ginger lilies belong to the genus *Hedychium*, a word derived from two Greek words: *hedys*, which means "sweet," and *chium*, which means "snow." While all ginger lilies belong to this genus, the term actually describes the most common ginger lily, *H. coronarium*, which is sweet smelling and has snow-white blooms that look like three-inch butterflies or little orchids. It multiplies enthusiastically and is one of the South's most popular pass-along plants.

The ginger lily that delights me whenever I walk out my kitchen door is *H. gardnerianum* 'Tara', a more striking plant than the common *coronarium* but not nearly as aromatic. A dozen or so additional species exist, and enterprising breeders are turning out cultivars that are pink, yellow, raspberry, and orange.

Ginger lilies are herbaceous perennials, which means they die back to the ground at the end of their season and re-emerge the following year. Ginger lilies are supposedly hardy only to zone 7, so gardeners in colder climates dig them up and bring them indoors for the winter. What a nuisance.

However, ginger lilies may be hardier than commonly thought. I read about a fellow in zone 5 or 6 who was given some ginger lily rhizomes, which he threw under a shrub until he could figure out what to do with them. I have been guilty of such negligence myself. One day he realized temperatures were dropping fast and a freeze was imminent. He pitched a pile of mulch over the rhizomes, and they not only survived but grew spectacularly the following summer. Often ignorance is bliss.

However, ginger lilies are not meant for snow and ice. They are tropical in appearance, fragrance, and aura. The British have been growing them since the 1700s, calling them "butterfly gingers" or "garland flowers," leading me to believe they brought the first rhizomes from the Hawaiian islands, where leis bestowed upon visitors are made of ginger lily blooms.

Though you are apt to catch the almost cloying scent of ginger lilies before you see them, their physical presence is impressive. The stalks are four to five feet tall, and as the plant matures over the years, stalks emerge from large rhizomes in clusters. Usually ginger lilies are relegated to the back of a sunny border, but I am thinking of setting a 'Tara' in mid-border as a focal point or exclamation mark.

Fortunately, breeders are tinkering with ginger lily size as well as color and fragrance. Next summer my garden will include *Hedychium* 'Luna Moth', which grows just thirty inches tall and has slightly spicy-scented large white and pink blooms. A ginger lily this size would be ideal grown in a container that could be moved around strategically to scent the scene.

Speaking of *H.* 'Luna Moth', one of my sons asked for some ginger lilies for his garden after he saw a real luna moth fluttering around a ginger lily in a neighboring yard. He and his family were entranced by this large and beautiful creature sipping nectar in the moonlight.

Ginger lilies are perfect pollinator lures with their bright flowers, almost indecently prominent stamens, and exotic fragrance. They are a sensual delight to butterflies and moths, which pick up pollen on their wings as they hover over the flowers and dine on nectar.

Large-flowered ginger lilies tend to have two to four flowers, while small-flowered ginger lilies may have as many as fifty. Each flower lasts a single day, but the inflorescence or cluster will bloom three to four weeks.

My common white ginger lilies, passed along to me by a generous friend, were planted in shade, where they have remained. All these years they have fallen over after blooming, as if they had given their all in the effort.

After observing the orange ginger lily bloom so flamboyantly in the sunny border outside my kitchen door, I plan to move all those neglected ginger lilies into locations where they will get at least four hours of sun each day. They need to be placed where their fragrance grabs attention, perhaps under a window that is opened on summer nights or next to the door visitors enter.

Ginger lilies thrive in moist, well-drained, humus-rich soil. Like iris, rhizomes should be lifted and divided every few years, which should provide ample ginger lilies to enjoy and share. New or divided rhizomes should be planted just one or two inches deep and two to four feet apart. Mulch them with aged manure or compost.

Ginger lily rhizomes are indeed gingery and edible. Slice off a smidgeon and throw it in the curry or spice cake. Attractive flowers, exotic fragrance, piquant flavor. I suspect the leaves rustle sensually in the breeze. *Hedychium* is one of those plants that has it all.

Doing Flowers and Doing Good

Not long ago I enlisted in the new flower guild at my church. About ten of us take turns "doing" the altar flowers for Sunday services, and so far, the guild has been a success. Church members have been generous with their compliments about the arrangements, taking particular interest because they usually know who has created them. If there have been any critics of our arrangements, they have kept their opinions to themselves. The Christian spirit lives! If only all church functions were so blessed.

We guild members have enjoyed our creative efforts, and, I think it is safe to say, we have learned from our mistakes as well as from our fellow guild members. Making two almost identical arrangements can be tricky. Do you do one and then another just like it? Or do you do them both, stem by stem, at the same time?

I have learned that arrangements must be shorter than the brass cross on the altar, but large enough to make a statement. Small flowers and fillers that spiff up table arrangements get lost when viewed from a pew. Many of the richest colors, such as burgundy and red, do not show up against the dark wood behind our altar.

Bright colors, especially yellows and white, sing out all the way to the back of the church. When I do arrangements, I strive for loose and airy, as if the flowers were still in a garden. However, when I take a quick look from the communion rail, they seem "overarranged" and always too short. A good lesson in striving to improve oneself.

I like the guild's flower arrangements because they are as distinctive as the ten of us. Each woman (though the guild is open to both sexes, we are solidly female) brings to those brass urns her own favorite flowers and personal judgments. Our "stems" may not be as showy as those from the florist, and our arrangements may be less than professional, but they are done for love and with love, and you cannot beat that.

As a result of this flower guild experience, my gardening world has expanded, and that is always a good thing. I look at my garden (and my friends' gardens) differently, continually on the prowl for flowers that will show up from the very last pew.

When it is my turn to do the flowers, I want to cut them from my own garden. I wish this zeal were all for the glory of God, but I confess to a touch of vanity. I am not usually a worrier, but I often dream about walking into church Sunday morning to find my arrangements have become bunches of wilted stems. That is where false pride will get you.

Almost all summer I have had a bumper crop of tall, straight-stemmed daisies (*Leucanthemum × superbum* 'Becky'). Becky must be the most dependable flower in the gardening world. Not only does this perennial last a long time in a vase and have a June-to-September blooming season, Becky continually regenerates herself by producing offspring at her base. One determined yank, and the gardener has a whole baby Becky with roots attached, ready to start a new family.

I also possess several clumps of a nameless helianthus scattered around the borders. These are daisy look-alikes, but instead of white petals with yellow centers, helianthus is solid gold. Like Becky, they bloom all summer long and are perennial and carefree, even without a pedigree.

When summer perennials begin to fade, swamp sunflowers (*Helianthus angustifolia*) save the day. Two clumps that began as a single pass-along from a friend are by late summer six feet tall and six feet wide. In October they will be a mass of gold.

As a result of this flower guild venture, I find myself making careful notes in my garden calendar about bloom times. I will be pretty sure that the Tardiva hydrangeas will be blooming in August. So will small white gladioli. Yellow patrinia (*Patrinia scabiosifolia*) blooms and blooms and blooms in July. White patrinia waits until September.

Thinking ahead is the key to keeping home-grown flowers available for arrangements. With fall in mind, I purchased two Mexican bush sage plants last spring, knowing their long velvety purple blooms will be stunning as the summer garden comes to a close. For the first time ever, I have started snapdragon seeds for cool-weather arrangements. In the fall I will sow plenty of larkspur for early spring bouquets. I am ordering a hundred Dutch iris for early spring arrangements—all of them blue, or maybe half blue and half white.

Of course, there are yellow Dutch iris as well, and bronze. Perhaps I should order two hundred.

While doing Saturday errands in the countryside, I stumbled across a field of flowers growing in long rows like crops. Naturally I stopped to visit the gardeners who were weeding and discovered that this contented couple had decided to spend their years of retirement growing flowers for wholesale florists. They had rows of paniculata and mophead hydrangeas, *Sedum* 'Autumn Joy' (still creamy white before turning shades of rose), tuberoses almost ready to bloom, white phlox, and stalks of fuschia celosia. Earlier in the summer they had had dahlias, and I could see remnants of the crocosmia crop.

They have had their share of disappointments. What gardener does not? They have been unable to cultivate because their soil is too wet. They were struggling with a field full of weeds that had gotten ahead of them. The deer had chomped their sunflowers to nubs.

But obviously they are having fun in this enterprise that is completely foreign to their former lives as college professors. I admire their spirit of adventure, their delight in working with plants, and their sense of accomplishment. I envy their initiative in not thinking they are too old to try something new and risky. They are doing exactly what gardeners do, though on a grander scale than most of us. They grow beautiful flowers for others to enjoy, and like every gardener I know, they themselves continue to grow in knowledge, experience, and satisfaction.

A Church Lady's Thoughts

Try as I might, I could not keep my mind on the service at church. I was so embarrassed by the behavior of my hydrangeas, sitting there on the altar for all to see. Sort of like having a loudly yawning child in the cherub choir . . . and not a thing you can do about it until the service is over.

I did not have my glasses with me, so I could not be sure why the two arrangements looked so different, but I knew something was wrong. One looked fine; the other appeared shriveled and unbalanced. Fortunately, I attend the earliest service, so as soon as the congregation was blessed and sent on our way, I went up to the altar, took the offending arrangement into a workspace, and did some repair work. Actually, just one bloom had shriveled, and it was replaced by another bloom that was perfectly perky.

This is the surprising part. As I was rearranging, two members of the altar guild raved about how beautiful the flowers were and how they had admired them throughout the service. (I hope our pastor does not worry about our lack of focus on important matters. His sermons are thought provoking and inspirational, much worthier of our attention than vases of flowers.) The offending hydrangea drooped because it was not properly inserted in the Oasis, the rectangular block of absorbent foam that flower arrangers use to keep stems in place. But hydrangeas can be tricky even when they are in adequate water. I have seen whole vases full of them fall over in a faint in a matter of hours. I have also enjoyed bouquets of hydrangeas for a week and more.

I cut hydrangeas with long stems either early in the morning or in the evening after the sun goes down and immediately plunge the stems into water. I bring them inside and recut the stems underwater. If I am using Oasis, I let the hydrangeas sit for eight to twelve hours in water before inserting them in the container.

I do not tinker with the colors of hydrangeas, though I have a spectrum of bloom hues: white, pale blue, deep blue, pink, and rose.

One of my favorite hydrangeas, 'Penny Mac', has been pink since I planted it twenty years ago. When visiting another garden, I realized 'Penny Mac' is considered a blue bloomer. Mine happens to be next to our old pump house, and I assume the cement has leached and made the soil alkaline.

'Penny Mac', like other hydrangeas that bloom on both old and new wood, usually flowers until Thanksgiving. Hydrangeas were once "a southern shrub," but new developments have created cultivars that are hardy almost to the Canadian border. Hydrangeas that bloom only on old wood (last year's growth) are out of luck if there is a late freeze that nips all the buds. Reblooming hydrangeas get a second chance, setting buds on new stems that emerge in spring.

If you want deep blue hydrangea blooms, you need acidic soil. A prominent hydrangea grower suggests a solution of one-quarter ounce of aluminum sulphate and one-quarter ounce of sulphate of iron mixed into one gallon of water. Apply up to two gallons in spring and fall. Sounds too much like chemistry to me.

Or look for acidic fertilizers labeled for camellias, azaleas, and rhododendrons. If you want pink hydrangeas, dose your plants with lime to increase alkalinity. White hydrangeas will be white no matter what you do, and you should be glad.

Personally, I prefer to let nature take its course and be surprised with the results, which are always pleasing. I have about thirty hydrangea shrubs in my garden and squeeze a couple more in every year. I remove hydrangeas that are less than stellar and replace them with new cultivars. However, some of my favorites have been in my garden thirty years and are covered with blooms every year.

I am trialing three hydrangeas for a plant production company, all of them in rich shades of pink from rose to fuchsia. They are supposed to retain their color no matter what soil they are growing in. Hydrangeas are hot in horticultural circles, so be prepared for many developments ahead.

Clip off blooms as they fade. You never know whether they will rebloom later in the summer. A gardener's life is full of surprises. Reshape shrubs and remove dead branches in midsummer to allow plenty of time for new stems to emerge and harden.

Drying hydrangeas is easy. Cut them from the shrub when they are fully mature, just on the cusp of crispness. I have never had luck with lacecaps, but I dry mopheads, panicles (such as 'Tardiva'), and my favorite, the oft-mentioned *Hydrangea arborescens* 'Annabelle', a pristine white mophead that dries to a pale green.

I gather a few hydrangeas of varying stem lengths and fasten the stem ends with a rubber band. Then I slide the rubber band over a nail and let the flowers dry upside down in a dark, dry storage area. I have heard of people drying hydrangeas successfully in the trunk of their cars. Sometimes I just stick them in a vase and let them dry that way.

I love dried hydrangeas for arrangements, frequently mixing them in with fresh flowers. And I always use them to decorate my Christmas tree, poking them in among the branches. Sometimes I spray them gold or silver but more often leave them au naturel.

Praise Be for the Good Guys

As soon as I finished reading *The Great Deluge* by Douglas Brinkley, a detailed history of the first week in New Orleans following Hurricane Katrina, I could hardly wait to write about it. Alternately depressing and inspiring, the book examines extraordinary generosity and courage on the part of rescuers and medical personnel, incredible snafus caused by small-minded bureaucrats, and deliberately evil behavior of thugs, including members of the police force as well as hoodlums victimizing the weak.

The Great Deluge is the story of countless heroes and villains, but a subplot that excited me is a small footnote in the grand epic. Covered with filthy, stagnant water that generated millions of mosquitoes, the entire Gulf Coast seemed destined for an aftermath of disease and death. Here's the neat part: a zillion dragonflies swooped in to lay their eggs on the surface of the water. As soon as the larvae emerged, like insatiable machines they began consuming mosquitoes and mosquito larvae.

The plague never happened. Nature had delivered a terrible blow to the people of the Gulf states, but, as if sensing enough was enough, nature then delivered a miracle, saving countless lives via hordes of fierce-looking bugs with whirring wings and gargantuan appetites.

This same miracle happens in our gardens if we let nature take its course. If you have a water garden or boggy areas, you have dragonflies and should be grateful. We all should be grateful.

At least 98 percent of insects are beneficial to our gardens and to us. When we spray indiscriminately, we kill the good guys along with the not-so-good guys. When the good guys are gone, we open our gardens to chewers and chompers, which, of course, we spray. The beat goes on . . . and the bad guys win.

Less miraculous but closer to home, I discovered something surprising in my own garden last summer. I realized that out of perhaps a thousand plants in my garden, only one was noticeably affected by some insect. I do not know who the culprit was, but he chomped away at the foliage of a dwarf mock orange I had planted the year before. Not another plant was damaged, only this single specimen. I examined the foliage and found no clues as to who the chewer was. I cannot regard him as a villain. He simply could not stop himself once he started on that mock orange. I have had the same experience myself with chocolate pound cake.

My problem was solved quickly and simply without any damage to the environment, myself, or the bug population. I yanked the mock orange out of the ground and deposited it in a brush pile. Life is short, and there are plenty of other plants to be purchased.

I cannot remember the last time I used any kind of insecticide. I believe in letting bugs and plants tough things out . . . and letting the strongest survive. As a result, I not only have a diverse and numerous collection of plants; I have a diverse and numerous assortment of insects, and no single species gets out of hand.

It is possible to purchase predators and parasites, though I have never had to do so. No single beneficial takes care of all the problems in a garden, so if you plan to import your beneficials, do some research. It is a fascinating and addictive subject. For instance, lady beetles are effective predators, devouring mealybugs and aphids. They are collected in winter and need refrigeration until you are ready to disperse them in the garden. Do not count on all of them settling in to stay, especially if there are insufficient victims.

Lacewing larvae are effective predators, purchased as eggs, which limits their ability to migrate as soon as they are let out of the mailing container. Lacewing larvae look like tiny alligators and are voracious eaters with a taste for mites, aphids, and whiteflies.

Minute pirate bugs attack thrips, mites, aphids, young caterpillars, and many other pests, giving you the most predatory bang for the buck. They tend to stay around a garden as long as food is available and, as a bonus, are efficient pollinators.

I know there is a risk in my laid-back attitude toward insects, but it has worked wonders for me. Compared with the risks of insecticides, respect for and reliance on beneficials to manage the battle is a sure-fire winner.

August and the Lilies Are in Bloom

I greet with glee the increasing collection of Formosa lilies (*Lilium formosanum*) in my garden. Also called Philippine lilies or August lilies, their eight-inch trumpet-shaped blooms make them look like giant Easter lilies with blooms bending downward rather than facing forward. When the blooms fade, I ignore the fact that they look disreputable, sort of like damp Kleenex. Not a pretty sight, but I do not even think about deadheading. The real magic occurs after the blooms fade and seedpods form.

The seedpods are four- to five-inch apple-green rods that, like the blooms, face downward, but as they dry they turn upward and become a shiny golden beige. They expand as they dry with separate chambers, each packed with hundreds of Formosa lily seeds. When the pods are completely crisp and their upper edges flare, they look like golden candelabra. I like to cut long stems of the candelabra to use for dried arrangements and Christmas tree decorating.

Whenever you and the pods are ready, cover a counter or table with newspaper, and shake the pods gently over it. Before you are the makings of a lily plantation, and the pods are still in pristine condition. I keep a jar filled with Formosa lily seeds to distribute wherever gardeners gather. I throw some on the ground where I want Formosa lilies to grow in my garden, keeping in mind that they will become very tall and need staking or the support of other plants.

But I also start some seeds in a tray of damp vermiculite, just as I sow any seeds indoors. I press the seeds down, ensuring that they make firm contact with the vermiculite. Keeping the vermiculite consistently moist, I leave the flat somewhere outdoors or in the laundry room, out of direct sunlight. When the grasslike sprouts emerge, I put them under grow lights or someplace they will get at least six hours of sunlight daily.

When the blades are a few inches tall, I pot them up separately until they look like lilies, about five or six inches tall, and then I either put them out into the garden or continue growing them in the cold frame or greenhouse for plant sales and giveaways.

Formosa lilies were found in Taiwan in 1858 and brought to England in 1881. I suspect they were not a success in England or anywhere north of the Mason-Dixon Line. Formosa lilies thrive in the heat and humidity of southern gardens (blooming in August to make their preference clear) and actually rot in cooler climates.

I think Formosa lilies look best springing upward through masses of foliage and flowering plants, such as salvias, coreopsis, cleome, Mexican sunflowers, phlox, coleus, helianthus, and other cottage garden plants that are still blooming when the lilies do. I also like them tucked in among sun-tolerant hydrangeas, conifers, abelias, and other shrubs that will contribute to the lilies' support.

I have never been good about staking plants before they fall over. A trick I have learned over the years is to restrain myself and not cut down castor bean plants and other tall plants that have strong, stalky stems. The dried stems (without side branches) are handy for staking—as well as for providing landing sites for birds and dragonflies.

Like clematis, Formosa lilies like their roots cool but their upper bodies in the sun. When lilies are established enough to be transplanted and more than a foot tall, I dig holes deep enough so that I can put the root ball a foot or so down in the ground. Doing this makes the stems stronger since, like tomatoes, the lilies form roots all along their central stems if they are underground.

My Formosa lilies are scattered around the garden without rhyme or reason. I really must do something about improving my sense of garden design. I read an article years ago describing a small cottage in Texas, tucked into some piney woods. Around the house, in the yard, along the roadside, and even in the woods were thousands of Formosa lilies in full bloom. I do not know what happens there the rest of the year, but August must be some extravaganza.

Another lily I enjoy from midsummer on is the rain lily (*Zephyranthes* 'Labuffarosa'), considerably smaller than Formosa lilies but equally pest free and undemanding. Rain lilies bloom after a good rain. Otherwise, they sit around like clumps of grass. The flowers are about three inches across and pink. Unlike Formosa lilies, rain lilies should be planted with their bulbs just below soil level. They like sun (though they need rain to bloom) and good drainage and look best planted in clusters. Their round seedpods turn black as they dry and then bulge open over a period of days. I help out by scattering some seeds directly on the ground around the mother plant and also plant them in flats of vermiculite, following the same process I do with Formosa lilies. It works.

It has been a long hot summer, but I notice the air is cool now when I go out to get the paper in the morning. The school buses are on the road, so fall is not far off. This transition to fall has always been my favorite gardening season, a time of abundance and surprises that remind me how lucky I am to be a gardener.

Intimate Spaces

Like dresses and shoes, gardens go in and out of style. When we built our house in the early seventies, sprawling lawns were à la mode. So were foundation plants lined up, single file, around the perimeter of the house. A shrub or tree might be placed here and there, often inappropriately in full sun, as a specimen. What were we thinking?

What I like most about gardens in the first decade of the twenty-first century is that they are people centered, meant to be entered instead of observed from the periphery. They are intimate, reflecting changes of seasons and the personality and taste of the gardener. Intimacy is inviting and comfortable, with secluded places to sit and savor.

Entrances create intimacy. Entrances to my back garden and an entrance to what used to be my wild garden are all arbors. A garden I love, unfortunately not my own, is entered through a tunnel of three connected arbors covered by New Dawn roses. I yearn for a tunnel of my own.

Doors also create a sense of seclusion and invitation, perhaps because they open and close. A friend set up a glass-paned door between her front garden and a water garden at the side of the house, enclosing the water garden but not completely separating it from the rest of the landscape. This same friend separates each area of her garden with an entrance gate . . . creating garden rooms by announcing a change of scene.

Another gardener set up a rustic wooden door to separate her garden from the woods in back of her house. The woodland, shared by neighbors, is still visible, but her own garden seems enclosed just by the presence of the door. Unfortunately, the door does not exclude deer that nibble this friend's prized shrubs. It would be more efficient if a fence were attached . . . but not nearly as whimsical.

My garden is spread hither and yon all over a suburban acre lot. I have added some privacy by hedging around the back and sides and gained intimacy by dividing up spaces. I do not have garden rooms. I am not organized enough to achieve these—but about fifteen years ago, I built an island to break up the backyard and hide the back border so that it is unseen until I walk through one of two entrances. The island, a thirty-foot-long oval (more or less), was built in a single day under a large hickory tree. It began as a patch of sun-starved lawn that I covered with newspaper, eight or more layers, to deprive the grass and weed seeds of light needed to thrive.

I had ordered a truckload of compost and somehow, shovel by shovel, wheelbarrow by wheelbarrow, managed to unload it on top of the newspapers. Obviously, it would be easier and wiser to get someone to do this for you, well worth the expense or bribery. As I recall, the compost was six to eight inches deep, so I had created a bed slightly higher than the lawn around the island. If I had it to do over, I would double the compost. I eventually covered the compost with a thick layer of mulch: shredded leaves and coastal Bermuda hay (a hybrid grass that does not reseed). I did not use pine straw because I wanted the mulch to decompose quickly, providing me with rich, friable soil in a hurry.

I cannot remember whether I planted right away or waited until the newspaper turned into compost. I probably did both. If I planted right away, I would have cut holes in the newspaper layer and inserted the plants.

I planted assorted shrubs in the center of the island: hydrangeas, fothergilla, clethra, and variegated aralia. In front of them, I planted smaller shrubs, ferns, hellebores, acanthus, and rue. And in front of these I planted assorted groundcovers and small plants such as ardisia, alchemilla, creeping Jennie, creeping raspberry, forget-me-nots, and other shorties.

Other than adding mulch and plants, I have never reworked this island. The initial labor of placing the newspapers and unloading the compost was done once and never again. I lime the island when I lime the rest of my garden and have added a mixture of organic amendments occasionally. I do not recommend this haphazard schedule . . . but I have to be honest. I am a loose gardener.

When I am asked to make suggestions about other people's gardens, I recommend that we go inside the house and look out from the kitchen sink, the dining areas, the home office, the family room . . . the places they live and look out windows. Doing this not only allows us to design pleasant views, but it ties the garden to the house.

The butterfly garden just beyond my family room window is part of my daily life, even on the rare days that I stay indoors. From the kitchen sink I choose to ignore the sad-looking lawn and feast my eyes instead on my island. Or, looking to the left, I admire a crepe myrtle underplanted with elephant ears (*Colocasia* 'Illustris') and Siberian iris.

I like views that incite action and invite communion with nature. Place a bird feeder where you can see it from your favorite chair; hang a hummingbird feeder; set up a birdbath or basin of water; fill the area with plants that attract butterflies, bees, birds, and hummingbirds. Moisture and insects will lure frogs and lizards.

Intimacy is easily achieved if you let go of the rules and the expectations of others. Make the garden your own, establishing places to be alone and to share with friends. Allow your garden to give you peace and awareness. I know of no better reason to be a gardener.

The Year of XXL

This is the year of big. And I mean BIG. As a result of plentiful rain, plants in my garden are XXL this year. I suspect they are actually the sizes they are supposed to be every year. They are finally reaching those exaggerated heights the catalogs claim.

For instance, in the corner of my mixed border is an expanding grove of *Canna* 'Australia' that is at least ten feet tall. I am not kidding. In other locations it is just five feet tall, which is what I expect and, in some respects, prefer. However, the ten-foot-tall crowd gets the attention, especially when topped with fire-engine-red blooms.

The leaves on 'Australia' are eighteen inches of burgundy black, which, so far, have not faded. I would have expected the dark foliage to disappear into the dark green ligustrum hedge behind them, but the leaves are translucent enough to let light come through. I will probably move 'Australia' next year and stick to *C.* 'Bengal Tiger' in front of the hedge, but I am grateful for small favors . . . or, in this case, large ones.

'Bengal Tiger' has not reached unusual heights this year. In fact, mine may not be as tall as they were last year. Go figure. This is my favorite canna and, until 'Australia' came my way, the only canna I grew. The long leaves are green and yellow with a maroon edge. The blooms are as orange as pumpkins.

I have only recently come to appreciate cannas. I thought the plain green ones with red flowers looked fine in highway medians but not in my backyard. The foliage seemed drab and the flowers blowzy and disorganized. However, once the variegations started showing up in the marketplace, I welcomed them into my borders. The flowers are still blowzy and disorganized, but that foliage and upright structure are irresistible.

When the canna foliage begins to look tattered, cut the stalks to the ground and let them regrow. I learned this tip from a friend who creates enormous floral arrangements for special events. She grows and harvests her cannas like a renewable crop, so she is assured of a continual supply of fresh, colorful foliage.

Colocasia antiquorum 'Illustris' changed the way I think about elephant ears with its deep burgundy foliage streaked with green. Maxing out at about thirty inches, they make an emphatic midborder punctuation mark.

No stopping at thirty inches for *C. esculenta* 'Burgundy Stem', which approaches five feet in my garden and could reach seven. The satiny green leaves are over two feet long, and the glossy stems are deep purple. This specimen is so massive, I am never sure where to place them or what plants will accompany them. Sort of like working with a superstar who overpowers everyone else onstage.

The Joe Pye weeds (*Eupatorium maculatum* 'Gateway') have never reached the six-foot grandeur I had hoped for. However, they are as tall as I am and even wider. They should be in full bloom within a week or two, and I look forward to the show of rose pink blossoms. Earlier in the season I pinched some of the side branches back so that they will produce smaller blooms, but more of them. The top blooms should go for broke, reaching seven to eight inches in diameter.

Some of the orange-red Mexican sunflowers (*Tithonia rotundifolia* 'Torch') are five to six feet tall, and their bright yellow centers are already the favorite landing pads of assorted butterflies. If you are growing these annuals (and you certainly should), be sure to deadhead, or they will stop blooming. In fact, deadhead all annuals and perennials regularly, or cut back the plants so that they will continue to rebloom until fall.

My favorite daisies, *Leucanthemum* × *superbum* 'Becky', are waist high this year. I cut a dozen for an arrangement early this morning. The stems of 'Becky' are sturdy, so the large flower heads remain upright in the garden or in a vase instead of flopping over like most shastas. 'Becky' was chosen as the 2003 Perennial of the Year, so I am obviously not her only admirer.

My own BIG plant of the year is *Vitex negundo*, commonly called chaste tree. I do not know why. This tree, left to its own devices, could grow to twenty feet, but I cut mine back to keep it just a head taller than I am. I want to look right at, not up at, the violet-blue blooms that tempt me to rid myself of those weedy butterfly bushes and plant vitexes instead. What stops me is that butterflies do indeed prefer buddleias, though the bees, like me, lust for vitex.

V. negundo is a split-leaf vitex. *V. agnus-castus* has hand-shaped leaves. They are equally floriferous and free of pests (unless you mistakenly think of bees as pests). The blossoms make absolutely exquisite cut flowers. To keep the blooms coming, cut the stems back severely as you deadhead.

So far, so good this summer. June was wet and not nearly as hot as June can be. I suspect that when we hit a dry spell, our plants will droop quickly, spoiled by the easy life they (and we) have been leading. In the meantime, enjoy the cool mornings, the lush growth, and your own good fortune in being a gardener.

Short Stuff

After gloating about the exceptionally large and sturdy big shots in my garden this summer, I got my just deserts. The next storm humbled many of these prized behemoths, flattening them to the ground, never to rise again of their own accord. After a day or two of muttering to myself about pride going before the fall, I clipped those ten-foot cannas to the ground, left the tithonia to turn herself around and upward, and propped up the colocasias.

I turned my attention to the front of my borders, to the plants that grow sensibly close to the ground, never risking their lives by raising their heads higher than twelve inches or so. These are the plants that live along the margin between lawn and borders. Some of these plants could be groundcovers if I let them spread outward, but I choose to limit them to informal rows along the edges. My favorites are perennials that require little care other than pulling out the wayward. They thrive in full sun or full shade and sometimes in both, and they never need propping up, let alone staking. In other words, effective edging plants are about as obliging as plants can be and provide a finished look to the mixed border.

Some gardeners choose to edge with a single plant variety from one end of the border to the other. I often see impatiens and vinca used this way as well as liriope.

I prefer to mix it up. I have planted about ten attractive edgers, repeating them along the borders, not in any particular order but assigned randomly according to artistic eye and gut feeling.

For example, along one side of my shady island I grow lady's mantle, lamb's ears, *Veronica umbrosa*, carex, creeping raspberry, forget-me-nots, ardisia, creeping Jennie, and pennyroyal. Along the edge of a sunny border, I grow prostrate veronica, lamb's ears, creeping Jennie, dwarf coreopsis, oregano, coleus, sedums, and prostrate goldenrod.

Plants that grow in both sun and shade are planted in both borders. But even plants that appear only along shady edges or sunny edges are repeated for continuity.

Among the sun lovers, one of my favorite edgers is dwarf coreopsis, which forms a neat six-inch-tall clump of dark green foliage and slightly taller, golden daisylike flowers from early spring until frost. It is not a breathtaker, but it is dependable, generating additional plants around the crown, making it easy to divide without even digging up.

Dwarf veronica (*Veronica umbrosa* 'Georgia Blue') forms a mat of tiny evergreen foliage, and at about the same time as daffodils begin to bloom, it is covered with tiny blooms that can only be described as royal blue. Veronica flowers best in sun but will grow in shade.

Lamb's ears (*Stachys byzantina*) is happy in sun or shade. Its name comes from its large woolly, soft gray leaves that children love to stroke. I do, too. This foliage grows about twelve to fifteen inches tall. Some lamb's ears flower, but the best does not. It also does not flop over or shrivel in the heat. This paragon is *S. byzantina* 'Helene von Stein' and is the one you want growing along your edges. No problem to propagate. Lamb's ear offspring generate around the crown and can be pulled out and planted elsewhere in a jiffy.

Years ago, a packet of forget-me-not seeds (*Myosotis sp.*) arrived in the mail, and I planted them in an empty mushroom container filled with vermiculite. When the seedlings emerged, I potted them up and pampered them for about a month until they looked hale enough to be put outdoors. I planted them along the edge of my shadiest border, where they have lived happily ever since, covering themselves in early spring with tiny blue flowers.

The original plants continue to spread outward so that after they finish blooming, I am able to move a clump to another shady spot. I suspect they also reseed since occasionally I discover seedlings a foot or so away from the mother clumps.

Golden creeping Jennie (*Lysimachia nummularia* 'Aurea') thrives in sun or shade and could, I suppose, be considered "rampant." Who cares? This evergreen (or evergold) perennial is easily controlled by pulling up and planting elsewhere. Jennie lightens up the garden wherever she goes, and I like to let her wander out into the grass. I have never been an admirer of straight edges, explaining that C in geometry that still rankles after all these years.

Probably around the same time as I planted those forget-me-not seeds, I came into possession of Bowles' golden sedge (*Carex elata* 'Bowles' Golden'), and I have been dividing it ever since. Carex forms a tussock or clump of golden yellow grass, twelve to fifteen inches tall. Like taller ornamental grasses, carex adds texture and movement to the border.

Carex plants divide easily just by digging up the entire clump and separating it into several smaller clumps. Give carex sufficient moisture, and it will thrive in sun or shade.

In my garden, lady's mantle (*Alchemilla mollis*) is happiest in shade, but given sufficient moisture it holds its own in full sun. Lady's mantle has sprays of yellow flowers, but it is the foliage that grabs my attention. The pale gray-green leaves have rounded edges and a crinkled surface that catches dewdrops, making a trip out to the garden early in the morning well worth the effort.

Like all of these edging plants, lady's mantle is easy to divide just by a little digging around the crown to discover rooted offspring.

Front-of-the-border plants are short in stature but significant in effect. They provide a finishing edge to the landscape, zestfully reproduce, and, just like those more flamboyant megaplants in the back of the border, they add shape, texture, and color to the border.

And, when the downpour comes, they continue to mind their posture, standing up and doing their job.

My Garden Overfloweth

Though the garden of my dreams looks like a lush, overflowing, diverse bouquet, I rarely bring flowers into my house to make real bouquets. After occasional stabs at domestic elegance, I have come to the conclusion one either is or is not a "nester." I am with the nots.

I keep things habitable and comfortable, but Martha Stewart I am not. I will never float flowers in the soup or furnish perky little posies in the guest room. Occasionally I pop one or two interesting blooms into a small vase near the kitchen sink, but that is the extent of my interior decoration, horticulturally speaking.

I do, however, enjoy providing flowers for other people to arrange, and I make an effort to have something suitable for a vase just about any time of the year. When I "do" flowers myself for church or parties, using flowers from my own garden is not only frugal but gratifying, gloat-worthy even, especially when folks ooh and aah.

Spring is the easiest: just plop some azaleas and spirea or viburnums together and you've got a bouquet. For extra pizzazz, plant lots of Dutch iris bulbs in the fall for spring blooms. Dutch iris are inexpensive and, unlike bearded iris, blooms last a week or so, cut or uncut.

In summer, of course, hydrangeas are abundant, and it does not take many to fill up a vase. I especially like white mopheads and the snowy cone-shaped blooms of panicle hydrangeas (*Hydrangea paniculata*). Panicle hydrangeas bask comfortably in sunlight, and most bloom on new wood in mid- to late summer. The blooms are long lasting (up to two months on the shrub) and require minimal skill to grow or arrange. My kind of cut flower.

Summer annuals I count on for cut flowers are tall zinnias, preferably red, and even taller bright orange Mexican sunflowers, which reach five feet or more by midsummer. A summer storm may topple the massive plant, but as branches hit the ground, let them be. The stems head skyward and keep on blooming.

My favorite perennials for cutting are easy to grow, drought tolerant, and, if deadheaded, will bloom for long periods. Coneflowers are four feet tall in my garden by mid-June. I have grown purple coneflowers (*Echinacea purpureum*) my entire gardening life, but somewhere along the line I added 'White Swan' to the array and like it best. Coneflowers are easily divided, and they can be started from seeds left to mature on the plant. I let purple coneflowers reseed themselves, but I gather seeds from 'White Swan' and germinate them in pots to be sure I have enough.

Last fall orange *Echinacea* 'Art's Pride' joined the coneflower palette. 'Art's Pride' is not nearly orange enough to suit my gaudy taste, but it is slightly scented, sort of like herbal tea, if you get your nose right into it. I am hoping that this is just the beginning of orange coneflowers. Can red be far behind?

Though fond of salvias in the garden, I have never found them to be satisfactory cut flowers with the exception of Mexican bush sage (*Salvia leucantha*). This is a most accommodating bloomer whose straight or slightly curved stems arrange themselves in a tall vase or Oasis-filled bowl. No skill required. Just remove lower leaves and plunk the stems in place.

Mexican bush sage reaches four to five feet in height by midsummer. Its woolly, pale sage green foliage makes a handsome foil for vibrant midborder flowers. Then, in late summer, it comes into its own with twelve- to eighteen-inch-long spikes of purple or purple and white blooms and continues to flower until a decisively hard freeze.

Supposedly hardy in zone 7, Mexican bush sage does not return reliably in my zone 8 garden, so I always propagate several stem cuttings and carry them over the winter in a sheltered spot. I transfer them to pots in early spring, and they will be ready for the garden when I am ready to plant.

Not as long lasting in the vase as Mexican bush sage, *S.* 'Red Neck Girl' is even more spectacular. It grows even taller and wider in the garden, an absolutely splendid plant with thick burgundy stems and fifteen- to twenty-inch butter yellow panicles.

For some reason, patrinia is scarce in gardens I visit unless I bring a pot of it with me and nag my host to plant it immediately. I am crazy about *Patrinia scabiosifolia*, which begins blooming in late June in three- to four-inch clusters of tiny yellow flowers on stems three to four feet tall.

Once established, patrinia is long lived as well as long blooming if deadheaded. After it finishes flowering in late summer, I grub around the basal foliage to ease out baby plants for potting up, providing plants to share when I find it missing in other people's gardens.

While fall is the best time to plant perennials, especially in the South, take advantage of end-of-season sales and replant newly purchased perennials, whenever you find them, in pots large enough to accommodate growth. I use a combination of two-thirds potting mix and one-third compost or rich garden soil.

I put repotted perennials where they will get morning sun and afternoon shade. I give the same treatment to perennials I divide over the summer. I know. I know. I am supposed to divide spring bloomers in fall and fall bloomers in spring, but I may not be in the mood during the proper season. Rule breaking is not hard, once one gets the hang of it.

My cutting garden is scattered throughout mixed borders that meander around my yard, and that is the way I like it. Shrubs, annuals, and perennials are there for the picking, and in the meantime, they contribute diverse colors and textures to the garden . . . which looks, as it should, like a grand and overflowing bouquet.

A Gardener's Harvest

No matter how old we get or how busy we are,
our lives are enhanced by growing.

It's All about Wow Power

If you continue to garden into what I choose to call "late middle age," the garden of your dreams is likely to turn into a nightmare. You are plagued with guilt because you have not cut back dead stalks and foliage, never got around to deadheading, forgot to move the bulbs, neglected to pull out rampant vines. When did the garden get so big? And so demanding?

I have spent my gardening life looking for ways to make things easier. Instead of tilling, I layer newspapers, compost, and mulch. The newspapers (at least eight sheets deep) suppress weeds, the compost adds humus and nutrients, and the mulch keeps soil moist and, as it breaks down, adds even more humus and nutrients.

As a result of this layering process, I never till, I have only an occasional weed to pull out of my moist, nutrient-rich soil, and I fertilize only when a plant looks needy. Because of the diversity of my plant choices and the health of my soil, I never use insecticides or fungicides. If a plant looks sick, it leaves the premises and winds up on the burning pile.

As gardens go, mine is easy to maintain. I have reached the point, however, when it is more than I can manage. I like to travel, write, speak, spend time with children and grandchildren, have lunch with friends, read, and do all the other things that make life enjoyable. As a result, my garden is unkempt. Actually, it is a mess.

I have too many plants. I cannot believe I am saying this, but it is true. The smart thing to do would be to eliminate sections of my garden, but I like them all: the back border, the island, the butterfly and hummingbird garden.

The solution? Fewer and bigger plants. My attention is drifting from perennials and annuals and focusing on shrubs: flowering shrubs, conifers, glossy evergreens with berries. It is amazing how many shades of green exist, how much variation and texture there is in foliage. And for color, blooms to cut, and scents, flowering shrubs supply them all.

Think of your space in this way. A single moderate-sized mature shrub fills a lot more area than a dozen or so annuals or perennials. A shrub provides mass, texture, color, and perhaps blooms or berries for good measure. The shrub stays in its space for years, needing only occasional pruning, sufficient moisture, and adequate nutrients (provided by mulch that turns into compost and invites earthworms and microorganisms to help with the process). Unlike perennials and annuals, shrubs do not require continual planting, deadheading, dividing, and cleaning up.

The time comes when even minimal maintenance is too much. The happy news is that selected shrubs can provide a bower of flowers (and berries), foliage that varies in texture, and shades of green, chartreuse, and burgundy.

In winter, the drabbest of seasons, we can enjoy the blooms of witch hazels, daphne, flowering quince, viburnums, and mahonia.

Do not make the mistake of thinking spring belongs to azaleas. The first spring shrub to bloom in my garden is pearlbush (*Exochorda racemosa*), followed by early spireas, mock orange, viburnums, loropetalums, Virginia sweetspire, fothergilla, and sassafras.

When shopping for shrubs, I weigh their pleasure quotient. After all, they will be with me for the long haul. How long do they bloom? Is the foliage attractive? Do their limbs have a structural element (such as shaggy bark or contorted limbs) so they are interesting when naked? How long (in months) do the plants have "wow power"?

My favorite shrub, with twelve months of wow power, is Mexican orange (*Choisya ternata* 'Sundance'), which blooms in spring and sporadically through summer and keeps its golden foliage year-round. You will probably need to order by mail or, even better, ask your local nursery to order it for you.

Another shrub with twelve months of wow power is *Lespedeza thunbergii* 'White Fountain'. Cut to the ground at the end of winter, new growth emerges from the soil looking like little asparagus. By midsummer, the shrub is six feet tall. Small white blooms cover the branches in late summer, making it a stunner at night. In fall, the foliage turns lemon yellow, and when the leaves fall, the plant is a vase of slender branches that move upward in midwinter and cross, like a haystack or pair of hugging friends.

Instead of toiling over perennials and annuals, dig a hole for each potted shrub, no deeper than the plant sits in the pot and two to three times as wide as the pot's circumference. If you garden in clay, you should add compost to encourage the roots to grow outward. If you garden in sand, your plant's roots will move quickly into the surrounding soil.

If the plant is root-bound, take a knife and slice the sides or massage the roots until they spread out. Place the plant in a hole, being sure it sits no deeper than it sat in the pot. Fill in the space around the roots with the soil you have dug out.

Am I suggesting that you rip out all your perennials? Not at all. Keep your favorites and enjoy them. Add some choice annuals where you need quick color.

But remove from your life and your garden the troublesome tasks that make you feel guilty or resentful. Do not ever say that you cannot go to the movies, travel to England, have lunch with a friend, or visit a garden because your garden needs spiffing up. Life is short and should be sweet, especially for gardeners.

Who Makes These Rules?

One of the most important lessons I have learned as a gardener is to be skeptical about rules and experts. More than once I have blundered into success as a result of ignorance. No one told me, "You cannot grow that here," that age-old dictum gardeners have heard since the first cavewoman discovered that plants grow from seeds gathered from plants.

Lady's mantle (*Alchemilla mollis*) is not only a dawdler when it comes to germination, requiring up to thirty days for the first seedlings to emerge, it also will not tolerate the excessive heat and humidity of southern summers. At least that is what the manual says.

Twenty years ago, I blithely scattered lady's mantle seeds over a small flat filled with moist vermiculite. I placed the flat in a warm place (warmer than the prescribed sixty to seventy degrees), and in a week, seedlings started popping up. I raised the seedlings to small plant size and planted them at the edge of my shady island bed.

I still have several of those lady's mantle plants, and they seem reasonably content in my hot and humid garden. Granted, they do not bloom as enthusiastically as they might in cooler temperatures, but the foliage, pale gray-green and pleated, holds up well and catches dewdrops that sparkle in the early morning sun. With lady's mantle, the leaves are the best part.

Perennial forget-me-nots (*Myosotis sylvatica*) are rarely seen in southern gardens, but they have been in mine year-round ever since I tossed a packet of seed, again over moist vermiculite, and raised a tray of happy little plants. I did not know (and neither did the seeds) that forget-me-nots must be germinated in the dark and are highly susceptible to that seed sower's curse: damping off.

I now have many clumps of blue forget-me-nots that bloom early in spring and remain in tidy little bunches throughout the year. Myosotis reseeds in surprising places, both sunny and shady, and I welcome them. They are perfect for potting up and giving to rule-following friends who would never risk sowing forget-me-nots in their own gardens.

I know Southern gardeners who grow magnificent peonies and lilacs and lily of the valley as well as heaths and heathers, in spite of the warnings that it is just too hot and humid here in the South. They are smart enough to figure out ways to provide the essential "chilling hours" or, like me, they blunder into happy accidents where plants flourish in spite of expert advice. Sometimes it is good not to know any better.

One gardener who did not believe the experts is Stan McKenzie (Stan the Citrusman), who was inspired to try growing citrus plants in Scranton, South Carolina (zone 8a). He not only provided himself with oranges, lemons, and grapefruit, but McKenzie Farm nursery has flourished, and he now grows over sixty types of hardy citrus plants he sells to customers throughout the United States.

Another plantsman who pushes the horticultural envelope is Tony Avent, owner of Plant Delights Nursery in Raleigh, North Carolina. Avent takes pleasure in thwarting the rules head on. On a berm built up around the perimeter of his personal garden and in the display gardens throughout the nursery, Avent grows shade plants in the sun and sun plants in the shade. He plants succulents next to hellebores. Now that takes nerve.

What he has discovered is that just because a plant is "shade tolerant" it does not mean that the plant will shrivel in the sun. A sun-loving plant may be equally happy (or almost as much) in partial or even full shade. Avent has disdain for labels that restrict plants to specific growing conditions and limit a plant's use to specific site conditions when it will flourish in less-than-ideal sites.

"Plants can't read," Avent tells anyone who will listen. Plants do not know the rules or the restrictions or recommendations and are willing to do the best they can wherever they are, good advice for us all.

Even more irritating than experts who assure you that you cannot grow (fill in the blank) in zone 8 or 10 or 4 are the experts who insist you cannot grow roses or tomatoes or dahlias without chemicals. We know that roses, tomatoes, dahlias, and all other plants were grown for centuries without insecticides or fungicides. So why do so many gardeners stubbornly assume it can no longer be done?

I am not against all rules and restrictions. I obey the reasonable ones, especially those that protect me and the rest of the world. In fact, I loathe those who thoughtlessly break important rules and disregard the rest of us.

But we garden for fun, for the sheer joy of being outside and improving our environment, growing beautiful plants and delicious food. Our limits are boundless, especially if we keep the instruction book hidden from our plants and perhaps from ourselves as well.

Surprise, Surprise

In my former life, I taught English to high school students, and the best part of the job was the variety of experiences. No classes were alike; no students were alike (except in certain puzzling characteristics—we're talking teenagers here); and no day was like another. My life as a teacher was full of surprises. In retrospect, most of the surprises were pleasant. A few were disheartening. All of them were learning experiences. Just like gardening.

You might think that after thirty years, my garden would be complete and pretty much the same year after year. Not true. Conditions change. For instance, for five years we have moaned about and contended with drought conditions. This year I am surprised to hear ungrateful wretches complaining about too much rain. I am not among them.

A gardener's life is full of surprises, and, as in teaching, these unexpected occurrences are what keep life interesting.

Last spring I was bowled over by geum, a perennial I had never met. A perennial nursery in Oregon sent me a geum as part of a plant collection to try out (one of the perks of being a garden writer). After letting it increase in size a bit in a pot, I tucked the geum into the garden and, I confess, forgot it.

Talk about surprises. Last spring, out of a clump of matte green lobed foliage came a bevy of bright orange blooms. This plant continued to flower for about a month, a remarkable performance for a perennial. The geum sent to me is *Geum* 'Fireball', and I hope it will like being divided because I surely want more.

A newer geum listed in the nursery's wholesale catalog is *G.* 'Werner Arends' but, alas, they did not include it in this year's goody package. I hope to find it at a local nursery.

Here is what you can do to help. Mention *Geums* 'Fireball' and 'Werner Arends' to your local independent nursery, and ask to have some available next fall during perennial-planting season. Geums are hardy in zones 5 through 9. Their foliage, even when the blooms cease, has what the catalog calls "a neat rosette habit," and the flowers are semidouble. Orange is the color we want.

In the same group of plants sent by this generous nursery were several heucheras (coral bells or alumroot), and I wondered just how many heucheras does a garden need? Well, surprise, surprise . . . it needed this one: *H.* 'Amber Waves', with ruffled amber-gold foliage. It also has light rose-colored flowers, but who cares? The foliage on its own is nifty.

Another surprise has been campanula (bellflower), an extraordinarily large and varied family I fell in love with in England but was assured would not tolerate our heat. The one in my garden is *C. punctata* 'Cherry Bells', obviously a wanderer, but that is okay with me. The catalog calls the flowers red, but they are pink in my sunny border, and that is okay, too.

But not all surprises bloom. My favorite "grass" is *Carex* 'Sparkler', and my second-favorite is *C.* 'Bowles Golden', two plants in the same family that look completely different. *Carex siderosticha* 'Island Brocade' looks like neither of them. 'Island Brocade' has strappy, bright green gold-edged leaves that will spread out and spill over, a growing habit I much admire at the edge of the border or in a container.

The nursery's catalog recommends 'Island Brocade' combined with *Colocasia esculenta* 'Black Magic' (truly black elephant ears), which sounds like a winner to me. The same catalog advises us to bring in colocasia bulbs for winter storage. Here is a pleasant surprise: colocasias do not need such pampering. When cold weather arrives (and it will), just leave colocasias in the ground where they are, and they will reappear in the spring. I hope.

The shade garden has also surprised me this summer with two pulmonarias (lungworts), which are new to my garden. Mine have not bloomed (and perhaps never will), but I forgive them, though I cannot identify them with certainty until they do. Both varieties have dark green foliage streaked and blotched with silvery white, every bit as handsome as temperamental hostas.

Here is the best surprise: deer and slugs dislike pulmonaria, probably because the foliage has the texture of coarse and slightly hairy sandpaper. Here is the bad news: pulmonarias are subject to chlorosis, or iron deficiency, but that can be fixed with the right amendments.

However, too much fertilizer can kill them. The worst news is that they may be touchy about heat and humidity, but to my surprise, they have done fabulously this very damp summer.

Of course, as in the classroom, not all surprises in the garden are happy ones. The cannas fell over, some of my first year baptisias look unhappy, and my yellow clematis that I discovered in England never bloomed.

Occasionally I am surprised by the disappearance of plants and wonder where they went and how I could have prevented their departure. (As I recall, this happened with students, too.) Lobelias are always departing from my garden. Even invasive cypress vine has left the premises. For no apparent reason, my only Japanese maple expired last winter.

On the other hand, Joe Pye weed (*Eupatorium* 'Gateway') has outdone itself this year, and I am thrilled with its abundant size and longevity of bloom. This is another plant (with slightly scratchy leaves) supposedly shunned by deer. Bright orange butterfly weed (*Asclepias tuberosa*), which previously has bloomed once and quickly set seed has, as a result of judicious deadheading, bloomed all summer long and is still flowering.

As in teaching and life in general, we learn from our failures but wisely focus on our successes. That is where the fun is. As gardeners, we know that some things cannot be explained or prevented. Surprises happen, and aren't we glad?

Gardening Goofs: Let Me Count the Ways

This may be the best advice one person can offer another: "Learn from the mistakes of others. You can't live long enough to make them all yourself." If only we were wise enough to heed these words of Eleanor Roosevelt, but I do not know anyone who does. We continue to make our own mistakes, pay the penalties, and, all too often, do the same thing over again.

Years ago, a friend and I were wandering around a public garden when we spotted the cutest little groundcover with variegated foliage shaped like Swedish ivy. In the cracks of the pathway, small plants had emerged, begging to be adopted. We eased the little plants out, placed them in plastic bags we happened to have in our purses, and took the plants home to our gardens. As soon as those roots hit soil, they were off and running, which is why this groundcover is commonly known as "runaway robin."

Glechoma, the common name for runaway robin, continues to be the plague of my garden. A horticultural Godzilla, it has consumed the lawn in the middle of my mixed border, eased into the grass between the garden and the house, and covered what used to be my wild garden. Most of the foliage is now solid green, but occasional variegated leaves remind me why I was tempted.

I learned my lesson with runaway robin. However, while the lesson was sinking in, I planted passiflora vine, five-leafed akebia, autumn clematis, lamium, and houttuynia. Notice the pattern here: I am a glutton for rampant vines and punishment. They are all still with me in varying amounts. I suspect I will have to move . . . perhaps to another state . . . to rid myself of them.

No sooner had I decided thirty years ago that I wanted to be a gardener than I made a critical blunder, not as pervasive as the vines, but goofy nevertheless. My first gardening adventure was an herb garden I located in the back corner of our acre lot. As a result of the distance and the garden's inaccessibility, I forgot all about it, never gathering herbs or involving my small children in the miracle of a well-tended garden.

A year or two after the herb garden fiasco, I started a cutting garden across the back of our lot . . . equally dumb and distant. I planted perennials all the way across it before coming to my senses. Like the herb garden, my cutting garden was out of sight and out of our daily lives. I may be a slow learner, but I eventually caught on. It is best not to include anything in your garden that is going to make life more difficult . . . unless, of course, it has redeeming features. Some problems, like puppies, are worth the effort.

I also learned that gardens should be located where we can appreciate them as we go about our lives. They should be visible from windows where we sit and eat and do chores. They should be placed where we pass them on the way to the car or the mailbox.

When my young sons goofed up, setting fire to the foundation shrubs, for instance, or backing into a brother's car, I asked them, "What did you learn from this experience?" They hated this question, which led me to believe it was a useful parenting tool.

Now I ask myself (and occasionally my husband) this same question . . . which just goes to show, after all these years, mistakes continue to be made, and there is always plenty to be learned.

Fleeting Pleasures

For twenty years and maybe more, I used an old clothesline as a trellis for Lady Banksia rose at the sunny end and for autumn clematis at the shady end. The clothesline was a relic from pre-dryer days, and I decided to make use of its solid structure.

The yellow Lady Banksia rose bloomed with gusto in May. I cut her back as she finished blooming, and she spent the remainder of the summer and fall growing long whips that shot out in all directions, like a very bad hair day. The autumn clematis bloomed with the same abundance in late summer, even though the trellis was deeply shaded by a mature hickory tree. By midsummer, the two vines met in the middle of the clothesline, making a frame for the mixed border beneath. I never planned this picture, but it has been one of the most effective characteristics of my garden.

Alas, the vignette met its end when an ice storm struck and the clothesline was flattened by the accumulation of ice. Lady Banksia came toppling down, and the clothesline support pulled out of the ground. Twenty years and a load of ice were all it could take.

I had hoped to leave the mound of rose canes and let them bloom before tidying up. That's the kind of person I am. But I summoned my grit and bid adieu to the mess. It was time to say good-bye. Besides, I had been yearning for a tunnel made from a series of arbors, and the elimination of the rose and clothesline opened up space, though I still do not have a tunnel. I miss that abundance of yellow blooms in May, but it was time for a change.

That is how gardening is. Nothing is permanent, not even the gardener. We must focus on the pleasures of the moment before they (and we) move on.

For over thirty years we had a cottage on the Outer Banks of North Carolina. When we bought the property it was part of a maritime woodland, and fortunately, everyone in our little community carefully preserved every tree we could when building our houses. When Hurricane Floyd ripped through our yard, we lost four dramatically twisted old cedars.

Hurricane Isabel finished the job. We lost four more cedars, the last of our shade, and our yard became a sun-baked patch instead of a shady woodland. Mother Nature taketh away, but look what she giveth. No human being planted those cedars—or the wax myrtles and yaupon hollies and red bays. We borrowed them for thirty years and were glad of their company.

Sweet Annie (*Artemisia annua*) is a little-known, richly aromatic herb that begins life as the tiniest seedling and grows to five or six feet by midsummer. A mature sweet Annie looks like a soft, feathery Christmas tree. Late in the summer it forms masses of tiny beadlike flowers, and in the fall the foliage turns bronze. I hang cut stems upside down or leave them upright to dry for arrangements, or I shape the stems into wreaths.

You will probably not find sweet Annie at a garden center, but she is an enthusiastic reseeder. For years, through no effort of my own, I grew enough sweet Annie to fill bouquets, make wreaths, and donate to plant sales. I planted that first crop of sweet Annie in the back corner of the yard, but she appeared everywhere the following year and for years after that. Seeds dropped to the ground and germinated, another gift from Mother Nature.

However, my luck ran out a few summers ago, and not one sweet Annie emerged from the ground. Who knows why? I endured a summer without sweet Annie, and that was all I could take. I purchased two packets of seeds, a tall variety I had grown all those years and another, shorter version, *Artemisia annua* 'Cramer's Yardstick'. With luck I can look forward to sweet Annie for years.

If you have a wreath of sweet Annie, you can probably strip the seeds (those beadlike flowers) and toss them over bare soil. I have two wreaths that are at least ten years old. They still have remnants of sweet Annie scent, and the seeds may very well be viable.

The same thing has happened to cypress vine and annual red salvia that popped up on their own year after year. They disappeared without announcing their plans to me, leaving me for at least a season without them.

The loss of a clothesline, trees, or reseeding annuals reminds us that a garden is full of fleeting pleasures to be treasured while we have them, missed when they leave, and eventually replaced by new joys.

Sweet Surrender

I have discovered the secret of "sweet surrender." It means giving up something you have put up with for a period of time but would be happier without. Like a girdle.

Remember those rubberized peel-on instruments of torture? When did women come to their senses and say, "No more"? How was the decision made by so many women in such a short period of time? When I was a teenager, adult women wore girdles. By the time I was a young mother, girdles were gone. And not a moment too soon.

That is what I believe sweet surrender is about. We tire of something that is uncomfortable or tedious or damaging and, one by one, we declare independence. We choose liberation over the norm or the expected. And it feels wonderful.

The house we live in was built in the early seventies, a long ranch-style stretched across a wide suburban lot. In front of the house was a row of evergreen shrubs, and in front of the shrubs was a lawn out to the street and across the lot from edge to edge. Everyone on our street had the same kind of lawn, sprigged by hand, watered, admired, and mowed when we could have been doing something fun.

At the turn of the millennium, wise people came to their senses and just said no to manicured lawns that take too much time, money, water, and effort to maintain. Naturalized areas became stylish—large islands of shrubs and trees, mulched with pine straw, covered areas that had been dedicated to lawn. Notice how these naturalized areas expand. The ratio of lawn to mulched areas reverses as homeowners wisely surrender pristine lawns in favor of leisure, thrift, and family.

One of my sons lives in a neighborhood with a lake on one side and a golf course on the other. Landscaped yard after landscaped yard look pretty much the same with lush green grass, a little "naturalized" area, and a twisted driveway that challenges one's backing skills. The same six plants are arranged differently from yard to yard, but the landscapes wind up looking the same.

Mavericks moved into the neighborhood and planted a garden in their front yard, full of interesting shrubs, trees, ferns, and perennials. The colors and textures were a fabulous counterpoint to the look-alike landscapes up and down the street. I imagine these folks saying, "Lawn? A row of shrubs? A few trees? Forget it . . . we want a garden we can enjoy." I loved it. The neighbors hated it.

The mavericks moved recently. New people bought the house and razed the garden. The yard now fits the neighborhood pattern. Some folks are just not ready to surrender the tedium of a manicured lawn and sculpted shrubs, perhaps because the tedium is endured by a lawn service, not the owners themselves.

On the other hand, friends of mine who have the most magnificent private garden I have ever seen could not grow grass in a shady area patchily covered with moss. After numerous attempts to grow grass, they surrendered and now have a velvety moss lawn that is a delight to see and to walk across barefoot.

Some people who move to the beach or the mountains or desert have trouble surrendering the landscape patterns of their previous residential areas. They want the same green lawns, clipped hedges, and favorite plants they had "at home" in spite of the fact they have chosen to move to a different kind of environment, presumably to enjoy a more leisurely lifestyle.

They want to get away from it all . . . but not quite all. They still want boxwoods or lilacs or peach trees and are willing to go to great lengths to grow them. How much easier it would be to fall in love with wax myrtles and yaupon hollies or conifers or agaves and create landscapes with plants meant for the area.

When I speak to gardeners, I sense a wave of surrender. I see nodding heads as I explain why I do not use insecticides. I am asked questions about how to deal with infested plants without poisoning the environment and ourselves. As I sing the praises of beneficial insects, I see more nodding as I plead with audiences to let nature take her course.

Sweet surrender indeed. Many of us have disposed of fungicides and insecticides because they make no sense and we do not want them in our yards, our children's lungs, or our water systems. And what do you know? Flowers bloom, foliage thrives, vegetables and fruits flourish as well as or better than they did with all those killer sprays.

What to do with a plant so badly infested you cannot bear to look at it? Or you are fearful its blight will spread? Pull (or dig) it up and get rid of it. Burn it or bag it and dispose of it. Buy something else to fill the space.

You can fight whitefly the rest of your life, or you can cut down those gardenias and plant something else. I have an old species gardenia (in contrast to a fancy hybrid) that grows in dappled shade, consistently free of whiteflies. Sometimes progress calls for moving in reverse.

My friends with the moss lawn were plagued with Japanese beetles. They identified the "magnet plants" that attracted these critters and cut two treasured flowering cherries to the ground. It pains me to think about it. But they surrendered the trees in favor of their sanity and health, and it worked. The Japanese beetles chomp elsewhere now, preferably in another state.

A friend who has been active in the Backyard Habitat program since she discovered it fifteen years ago tells me she senses victory when a gardener says, "Oh good. Something is eating my parsley." Such a gardener happily surrenders an unblemished parsley (which will regrow) for a well-nourished caterpillar about to become a butterfly. Who wouldn't?

Sweet surrender is about trade-offs. Which is better: a firm rear end or comfort? A pristine lawn or time with your family? Unnibbled parsley or butterflies? Bug-free foliage or the environment?

Once the decision is made, the sweetness of surrender is apparent. Liberated and relaxed, free of guilt, you will have one more question to ponder: "What took me so long?"

INDEX

Abelia spp., 25, 39; 'Confetti', 125; 'Sunrise', 125
Abelia chinensis, 20, 39–40
Abelia × *grandiflora*, 39, 124–25; 'Compacta', 125; 'John Creech', 125; 'Little Richard', 125; 'Rose Creek', 12, 40, 125
Abelia parvifolia 'Bumble Bee', 125
absence, and gardening, 168–70
accidents, and gardening, 27–29
Aesculus pavia, 136
age, and gardening, 214–16
ajuga, 50
akebia, 223
Alchemilla mollis, 84, 94, 154, 208, 217
allium, 99, 148
aloe, 163
alpine gardens, 18
alstromeria, 95
Alternanthera spp., 15, 59–60, 132–33; *dentata* 'Rubiginosa', 59–60, 132–33; 'Purple Knight', 166
aluminum, 91
American holly, 148
amsonia, 148
anemone, 148
angelonia, 133
anise sage, 135
annuals: planting, 120; potted, 157; propagating, 132–34
applemint, 25, 55, 131
Aquilegia spp., 48; *canadensis*, 115; 'McKana's Giant', 72, 114
arbors, 200
arborvitae, 66
aromatherapy, 52
Artemisia spp., 134, 148; 'Powis Castle', 154
Artemisia annua: 'Cramer's Yardstick', 226; 'Sweet Annie', 154, 226
Artemisia lactiflora, 34, 154
Artemisia ludoviciana 'Silver King', 154
Asarum minor, 107
Asclepias tuberosa, 11, 25, 47, 125, 140, 148, 175, 221
asparagus, 121–22
asparagus fern, 166
Aspidistra elatior, 83, 88, 106–7
Aster spp., 50, 146; *carolinianus*, 146; 'Fanny's Fall Aster', 146; 'Purple Dome', 146
Athyrium nipponicum, 154
aucuba, 48, 69, 148

August lily, 67, 99, 197–99
autumn, 23–69; end of, 67–69; planting for, 144–46
autumn clematis, 223
autumn crocus, 45
autumn fern, 83, 156
Avent, Tony, 218
azalea, 27, 209; pH and, 89; pruning, 110–11

baby's breath, 95
bacopa, 128
banana shrub, 25, 54
Baptisia spp., 11, 51, 125, 148, 221; *australis*, 175
barberry, 15, 66, 148
barrenwort, 45
basil, 11; Genovese, 131; 'Siam Queen', 131
bay, 84, 131
bearded iris, 148
bear's foot hellebore, 85
beautyberries, 39
beautybush, 148
Becky daisy, 33, 47, 139, 190, 204
bee balm, 148
bellflower, 221
beneficial insects, 196
Bermuda hay, coastal, 65, 76–77, 161, 168
bones, 68–69
bottlebrush, 20
Bowles' golden sedge, 207–8
boxwood, 66; common, 148
Brinkley, Douglas, 195
Buddleia spp., 148; *davidii*, 20, 126, 169; tree-form, 81
bulbs: dividing, 114; planting, 95–96
butcher's broom, 45
butterfly bush, 28–29, 126, 169; tree-form, 81
butterfly weed, 11, 25, 47, 51, 125, 140, 148, 175, 221
bypass pruners, 76

cacti, 163
calcium, 89–91
calendar, 32, 62, 112, 160
Calibrachoa 'Superbells Tequila Sunrise', 166
Callicarpa spp.: *acuminata*, 39; *americana*, 39; *dichotoma* 'Issai', 39; *japonica*, 39; 'Lactea', 39
Calycanthus floridus, 25, 53
camellia, 103; tree-form, 82
Campanula spp., 221; *punctata* 'Cherry Bells', 221
Campsis radicans, 20–21, 136
candytuft, 94
Canna spp., 221; 'Australia', 203; 'Bengal Tiger', 203
cardboard, for mulch, 2–3
Carex spp.: *elata* 'Bowles Golden', 93, 207–8, 221; *siderosticha* 'Island Brocade', 221; 'Sparkler', 221
Carolina allspice, 25, 53
Cassia spp., 144; *bicapsularis*, 15, 28–29, 144–45; *corymbosa*, 28, 144
cast-iron plant, 83, 88, 106–7
castor beans, 11, 13, 15, 67, 145, 169
cat's whiskers, 58–59
cedar, 225–26
Chamaecyparis, 148
chameleon plant, 57
chaos, and gardening, 14–15, 17
Chasmanthium latifolium, 56
chaste tree, 12–13, 126, 204–5
Chinese abelia, 39–40
Chinese fringe tree, 53
Chinese juniper, 148
Chinese ligustrum, tree-form, 81
Chinese mahonia, 84

Chinese pistache, 37
Chionanthus spp.: *retusus*, 53; *virginicus*, 53, 173
chocolate mint, 55, 131, 162, 169
Choisya ternata 'Sundance', 15, 215
chokeberry, 148
Christmas, 95–97; tree ornaments, natural, 98–99
Christmas fern, 45
Christmas rose, 85
chrysanthemum, 47, 50, 67, 95, 145, 148; 'Gethsemane Moonlight', 145; 'Miss Gloria', 145; 'Ryan's Daisy', 145
church, flowers for, 189–91
cigar plant, 59
cinnamon fern, 156
citrus, 53
cleaning up, 24–26, 139
Clematis spp., 61–63, 221; 'Henryi', 62; 'Nelly Moser', 62; *paniculata*, 61; *pitcheri*, 62
Clerodendron bungei, 181
Clethra alnifolia, 53
cleyera, 80
close planting, 15
coastal Bermuda hay, 65, 76–77, 161, 168
Colchicum, 45
cold frame, 31, 50, 76, 96
coleus, 60, 132
Colocasia spp., 66
Colocasia antiquorum 'Illustris', 169, 178–79, 181, 202, 204
Colocasia esculenta, 178; 'Black Magic', 221; 'Burgundy Stem', 178, 204
color, 15; for autumn, 35–37; gray, 153–55; for winter, 83–85
columbine, 45, 48, 72, 114–15, 148
comfrey, 25
common boxwood, 148
compost, 2–4
coneflower, 25, 47, 67, 125, 148, 175, 209–10
confederate jasmine, 53
conifers, 68–69, 80; potted, 156; propagating, 101
container gardening, 17, 156–57, 166–67; lettuces, 30; small-scale, 127–29
contorted mulberry, 68
coppicing, 109
coreopsis, 148, 175
corydalis, 45
cow itch, 20
creeping Jennie, 15, 93, 207
creeping raspberry, 45, 55–56
crocosmia, 148
Cuban oregano, 151
Cuphea spp., 125; *ignea*, 59; *llavea* 'Bat Face', 59; *micropetala*, 59
cuttings, 9–10, 31, 50, 68, 160–61; hardwood, 100–101
cyclamen, 45, 48
cypress vine, 221, 226
Cyrtomium falcatum, 8, 83, 107

daffodils, 45, 48, 96, 109, 114, 118; 'Tete-a-Tete', 128
damping off, 74
Daphne spp., 12, 68, 86–87, 106, 109; *aureomarginata*, 86; *odora*, 53, 86; *rubra*, 86
daylily, 50
deadheading, 140, 161, 174–76
dead nettle, 24
deer, 141, 147–48
dianthus, 94
dill, 131, 135
Dirr, Michael, 78
DiSabato-Aust, Tracy, 176

diversity, and gardening, 16
dividing plants, 8–9, 50–51, 114, 138–39
dolomitic lime, 90–91
doors, in garden, 200
Dryopteris erythrosora, 83
dry shade, 44–46
Dutch iris, 190–91, 209
dwarf abelia, 12, 20
dwarf coreopsis, 207
dwarf iris, 128
dwarf mondo grass, 56
dwarf pennyroyal, 48, 56, 128, 130–31
dwarf spirea, 65
dwarf veronica, 207

Echinacea spp., 47, 175; 'Art's Pride', 210; *purpurea*, 25, 210; 'White Swan', 25, 210
economy, and gardening, 8–10
Edgeworthia spp.: *chrysantha*, 53; *papyrifera*, 84
edging, 92–94; plants for, 206–8
elagnus, 53
elephant ears, 64, 66, 169, 178, 181, 202
encore azalea, 27
English ivy, 162
English laurel, 68, 80, 157
entrances, 200
Epimedium, 45
Euonymus spp., 66; *alatus*, 36
Eupatorium maculatum 'Gateway', 11, 33, 177, 204, 221
euphorbia, 148
evergreen ferns, 83
Exochorda racemosa, 215

fairy garden, 128–29
false cypress, 148
false indigo, 175

×*Fatshedera lizei*, 106
Fatsia spp., 48, 66, 69; *japonica*, 45, 106
February itch, 108–9
fennel, 131, 135
ferns, 148; potted, 156–57
fertilizer, 119
fig tree, 68, 173
firecracker, 59
fish emulsion, 30, 74
flexibility, and gardening, 11–13
Florida anise, 25, 80
flowers: for arrangements, 209–11; for church, 189–91
forget-me-not, 128, 139, 207, 217–18
Formosa lily, 99, 197–99
Fothergilla spp., 35, 48; *major* 'Mt. Airy', 35
foundation planting, 64–66
fragrance, 52–54
frost, 67
fungicides, 16, 77, 228–29
Fusarium fungus, 118

gardenia, 53
gardening: beginning, 1–21; math skills for, 138–40; mistakes in, 223–24; rules for, breaking, 217–19; simplifying, 214–16; small-scale, 127–29; tools for, 75–77; trends in, 16–18
garden structures, 14–15
garlic chives, 131
gaura, 175
Geum spp., 148, 220–21; 'Fireball', 220–21; 'Werner Arends', 220–21
gifts, for gardeners, 96
ginger lily, 27, 53, 186–88
Glechoma spp., 108, 180, 223; *hederacea*, 57

goals, for garden, 2; versus planning, 5–7
goldenrod, 61
golden sedge, 207–8
Gordonia lasianthus, 157
Grancy graybeard, 53, 173
greenhouse, 31, 58, 75–76, 96, 103–4
groundcovers, 55–57; weeding, 162
ground ivy, 108
grow light, 74, 109

hardwood cuttings, 100–101
hay, coastal Bermuda, 3, 65, 76–77, 161, 168
hedges, 78–80, 200–201; double, 79–80
Hedychium spp., 27, 186–88; *coronarium*, 186; *gardnerianum* 'Tara', 186; 'Luna Moth', 187
Helianthus angustifolia, 175, 190
Helleborus spp., 12, 45, 84–85, 96, 109, 113–14, 148; *foetidus*, 85; *niger*, 85; *orientalis*, 84–85, 113
hens and chicks, 163–65
herbs, 130–31; for winter, 84
Heuchera spp., 15, 45, 50, 93, 175, 221; 'Amber Waves', 221
hibiscus, 15
hickory, 171–72
Hilton, Bill, Jr., 20–21
holes, 156–57
holly, 65–66, 95, 173; tree-form, 82
holly fern, 8, 48, 68, 83, 107, 156
hostas, 141
houseleeks, 163–64
Houttuynia spp., 223; *cordata*, 57
humus, 3
hyacinth beans, 67
Hydrangea spp., 25, 27, 41–43; aluminum and, 91; arrangements with, 192–94, 209; 'Dooley', 43; dried, 98; potted, 157; propagating, 160–61; pruning, 111–12, 119–20, 160; tree-form, 81–82
Hydrangea arborescens, 42; 'Annabelle', 42, 48, 111, 160
Hydrangea macrophylla, 41–42; 'Endless Summer', 27, 43, 48, 111–12; 'Penny Mac', 27, 41, 43, 111–12, 193
Hydrangea paniculata, 42–43; 'Grandiflora', 43; 'Limelight', 12, 43, 48, 160; 'Tardiva', 43, 48, 111, 133, 160
Hydrangea quercifolia, 43; 'Pee Wee', 125; 'Sikes Dwarf', 125

Iberis sempervirens, 94
imperial taro elephant ear, 181
Indian hawthorn, tree-form, 81
inkberry, 148
insecticides, 16, 77, 195–96, 228–29
insects, 195–96, 229
intimacy, and gardening, 200–202
invasive plants, 180–82
iron, 221
irrigation systems, 149–50
Issai beautyberry, 39
Itea virginica, 35, 48; 'Henry Garnet', 35–36, 105–6; 'Little Henry', 36, 106

Japanese anemone, 48
Japanese aucuba, 46
Japanese beetles, 229
Japanese fleece flower, 182
Japanese maple, 221
Japanese painted fern, 45, 156–57
Japanese privet, 78
Jefferson, Thomas, 85
jessamine, 61

Jewel of Opar, 15, 181–82
Joe Pye weed, 11, 33, 47, 148, 177, 204, 221

kerria, 148
kneelers, 96

lacecap hydrangea, 41
Lacy, Allen, xii
'Lady Banksia' rose, 225
lady's mantle, 84, 94, 154, 208, 217
lamb's ears, 11, 48, 84, 93, 96, 130, 139, 148, 153–54, 207
Lamium spp., 24, 45, 57, 162, 223
landscaping, 64–66
lantana, 66, 105
Laurus nobilis, 131
lavender, 84, 99, 128, 131
layering, 17, 48–49
leaf miners, 115
leafy greens, 183–85
leatherleaf mahonia, 46
leaves, shredded, for mulch, 3, 65, 76, 161, 168–69
leisure, and gardening, 2–4, 7, 12
lemon balm, 25, 131
lemongrass, 130
lemon marigold, 131
lemon verbena, 99, 130
Lenten rose, 84–85, 113
Leonotis leonurus, 11, 27–28
Lespedeza thunbergii 'White Fountain', 215
lettuce, 184–85
Leucanthemum × *superbum* 'Becky', 33, 139, 190, 204
Leyland cypress, 95
Ligustrum spp., 66, 95; *japonicum*, 78; tree-form, 81
Lilium formosanum, 197–99
lime, 89–91, 131
lion's ears, 11, 27–28
lion's tail, 28
lobelia, 221
loblolly bay, 157
location, and gardening, 224
loppers, power gear, 76, 96
loropetalum, 15, 66; 'Snow Muffin', 40; tree-form, 81, 125–26
love-in-a-mist, 30
lungwort. *See Pulmonaria*
lupine, 61
Lysimachia nummularia, 15; 'Aurea', 93, 207

magnesium, 90
magnolia, 45
Mahonia spp., 83–84, 109, 148; *aquifolium*, 84; *bealei*, 46; *fortunei*, 84
maintenance, simplifying, 214–16
male fern, 45
manure, 3
Mary's tears, 142
math skills, for gardening, 138–40
mazus, 128
McKenzie, Stan, 218
Mentha pulegium, 56
Mexican beautyberry, 39
Mexican bush sage, 31, 47, 50, 145, 155, 190, 210; potted, 157
Mexican orange shrub, 15, 215
Mexican petunia, 174
Mexican sunflowers, 13, 19, 67, 145, 204, 209
Michelia spp.: *figo*, 25, 54; *maudiae*, 54; *skinneri*, 54
Mickey Mouse plant, 59
milkweed, 135
millet, 'Purple Majesty', 72–73
minerals, 89–91
mint, 55, 148

Miscanthus spp., 148; *sinensis* 'Variegatus', 12
mistakes, in gardening, 223–24
Mitchell, Henry, xi–xi
mixed borders, 2, 5–6, 16; cutting back, 50, 67; and disease resistance, 65; and foundation planting, 65–66
mock orange, 25, 124, 196
mondo grass, 56, 93
monkey grass, 92
moonvine, 53
mophead hydrangea, 41, 98
moss, 18
mountain laurel, 148
mountain mint, 99, 154
mouse ears, 59
mulch, 3–4, 65, 76–77, 161, 214; for absence, 168–69
Myosotis spp., 207; *sylvatica*, 128, 217–18

nandina, 95, 148
narcissus, 95–96
nasturtium, 'Empress of India', 73
National Wildlife Federation, 21
native columbine, 148
native plants, 135–37
naturalized areas, 227
New England aster, 146
newspaper, for mulch, 2–3, 161
night-blooming cereus, 53
ninebark shrub, 15, 66
nitrogen, 30
northern sea oats, 56

oakleaf hydrangea, 125
Ophiogon japonicus, 56; 'Gyoko', 56; 'Kioto', 56; 'Nippon', 56
Oregon grapeholly, 84
organic gardening, 16–17
Orthosiphon stamineus, 58–59
Osmanthus fragrans, 38, 87; 'Aurantiacus', 38; 'Fudingzhu', 38, 87; 'Nanjing Beauty', 87

painted fern, 154
panicle hydrangeas, 12, 98
pansy, 66
paper bush, 84
parsley, 131, 135, 229
Parthenocissus quinquefolia, 36, 182
passiflora, 223
Patrinia spp., 139, 190, 210–11; *scabiosifolia*, 34, 190, 210–11
pearlbush, 215
Pennisetum setaceum 'Rubrum', 166
pentas, 133
perennials: for cutting, 209–10; cutting back, 50; deadheading, 140, 175; and deer, 148; dividing, 8–9; favorites, 47; potted, 157; propagating, 32–34; for spring, 125–26; tender, 58–60, 120
Petunia integrifolia, 134
pH, 89–91, 193
Philadelphus coronarius, 124; 'Variegatus', 124
Philadelphus × *lemoinei*: 'Manteau d'Hermine', 124; 'Snow Velvet', 124
Philippine lily, 99, 197–99
phlox, 175
Photinia × *fraseri*, 5, 78
Physocarpus opulifolius, 15
pineapple lily, 15
pineapple mint, 130–31
pineapple sage, 31, 50, 145; potted, 157
pine bark, 91, 161; shredded, 65
pine straw, 3, 65, 76, 168
Pistachia chinensis, 37
pittosporum, 80, 95

planning, 5–7, 32–34
planting: close, 161–62; delaying, 121–23; shrubs, 216
plants: big, 203–5; giving up on, 141–43; short, 206–8
Plectranthus spp., 31, 50, 60, 151–52; 'Athens Gem', 152; 'Erma', 152; *fructicosus* 'Purple Martin', 60, 152; 'Mona Lavender', 152; 'Purple Majesty', 152; 'Vanilla Twist', 152
plumbago, 148
pocketknife, 76
Podocarpus macrophyllus, 79
Polygonum cuspidatum, 182
poppies, 30–31
pots, 17, 156–57, 166–67
potting area, 76
potting mix, 9, 74, 166
powdery mildew, 63
privet, tree-form, 81
propagating, 32–34; annuals, 132–34; hardwood, 100–101; hydrangeas, 160–61; plectranthus, 151; succulents, 165; tools for, 76
prostrate crepe myrtle, 40
pruning, 24–26, 48, 109, 140; for absence, 169; clematis, 61–62; versus deadheading, 174–76; issues in, 110–12; in spring, 119–20; tools for, 76, 96
Prunus laurocerasus, 157
Pulmonaria, 94, 142, 148, 221–22; 'Milky Way', 142; 'Moonshine', 142–43; 'Raspberry Ice', 143; 'Silver Streamers', 142; 'Trevi Fountain', 142
purple fountain grass, 166

Queen Anne's lace, 25, 30, 61

rain lily, 198–99
rakes, 77
reblooming hydrangeas, 43, 48, 193; potted, 157
red buckeye, 20, 136
red cedar, 20
red-hot poker, 148
red salvia, 226
redtips, 5, 78
red-veined enkthianthus, 36
repotting, 8–9, 13
rice paper plant, 53, 84
Ricinus communis, 13, 145, 169
rocks, 18
Roosevelt, Eleanor, 223–24
rooting hormone, 10, 31, 33
rooting medium, 31, 33
rose, 122; 'Lady Banksia', 225
rosemary, 84, 95, 99, 128, 131, 148
royal blue salvia, 11, 25
royal fern, 157
Rubus calcycinoides, 55–56
rudbeckia, 47
rue, 84, 95, 131, 135, 155
Ruellia brittoniana, 33–34, 174
Rule of Five, 123
rules, breaking, 217–19
runaway robin, 57, 223
Ruscus aculeatus, 45
Rutus graveolens, 155

sales, on plants, 51
Salvia spp., 19–20, 31, 47, 50, 66, 134–35, 145, 148; 'Anthony Parker', 145; *elegans*, 145; *guaranitica*, 11, 19, 25, 135, 145, 174, 178, 180–81; *leucantha*, 145, 155, 210; *madrensis* 'Red Neck Girl', 67, 145, 210; 'Phyllis Fancy', 20, 67, 135–36, 145; *uliginosa*, 19

santolina, 130
Sarcococca spp., 87–88; *hookeriana*, 88, 157, 167; *ruscifolia*, 88
Sassafras spp., 20, 173; *albidum*, 36
seagrass, dried, 3
sea lavender, 95
seaweed, 161
sedge, 207–8
Sedum spp., 148, 163–64; 'Autumn Joy', 20, 164, 175, 191; 'Blue Spruce', 164; 'Goldmoss', 164; 'Green Mantle', 164; 'Ogon', 164
seeds: cold-starting, 101–2; Formosa lily, 197; gathering, 67–68; starting, 72–74, 108–9, 183–85
Sempervivum spp., 163–65; *tectorum*, 164
shovel, 77
shrubs, 38–40; cuttings from, 9–10; and deer, 148; for fall color, 35–36; flowering, 124–26; fragrant, 53–54; for hedges, 78–80; hydrangeas, 41–43; moving, 118–19; planting, 216; propagating, 32–33; pruning, 31; for simple maintenance, 214–15; as trees, 81–82; wildlife-friendly, 20; winter and, 86–88, 105
Siberian iris, 178–79
Skinner's banana shrub, 54
slugs, 141
small gardens, 47–49
Smith, F. Brian, 52–53
smoke bush, 66
snapdragons, 66, 95
soaker hoses, 150
soil improvement, 2–4, 44–45, 64–65, 161
solidago, 11, 148
southern magnolia, 53
southernwood, 131
spearmint, 55
spice bush, 148
spinach, 30
Spirea spp., 66, 209; 'Gold Flame', 15
spotted dog, 142
spreading plants, 180–82
spring, 117–57; anticipating, 108–9, 113–15
Stachys byzantina, 48, 84, 153, 207; 'Helene von Stein', 93, 130, 153
stem rot, 63
stonework, 18
stooling, 109
Stout, Ruth, xi
strawberry, 121
Stylophorum diphyllum, 25, 48, 107, 114
succulents, 163–65
summer, 159–211; maintenance for, 160–62; peak of, 177–79
summersweet, 53
surprises, in gardening, 220–22
surrender, and gardening, 141–43, 227–29
Sutera spp.: 'Giant Snowflake', 128; 'Glacier Blue', 128
swamp sunflower, 50, 175, 190
Swedish ivy, 151
sweet Annie, 99, 226
sweet autumn clematis, 61–62
sweetbox, 87–88, 157, 167
sweet potato, 134
sweet shrub, 53

Tagetes lemmonii, 131
Talinum paniculatum, 15; 'Kingswood Gold', 181–82

tansy, 25
tapestry hedge, 79–80
tea olive, 38–39, 53, 80, 87
thunder and lightning, 142
thyme, 84, 128, 130–31
tiger lily, 148
Tithonia spp., 145; *rotundifolia*, 13, 19, 204; 'Torch', 204
tomato, 122; 'Better Boy', 121; Costoluto Genovese, 72; 'Marianna's Peace', 121; 'Sungold', 121; 'Thessaloniki', 121
tools, 75–77
top tens, 47–49
Trachelospermum jasminoides, 53
trailing plectranthus, 151–52
travel, and gardening, 168–70
trees, 171–73; and dry shade, 44; pruning, 31; shrubs as, 81–82; wildlife-friendly, 20
tropical plants, 18
trowels, 76
trumpet creeper, 20–21, 136
tulip poplar, 20
tuteurs, 14

upright plectranthus, 151–52

variegated carex, 93
variegated privet, tree-form, 81
vegetables, 183–85
vermiculite, 73
Veronica spp., 148; *umbrosa* 'Georgia Blue', 114, 128, 207
Viburnum spp., 20, 48, 68, 80, 95, 209; *tinus* 'Spring Bouquet', 48, 109; tree-form, 81
Viette, Andre, 148
vinca, 24, 57; major, 45
vines, pruning, 24–26
Virginia creeper, 36, 182
Virginia sweetspire, 35, 48, 105–6
Vitex spp., 173; *agnus-castus*, 12–13, 126, 205; *negundo*, 204–5; 'Shoal Creek', 12–13; tree-form, 81

water gardens, 18, 47, 97
watering, 149–50
waxleaf ligustrum, 5; tree-form, 81
wax myrtle, 20, 80, 173
weeding, 50, 139, 161–62
Weigela spp., 125; 'Java Red', 125; 'Ruby Queen', 125
whitefly, 229
wild blue ageratum, 61
wilde dagga, 28
wild ginger, 107
wildlife-friendly gardening, 19–21; native plants for, 135–37
wild petunia, 33–34
winged euonymus, 36
winter, 71–115; color for, 83–85
winter daphne, 86
winter honeysuckle, 53
Wisteria sinensis 'Pride of Augusta', 53
wood shavings, 3
woods poppy, 25, 48, 107, 114

yarrow, 148

Zephyranthes 'Labuffarosa', 198–99
zinnia, 32, 209

ABOUT THE AUTHOR

By some genetic fluke, Margot Rochester emerged from a city-dwelling family as a passionate gardener. Born in Los Angeles and raised in various parts of California and New York, she likes to say she discovered gardening at a bookstore at the University of Michigan. After graduating, marrying, and moving to South Carolina, she started some serious digging in.

While admitting to her share of failures over the course of forty-plus years, her enthusiasm never wavered. Gardening is her passion. So is writing about gardens. She has been a freelance garden columnist for nearly twenty years.

In the midlands of South Carolina and on the Outer Banks of North Carolina, Margot lives with her husband of more than fifty years. Adding zest and joy to their lives are two sons, two daughters-in-law, five grandchildren, and two spoiled dogs.